AN ALTERNATIVE TO PSYCHIATRY

AN ALTERNATIVE TO PSYCHIATRY

Tuula E. Tuormaa

Foreword by
Professor D. Bryce-Smith,
PhD, DSc, CChem, FRSC

The Book Guild Ltd.
Sussex, England

The Book Guild Ltd.
25 High Street,
Lewes, Sussex

First published 1991
© Tuula E. Tuormaa 1991
Set in Baskerville
Typesetting by Kudos Graphics,
Slinfold, West Sussex

Printed in Great Britain by
Antony Rowe Ltd.
Chippenham, Wiltshire.

British Library Cataloguing in Publication Data
Tuormaa, Tuula E. (Tuula Elisabeth)
    An Alternative to psychiatry
    1. Medicine. Psychiatry
    I. Title
616. 89

ISBN 0 86332 583 1

In memory of my mother,
Tony Mead,
Kaija and Eeva

One of the most widespread diseases is diagnosis.
Karl Kraus (1874–1936)

CONTENTS

FOREWORD

C. P. Snow first drew attention to the 'two cultures' problem. This arises from the intellectual and conceptual gulf that so frequently exists between scientists on the one hand and politicians, sociologists and the like on the other. Tuula Tuormaa has in the present book tackled a related 'two cultures' problem concerned with human behaviour. One culture – currently dominant – sees social (i.e. sensory) factors as all-important determinants of behaviour and the various manifestations of abnormal behaviour such as crime, educational underachievement, and adverse reactions to stress. On the other hand, scientifically trained persons tend to see behaviour as a manifestation of the way the physical brain reacts biochemically to both sensory and non-sensory inputs, in conjunction with past inputs stored as memory, and past non-sensory factors such as biochemical and physiological effects of toxins and nutrient deficiencies on the developing fetal and child brain.

Nutrition, both current and past, is certainly one important influence on the way the brain develops and functions, and food allergies are sometimes primary factors in disturbed behaviour – hyperactivity in children for example. Unfortunately, these important points have yet to be adequately grasped by many professionally concerned with mental disorders. The present book, being written in a chatty style largely for the general reader is perhaps unlikely to appeal to those professionals who would prefer a more condensed and unemotional account couched in technical language; though there are in fact numerous references to the professional literature.

But the growing number of people becoming dissatisfied with, on the one hand, Freudian and similar psychiatric

9

approaches to mental disturbance in its many forms, and on the other the current medical emphasis on mere treatment by drugs of the symptoms of mental illness, will appreciate the emphasis in this book on nutritional and toxic factors. For this approach provides new insights to *causes,* and thereby points the way to more effective prevention and treatment.

Professor D. Bryce-Smith,
PhD, DSc, CChem, FRSC
Chemistry Department,
University of Reading, UK

ACKNOWLEDGEMENTS

First and foremost I would like to thank all those scientists, doctors and researchers whose names will appear in this book and without whom it would never have been written. I also wish to thank all those dedicated scientists, doctors and researchers, whose names I have failed to mention, but who have neverthless contributed to the production of this writing. I must stress here, that despite their invaluable help I alone am responsible for any errors of facts or judgement which may have crept into my conclusions.

I also wish to acknowledge my former teacher Mrs Kyllikki Penttilä for giving me self-confidence, The Mental Health Foundation for the initial research grant, my family firm Tukku-Tuormaat and Sinikka Butler for their financial help and the BMA Nuffield Library for supplying me with most of the research material. In addition I wish to thank the following publishers and authors for their kind permission for quotations:

American Heart Assocation, Dallas, Texas 75231–4599, USA.
    Kuller *et al.* Epidemiological study of sudden and unexpected deaths due to the arteriosclerotic heart disease. (1966)
American Journal of Clinical Nutrition, Bethesda, Maryland 20814, USA
    Williams R: Alcoholism as a nutritional problem. (1952)
    Lonsdale D. and Shamberger R.: Red cell transketolase as an indicator of nutritional deficiency. (1980)
American Medical Association, Chicago, Il. 60610, USA
    Gyland S.: Possibly neurogenic hypoglycaemia. (1953)
American Psychiatric Association, Washington DC 20005, USA

Greden J.: Anxiety or caffeinism: A diagnostic dilemma. (1974)
Association of Metropolitan Authorities, London SW1P 3BJ, UK.
Of little benefit (1987)
The Athlone Press Ltd, London NW11 7SG
Wilson G.: The hazards of immunisation. (1976)
Basil Blackwell, Oxford OX4 1JE, UK.
Scott A.: Pirates of the cell. (1987)
British Medical Journal, London WC1H 9JR, UK.
Addy D.: Happiness is iron. (1986)
Ashton H.: Benzodiazepine withdrawal: An unfinished story. (1984)
Cannon G.: Happiness is iron (Letter) (1986)
Catalan J. et al.: Benzoidazepine in general practice: Time for decision. (1985)
Lloyd G.: Medicine without signs. (1983)
Millard P.: Treatment for ageing brains. (1984)
Orr J.B.: The development of the science of nutrition in relation to disease. (1931)
The British Nutrition Foundation, London SW1X 8PG, UK.
Nutrition in medical education: Report of the British Nutrition Foundation's Task Force on Clinical Nutrition. Ed: J. Gray, (1983)
Food intolerance or food aversion: A joint report of the Royal College of Physicians and the British Nutrition Foundation. (1984)
CW Daniel Co Ltd., Saffron Walden, Essex CB10 1JP, UK.
Chaitow L.: Vaccination and immunization: Dangers, delusions and alternatives. (1987)
The Economist, London SW1A 1HG, UK.
Wyke A.: Pharmaceuticals: Harder going. (1987)
Health Plus Publishers, Phoenix, Arizona 85028, USA.
Airola P.: Hypoglycaemia: A better approach. (1981)
Journal of Alternative & Complementary Medicine, Bagshot, Surrey GU19 5AH, UK.
Quotations from the following issues: September 1984, January 1985, October 1985, August 1986, November 1986, May 1987, June 1987, November 1987 and May 1988
Journal of Nervous and Mental Disease, Baltimore, Mary-

land 21202–3993, USA.

Marks I. and Lader M.: Anxiety States (Anxiety Neurosis): A Review. (1973)

Keats Publishing, New Canaan, Conn. 06840, USA.

Pfeiffer C.: Mental and elemental nutrients. (1975)

1984/85 Yearbook of Nutritional Medicine.

The Lancet, London WC1B 3SL, UK.

Burnet F.M.: A possible role of zinc in the pathology of dementia. (1981)

Britain needs a Food and Health Policy: The Government must face its duty. (1986)

Bryce-Smith D. and Simpson R.: Case of anorexia nervosa responding to zinc sulphate. (1984)

Crook W.G.: Food additives and hyperactivity. (1982)

Horrobin D.F.: Schizophrenia: Reconciliation of the dopamine, prostaglandin and opioid concepts and the role of the pineal. (1979)

Osmond H. and Hoffer A.: Massive niacin treatment in schizophrenia. (1962)

Wynn V.: Vitamins and oral contraceptive use. (1975)

J.B. Lippincott Co, Philadelphia, PA 19105, USA

Spies T. et al.: The mental symptoms of pellagra and their relief with nicotinic acid. (Society for Clinical Investigation, 1938)

The McCarrison Society for Nutrition and Health, London W1M 4DR, UK.

McGarrison, Sir Robert: Nutrition and Health

MIND Publications, London SW1A 1HG, UK.

Major tranquillisers: The price of tranquillity.

Minor tranquillisers: Hard facts, hard choices.

Anti-depressants: First choice . . . or last resort?

Pilgrim D.: The myth of schizophrenia. (Openmind, 1988)

Lacey R. and Woodward S.: That's Life survey on tranquillisers. (1985)

National Medical Association, Washington DC 20001, USA.

Salzer H.: Relative hypoglycaemia as a cause of neuropsychiatric illness. (1966)

The Natural Medicines Society, Birmingham B16 8LA, UK.

Thomson C. and MacEoin D.: The health crisis. (1988)

New Scientist, London SE1 9LS, UK.
Martin P.: Psychology and the immune system. (1987)
The New York Academy of Sciences, New York, NY 10021, USA.
Roberts K. et al.: Respiratory alkalosis. (1957)
W.W. Norton & Company Inc., New York, NY 10110, USA.
Fenichel O.: Psychoanalytic theory of neurosis. (1945)
Pan Books, London SW10 9PG, UK.
Mackarness R.: Not all in the mind. (1976)
Parker House Publishing, California 94704, USA
Schauss A.: Diet, crime and delinquency. (1981)
Penquin Books, London W8 5TZ, UK.
Yudkin J.: Pure, white and deadly, (1986)
Plenum Publishing Co., New York, N.Y. 10011, USA.
Wilder J.: Psychological problems of hypoglycaemia. (The American Journal of Digestive Diseases, 1943)
Professional Books, Jackson, Tennessee 38302, USA.
Crook W.: The yeast connection. (1983)
Raven Press, New York, N.Y. 10036–2806, USA.
Cohen M. and White P.: Life situations, emotions and neurocirculatory asthenia. (Association for Research in Nervous and Mental Diseases, 1950)
Society for Environmental Therapy Newsletter, London WC1H 9DR, UK.
Rippere V.: The diet of psychiatric patients. (1982)
Smith F.: A basic guide to allergy. (1987)
Thorsons Publishing, Wellingborough, Northants NN8 2RQ, UK.
Randolph T.G. and Moss R.W.: Allergies, your hidden enemy. (1981)
Pfeiffer C.: Mental illness and schizophrenia: The nutrition connection. (1987)
Chaitow L. and Martin S.: A world without AIDS. (1988)

And last, but not least, my special thanks go to TBE, Sinikka, Jane and all my other friends for their help, understanding and support during my formidable task. Furthermore I particularly wish to thank Jane for her invaluable help in transforming my manuscript into comprehensible English.

I have written this book to serve only as a general information guide and a reference source for both professionals and non-professionals, hoping that this short overall survey will create more active interest for further scientific research into the nutritional aspect of both physical and mental health. I did not intend this book as treatment advice, only as a general information source when working with one's own health practitioner. Therefore, for obvious reasons, neither I, nor the publisher can assume any medical or legal responsibility for inappropriate usage of information contained herein.

1

THE NAME OF THE GAME IS THE NAME

Mental illness is the greatest single medical problem facing our health services, as almost one third of all National Health Service beds are filled by people with some sort of mental illness. In addition thousands of mentally ill people are living at home but going daily to psychiatric wards for treatment and support. An additional quarter of a million people have weekly or fortnightly appointments to see a psychiatrist in a general hospital psychiatric out-patients' department. There are also thousands of individuals who have been able to leave a psychiatric hospital, but are still in need of regular support if they are to cope with living outside the institution. Also nearly half of our massive prison population is thought to be in need of psychiatric treatment, not forgetting the majority of alcoholics, drug addicts and vagrants. (1) It is also believed that one in every six girls and one in every nine boys now at school can expect to spend at least one spell in mental hospital before they die. (2)

After reading all this mindblowing information I came to the firm conclusion that if this mental illness lark is allowed to get much more out of hand, there will soon be only a couple of 'normal' people left whilst all the rest of the folk will be regrettably away with the fairies. In short: 'Everyone's daft except thee and me, and even thee's a bit queer.'

Before I go on, I must stress that we are talking here about mental illness, not mental handicap, as these two are constantly confused and thrown together under the same heading. The vital difference is that if you are said to be suffering from mental illness, that means that you have started out in life being 'normal', but if a person is mentally handicapped, he usually suffers from birth with a kind of brain damage which can not be corrected.

The mentally ill are usually pigeonholed to the following diagnostic categories:

Depressive illness, which includes all such sub-groups of depression as endogenous, neurotic, obsessional, psychotic, manic, hysterical, agitated etc.

Anxiety neurosis, which includes such conditions as neurasthenia, effort syndrome, hyperventilation syndrome, phobias, agoraphobias and panic attacks.

Schizophrenic illness, which again consists of sub-groups such as paranoid, simple, catatonic, schizo-effective etc.

Affective disorders, which are said to be a group of psychiatric disorders which include anxiety states, depression, mania and hypomania.

Addictive disorders, which include alcoholism and other drug additions.

Confusional states, which include pre-senile dementia, Alzheimer's disease, transient confusion, arteriosclerotic dementia, toxic confusional states and senile dementia.

Miscellaneous psychiatric groups include epilepsies of all types, eating disorders such as anorexia nervosa, bulimia and sexual deviations. Also added to the psychiatric list are all sorts of bits and pieces like psychopathic personality, organic brain syndrome, hypochondriasis, and this little favourite of mine, the personality disorder.

Now that we have established what we are talking about, and furthermore that sanity nowadays seems to be more of a luxury than a way of life, it would be worth examining what could happen if any of us had the misfortune to get caught in this psychiatric web.

Kendell (3) studied Department of Health records of 1,913 patients admitted to psychiatric units and mental health hospitals in England and Wales from 1964 onwards, and who had been re-admitted on at least one further occasion before the end of 1969. The results showed the following: Schizophrenics tended to be re-diagnosed as depressives more often than depressives were re-diagnosed as schizophrenics. The four major psychiatric categories, depressive illness, schizophrenia, dementia and alcoholism all had a diagnostic stability of about 70%. But such categories as anxiety states, paranoid states, mania, personality disorders and hysteria, had a diagnostic stability well below 50%. Paranoid states tended to be re-diagnosed as schizophrenia, confusional states as dementia and anxiety or phobic states as depression. The conclusion was that these diagnostic changes seemed to be more often due to a change of doctor than any change at all in the patient's own condition.

Kaebling and Volpe (4) investigated psychiatric diagnoses of 218 consecutive re-admissions to the same psychiatric hospital in a seven year period and came across a surprising amount of diagnostic changes. For example out of 126 schizophrenics and schizoid personalities on re-admission, only 87 were given the same diagnosis again. They concluded however, that the diagnostic stability of schizophrenic reactions and depression seemed to be more constant than personality disorders or psychoneuroses.

Odegaad (5) compared the first and last diagnoses attributed to all patients admitted to Norwegian mental hospitals for the first time between 1950 and 1954 and subsequently re-admitted at any time up to 1963. The most significant finding of this large scale study was that many patients originally diagnosed as having reactive psychosis were subsequently re-diagnosed as having either schizophrenia or manic depressive illness.

Barbigian *et al.* (6) studied the diagnostic changes of 155 patients, all of whom had visited a psychiatric hospital on four separate occasions over a two year period. They found out that 51% of the patients had had a change of diagnosis between the broad categories of schizophrenia, affective psychosis, chronic brain syndrome and 'other'. They also made an interesting observation that when a patient first contacted public medical services he was diagnosed as being 'psychotic', but when the same individual went to visit a doctor privately, he was able to lose his psychotic label immediately.

Cooper (7) studied case reports of 200 patients admitted to mental hospitals in England and Wales on four different occasions between 1954 and 1955. He found that only 54% of these patients were allocated to the same diagnostic category on all four occasions and these changes, particularly involving neurotic illness, personality disorder and addictive groups were usually attributable to a change of a doctor rather than anything to do with the patient's mental condition. In conclusion it seemed to be evident that if the patient keeps the same doctor for all his admissions, he will also keep the same diagnosis, but if he wishes to change his doctor, the chances are about even that his diagnosis will also change.

These few samples show that at least in psychiatry, patients seem to be diagnosed and re-diagnosed depending on who happens to be the doctor at the time, not as it should be, depending on the patient's own condition.

I have personally gone through this 'diagnostic merry-go-round' to perfection. It all started in 1961 when I was studying fashion and dress designing at London's St Martin's School of Art.

It happened to be our lunch hour and we students were all gathered in the school cafeteria standing about in an informal queue while waiting to be served. Suddenly, completely out of the blue, all feeling of reality started to slip away from me. All faces and figures around me became very blurred, as if I was seeing them through a heavy fog. People's voices started to thunder at me as if I was hearing them through some sort of metallic tunnel. Soon my legs started to buckle under me, my heart pounded furiously, my whole body was covered in clammy sweat and I started to shake like a leaf. Feeling that I was quite unable to control myself any more, I let my tray drop and staggered through the crowd of gaping faces towards the door, where I am sure I would have collapsed, if one of my classmates hadn't come to my rescue in time. He got hold of me and half carried and half dragged me to the nearest chair, into which I collapsed shaking all over, whilst my whole body and nerves seemed to be humming away like electric wires. I really thought that I was going to die. Soon a taxi was called to take me home, as I really felt far too weak and feeble even to contemplate drawing or designing any more that day.

On arrival at my flat I just crawled into bed, where I lay quietly, utterly stunned and perplexed over the whole terrifying incident. My flatmate arrived eventually, to whom I poured out a detailed description of what a dreadful sensation had hit me suddenly while at school. My friend had always been very much of a no-nonsense girl, so my feeble protest against calling a doctor home to see me was soon overruled. After hearing my horror story, my dear old doctor poked me around a bit, took my blood pressure and what have you, and finally came out with the verdict that there was nothing really the matter with me, except that I was suffering from a bout of anxiety neurosis brought on by stress. The suggested treatment was 'to take it easy for a while' and a prescription of Librium.

I did just as the doctor ordered. I took everything as easily as I could and dutifully swallowed my Libriums, but to no avail. The dreaded attacks just continued bouncing on me repeatedly without mercy. They always seemed to descend when I least expected them. They came over me when I was in my flat, they came over me when I was out, they hit me during my art classes, sitting on the bus, standing on the bus, going shopping and coming back from shopping. In fact these attacks hounded me just every-where, only slightly varying in severity, and needless to add, they made my life sheer hell.

Finally I got so fed up that I decided to go and see my old doctor again and ask for a thorough medical check-up, as each day I had become more and more convinced that these dreaded half-fainting sensations had to have a physiological origin, as it was just inconceivable even to contemplate any more, that 'nerves' alone can make a person as ill as I really was. Unfortunately my old doctor didn't see it that way at all, he seemed even to get a bit peeved that I had dared to challenge his diagnostic capability and he soon sent me packing with my renewed prescription of Librium.

By now, however, I was really determined to have a thorough physical and laboratory check-up at any cost. As my doctor had refused, I made a private appointment to go and see a Harley Street specialist. This doctor was a pleasant man with a pleasant manner in pleasant surround-ings, but charged unpleasantly high fees. After listening with interest to my panic-laden background, he was immediately quite agreeable to conduct very extensive physical laboratory tests.

When the results finally came back, however, to my great disappointment, they all turned out to be 'normal'. I honestly don't know what kind of an 'illness' I expected them to find, but some sort of a 'proper illness' anyhow, as I was getting fed up to the back teeth of being told by the medical professionl that there was nothing whatsoever the matter with me, or at best that my dreaded attacks were only caused by 'nerves' or by some unidentified psychosomatic hiccough.

The sad realization that the whole medical profession were unable to help me at all, depressed me a great deal, for which I was offered a prescription of anti-depressants.

From them on time and my panic attacks just dragged steadily on. Only a couple of things changed: my prescription from Librium to Valium and my diagnosis from anxiety neurosis to personality disorder. These both came about when following my old doctor's advice I went to visit a psychiatrist. The psychiatrist and I didn't seem to see eye to eye from the start. Even though I felt that the medical profession had failed me by not finding out the true cause for my dreaded panics, there was no way in the world that I could be persuaded to believe that these attacks were caused because my father fought on the Russian front when I was a mere sibling, or because my dear brother was three years my junior. I let the psychiatrist know in no uncertain terms, that at least in my opinion, he was talking utter rubbish, which naturally didn't make me very popular. However, he decided to change my prescription from Librium to Valium, and according to my old doctor, the psychiatrist was also convinced that I wasn't suffering from anxiety neurosis at all, but from a personality disorder, and a bad one at that.

Whilst these various diagnoses buzzed around me, my own symptoms didn't seem to ease at all. Finally the attacks became so severe and so much more frequent that to my great sorrow and disappointment I had to give up my fashion studies. Naturally I became extremely depressed because of it, for which I was offered yet again a prescription of anti-depressants.

Because I was unable to continue my fashion studies in London, I really didn't have very much choice other than to return to Finland, where I started working for my father. Unfortunately the dreaded panic attacks came with me.

However, I had learned then through past experience that if I felt an attack coming on, I was able to curtail it sometimes by eating something sweet or having a quick sip of some alcoholic beverage. Therefore wherever I went I carried in my handbag, besides my Valium, several bars of chocolate and a quarter bottle of brandy. You can just imagine that it didn't took too long for my father to cotton on, to his horror and disgust, that he had sired into this world a proper trainee alcoholic, which naturally caused tremendous rows at home. However hard I tried to convince him that I didn't drink alcohol because I liked it, only for medicinal purposes, he just wouldn't hear of it. Finally the rows escalated to the point that neither of us could take it any longer, so I decided to return to London.

When I had been back in London for some weeks I realized to my great surprise and relief that my panic attacks were gradually diminishing and if they did bounce on me sometimes, they seemed to do it with some delicate sensitivity, leaving me just mildly stunned, not utterly shaken as before. I could say that I started to feel almost human again, which was just great news. So when British European Airways advertised for cabin crew, I decided to apply. I became an air-stewardess in 1964. I would be lying if I was to say that I felt a hundred per cent well during my flight career, but I felt well enough to do my job, even if it meant a hell of a lot of self discipline, plenty of sleep and rest between flights and of course chocolate bars and an occasional Valium now and again. Besides frequent feelings of tiredness and an odd feeling of dizziness I felt perfectly content and happy. This feeling of quiet contentment unfortunately lasted only about three years, when my first full-blown panic attack descended on me in its full horror whilst I was on an overnight stay in Athens. From then on there seemed to be no way whatsoever in avoiding them any more. Chocolates didn't help, Valium didn't help, nothing seemed to help. Finally the attacks became so severe and frequent that I had to hand in my resignation. I felt simply devastated. All my dreams of becoming another Christian Dior had already been crushed because of some sort of anxiety neurosis or personality disorder or whatever. Now my beloved flight career was cut short for the same obscure reasons. Naturally I became depressed as hell, for which I was offered a prescription of anti-depressants. The fact which depressed me even further, was the nagging inner conviction that one of these days the medical profession were bound to find out what really was wrong with me, but by the time that happened, it would be far too late as far as I was concerned. My life was already in shreds.

After resigning from the airline I really don't know what I would have done without my friends. They all rallied round and did their utmost to cheer me up and even succeeded to some extent. Furthermore, during my flying period I had made quite a few friends all over the world and when they heard that I had left the airline, I received invitations galore to come over and visit them, and even in some instances offers to stay as long as I would like.

The following thirteen years were then spent drifting from place to place and country to country. I didn't travel alone, however, as my panic attacks and Valiums insisted on coming along.

Even though the panic attacks remained the same, the medical diagnoses seemed to change from one country to another. In Bermuda I was said to be suffering from a mild form of epilepsy, in Canada I was told that I was an agoraphobic, in Lebanon I was diagnosed as suffering from a psychosomatic disorder, in Switzerland as having cerebral arteriosclerosis and in Sweden I was told that I was a schizophrenic. As far as I was concerned, I couldn't care less any more what sort of a label or diagnosis doctors preferred to tack on me, as long as I could be assured that at the end of my appointment I would be clutching in my sweaty palm another prescription of Valium. This happened in every country, except in Sweden.

My doctor in Sweden was a funny old stick. He just refused point blank to prescribe Valium without a second opinion, which I was to acquire from a psychiatric teaching hospital in Stockholm. I pleaded, fluttered my eyelashes and pleaded again, but he didn't falter. Because I wanted my prescription very badly, I didn't have any other choice than finally to agree with him. He telephoned the teaching hospital right away and an appointment was arranged in three weeks' time. This gave me a bit of a jolt, because I was painfully aware that I had only a couple of days' supply of Valium left. I aired this grievance to my Swedish doctor, who didn't seem to be the slightest bit concerned and dismissed me with an impatient grunt.

The following three weeks were the worst of my life. My whole body became a great mass of excruciating pains. My neck alone was so stiff and painful that I couldn't walk any more, because each time I placed my heel on the floor, the pressure seemed to shoot straight to my neck muscles, creating such a massive pain reaction that tears spurted out of my eyes. I couldn't walk, I couldn't sleep either because of the distressing aches and pains. My speech became an unintelligible blabber, because my tongue seemed to have swollen to twice its original size as well as becoming stiff and rigid. If I tried to walk ignoring the pain sensation I only managed to stagger about feebly because I was shaking uncontrollably all over. My eyesight had dimmed to the extent that I kept on bumping into furniture and door-frames, or into anything which was or wasn't in my way. It was not only my body which seemed to have been shot to pieces, my mind also started to crack up. All my perceptions, such as sight, sound, touch, hearing, smell, and even taste seemed to play tricks with me. I saw things which I knew were not there. I seemed to hear sounds which I knew were not real. I really thought that I was going mad. I was a physical and mental wreck. Most of the following three weeks were spent sitting in an armchair, eyes closed, fidgeting, or rocking gently back and forth. I must have been a sight.

When my appointment with the psychiatrist finally arrived, he diagnosed me as suffering from schizophrenia. However, in order to confirm the diagnosis, he wanted me to enter the psychiatric hospital as a voluntary patient for so called 'observation purposes'. I can't remember what my answer was, but it must have been polite enough, because on leaving his surgery I had in my possession a brand new prescription of Valium. Needless to add that as soon as I was back on Valium, my 'schizophrenia' was cured straight away. What I didn't know even then for certain, I only had a faint suspicion, was that I was now a 'Valium junkie', and if I was not able to get my regular daily 'fix' of the drug, the withdrawal symptoms showed themselves as schizophrenic symptoms. I can't help wondering, how many people are at present lingering in mental institutions and being treated for schizophrenia with major tranquillisers because they have at first been treated with minor tranquillisers. Never mind, at least the drug companies ain't complaining.

The title of this chapter is not my own invention, but Dr Cheraskin's (8) who has written a very thought-provoking article under this heading in *The Physician's Handbook of Orthomolecular Medicine*. The article explains how the majority of doctors usually arrive at their diagnoses. He points out that for example bleeding, when observed by a doctor is a sign, but when it is reported by the patient it is a symptom. However, symptoms, like signs, can eventually be fitted into specific syndromes which can then be clearly identified in terms of medical textbook descriptions. So in conventional medical terms it is only at this point that diagnosis is justified. Therefore it could be said that in the traditional practice of medicine disease does not really exist until diagnosis is established. Furthermore, if several organ systems or anatomical sites are involved the syndrome might, by exclusion, be assigned to a psychologic or psychosomatic category. In short, the more symptoms you have, the more likely you will be diagnosed as suffering from a psychiatric or psychosomatic illness.

Dr Crook (9) talks about the same subject in his book *The Yeast Connection*, and concludes: 'We doctors are taught to diagnose, classify and label diseases. And most of us feel if we can put a diagnostic label on each patient who comes to us, we have done our duty. Then we feel that we can relax because thereafter the task becomes easy. All we have got to do then is to get our medical books and find recommended treatment and then prescribe either drugs, surgery or psychotherapy.' He also adds that 'the psychosomatic concept' has allowed us doctors to pretty well eliminate the category "I don't know" in cases particularly associated with the component of anxiety and depression. This psychosomatic theory gets much emphasis in medical schools so that in making diagnosis of psychosomatic illness, not only do we doctors escape the erosion of ego associated with saying "I don't know", but we do so with a diagnosis that makes us feel very educated and medically sophisticated.'

As far as my own case was concerned, there really was a flurry of different diagnoses, as besides anxiety neurosis, psychosomatic disorder, alcoholism, epilepsy, agoraphobia, depression, personality disorder, cerebral arteriosclerosis and schizophrenia, I was also blessed later on with the following: hyperventilation syndrome, allergy, hypogly-caemia (low blood sugar) and finally Post Viral Fatigue Syndrome or Myalgic Encephalomyelitis, or ME for short.

You have to admit that this is a hell of a lot of diagnoses for one individual for the same group of symptoms. However, in the later chapters I will discuss each of them briefly, so you can draw your own conclusions as to whether so many diagnoses are really justified, or could they all be placed under the same diagnostic category.

2

ANXIETY NEUROSIS, HYPERVENTILATION SYNDROME, AGORAPHOBIA ETC

Sometime in the late 1970s I finally returned to England. My panic attacks were still bothering me, but what started to bother me even more was the inconceivable fact that during all these years of suffering this fainting sensation of mine had been thrown on to so many different diagnostic hooks. The more I thought about it, the more curious I became, as to how the same ailment could be described by so many different medical terms. After pondering over the matter and questioning both the medical profession and fellow sufferers, and getting nowhere, I finally decided to take the law into my own hands and start my own medical research. In 1982 I received a small grant from The Mental Health Foundation, which gave me the opportunity to begin a thorough and comprehensive research study on mental health issues. In order to work effectively, all I needed was a roof over my head, a great deal of time, and literally hundreds of books and research studies on the subject. I also needed a group of helpful doctors and scientists around, to whom I could turn whenever I felt I got stuck. I also needed someone who could appreciate my efforts and encourage me to carry on whenever I felt that I had bitten off much more than I could chew, which in fact happened at frequent intervals. Even though the encouragement was delivered in most bizarre forms like 'Stop whining and pull yourself together', or 'I can see that you are still sitting on your mushroom and gazing at Box Hill, but when is your book going to be finished?', I am eternally grateful. Thank you TBE. However, most of all I needed the money to live during my formidable task. The grant from

28

The Mental Health Foundation was very important, because it added credibility to my efforts and opened many doors which otherwise would have been closed, but the grant was small, only a three figure sum, which was literally spent in a matter of months. So in order to keep me going I took all sorts of part-time jobs, kept asking loans from my friends, relatives, and even strangers, which wasn't a very lucrative business at all, as my requests were turned down more often than not. On close questioning the reason seemed to be the same. Everyone thought that I was now suffering from some sort of megalomania or delusion of grandeur in thinking that I alone, without any medical qualifications, would be able to put forward any credible challenge to today's mighty medical machinery. I listened to my friends, and even agreed with what was said. However, I still felt that I had to carry on regardless of all opposition because I knew all the time in my heart of hearts that what I was doing was the right thing. At some state of the game my financial situation became so desperate that I didn't have a penny to call my own and had to face the simple fact that if I didn't get some financial backing soon, there was no way I could continue my work. Carefully weighing all the odds, I finally managed to scrape together enough courage to approach our family firm Tukku-Tuormaat for a loan and the outcome brought positive results. Thank you Eko, Isto, Pyry and Lasse. You literally saved my life.

Before I get to the actual nitty-gritty of the writing, I might as well tell you what I am trying to achieve with this book. I am trying to convince the medical profession and patients alike that nutritional intervention and counselling, not drugs, is the most sensible way to help people suffering from so called 'mental illnesses'.

Sir Almroth Wright, founder with Sir Alexander Fleming of the world famous Wright-Fleming Institute at St Mary's Hospital, London, once said that a new idea in medicine has to pass through three stages: 1) When it is regarded as ridiculous. 2) When doctors say, OK, it is possible, but where is the proof? 3) When everyone dismisses it as obvious. (!0) As I see it at present, the great majority of the medical world will consider my argument as quite ridiculous, but I am just hoping that after reading this book, at least a few people will say that it is just about possible, but where is the proof? That is good enough as far as I am concerned, because let us never forget that from small acorns the mighty oak trees grow.

Now we have got that little background saga out of the way, it is time to take a closer look at conditions which are known in today's medical vocabulary as Anxiety Neurosis, Hyperventilation Syndrome, Agoraphobia, 'Petit mal' Epilepsy, Schizophrenia and Alcoholism.

In my opinion one of the best descriptions of Anxiety Neurosis can be found in Mark's and Lader's well researched study: *Anxiety States (Anxiety Neurosis): A Review.* (11) Anxiety states are characterized by the appearance of many symptoms, but few signs. The main symptoms are:

Neurological symptoms: dizziness, faintness, headaches and hot and cold flushes.

Cardiovascular symptoms: palpitations and various chest pains.

Respiratory symptoms: hyperventilation, breathing difficulties, a choking feeling and an excessive need to sigh or yawn.

Musculosceletal symptoms: muscular tremors, pins and needles and a feeling of numbness in various parts of the body.

Gastro-intestinal symptoms: dry mouth, difficulty in swallowing, vomiting and diarrhoea.

Genito-urinary symptoms: urinary frequency

General and psychiatric symptoms: nervousness, irritability, apprehension, unhappiness, feeling of fear, weakness, excessive fatigue, insomnia and nightmares.

Two thirds of patients with anxiety states are women. The age of onset follows that of agoraphobia, which is usually in the mid-twenties.

When the panic attack occurs, the patient suddenly feels ill, anxious, weak and has palpitations, lightness and dizziness in the head (as opposed to true vertigo). He feels a lump in the throat and weakness of the legs and has the illusion of walking on shifting ground. He feels as though he can't breathe, or he may breathe rapidly to the point of hyperventilation. He fears he may faint, or die, or scream out loud or 'lose control' or 'go mad'. His nervous panic may become so intense that he may be rooted to the same spot for some minutes until the intensity diminishes. The seizure may last a few minutes or several hours. It may pass off leaving the patient feeling as fit as before until the next attack occurs the same day, or weeks or even months later, or he may feel apprehensive and tremulous throughout the day. The attack may occur only once in a few days or come in successive waves every few minutes and become so troublesome that the patient is confined to bed. In more chronic forms the course is typically punctuated by remissions and relapses of varying duration. The intensity of nervousness varies from paralyzing terror to mild tension. It may be mixed with mild feelings of depression or a desire to cry and even transient suicidal ideas. Breathing difficulties are common. The complaint may be 'I can't take deep breaths', 'I can't get enough air' or 'My breath keeps catching' and the patient may in fact show repeated catches in his breathing. The opposite problem of hyperventilation may also be found. Choking and swallowing feelings are prominent and may be intensified in crowds. These anxiety states can occur in a wide variety of psychological states. It is a common feature of affective and obsessive-compulsive disorders. It can also be found in schizophrenia and epilepsy. Phobic avoidance develops usually following a stuttering series of these anxiety attacks. First comes the avoidance of the situations in which the first attack was experienced which thereafter may gradually spread to include other situations for the fear that they too may precipitate a further attack, so that the patient may progressively restrict his activities until he is virtually confined to his home . . . That is, I believe, when this term agoraphobia will be tagged on to the poor blighter.

Some years ago, when my primary concern was to learn as much as I could about Anxiety Neurosis, Agoraphobia and other anxiety related disorders, it came apparent that several other names have been, and still are, in use for these conditions. Here are some of them: DaCosta's syndrome, Soldier's heart, Irritable heart, Effort syndrome, Cardiac neurosis, Nervous exhaustion, Neurasthenia, Neurocirculatory asthenia, Phobic anxiety-depersonalization syndrome,

Anxiety neurosis, Phobic anxiety state and finally Hyper-ventilation syndrome (11, 12, 13, 14, 15) When I finally managed to haul all that on board my brain's grey matter, I was able to appreciate fully why it takes so many years to become a proper doctor.

After I learned that this Anxiety Neurosis is supposed to be the same as Hyperventilation syndrome, my life took a new turning altogether, because unlike Anxiety Neurosis, which is thought to be primarily 'in the mind' and therefore practically impossible to investigate from a scientific point of view, this Hyperventilation syndrome was supposed to be a true physiological disorder, into which I then firmly dug all my wisdom teeth, sat in my study for eternity and just did not let go.

The first account in medical history about Hyperventila-tion syndrome was provided by DaCosta in 1871 when it became known as DaCosta's syndrome or Soldier's heart. (16) This happened when DaCosta was observing 300 soldiers in the army, all of whom seemed to suffer from similar symptoms. They got out of breath easily and couldn't keep up with their comrades. They were troubled with dizziness, palpitations, chest pains and shortness of breath. The nervous manifestations of this syndrome were primarily headaches, dizziness and disturbed sleep. Possi-ble causes for this were suggested as bad nourishment, lack of sleep, excessive alcohol consumption and even the pressure of straps and tightness of the military uniform.

DaCosta's syndrome was also found in civilian life. In fact, according to Wood (17) it was found to be more common in women than in men, so this Effort syndrome, Soldier's heart or DaCosta's syndrome in male soldiers was renamed either Respiratory, or some other type of Neuro-sis, when it was affecting a female civilian. Now I under-stand why there are so many neurotic females about, as every male 'effort' becomes automatically a female 'neurosis'.

Cohen and White (12) have given a good description of the Hyperventilation syndrome: 'The faint feelings and dizzy or nervous spells are disagreeable as they vary in intensity. They may consist of a giddy sensation while walking or standing, or the patient may feel so insecure as to hold on to a nearby chair or walk close to a building wall. The patient may be seized with an acute attack of choking, palpitations, overbreathing, chest discomfort or an awareness of fear that he may faint, fall, have a heart attack or die. On account of these feelings the patient may avoid church or cinema, or if he goes to the latter, he sits near the rear in order to ensure a hasty exit if necessary. Hot, stuffy rooms and crowded department stores are of special discomfort and are usually avoided by these patients. . . . A hyperventilating Agoraphobic, I said to myself, and soldiered on with the subject.

The symptoms of the Hyperventilation syndrome are the following: (13, 15)

Neurological symptoms: faintness, dizziness, unsteadiness, dimmed and blurring of vision, 'pins and needles', numbness and tingling in various parts of the body, intolerance to bright lights and loud noises, migraine and headaches.

Musculosceletal symptoms: muscle and joint aches or pains, cramps and muscle tremors.

Respiratory symptoms: shortness of breath, tightness about the chest, excessive sighing and yawning, non-productive cough, frequent clearing of the throat, asthmatic-like breathing.

Cardiac symptoms: palpitations, 'skipped beats', various chest pains often mimicking angina.

Gastro-intestinal symptoms: dryness of the mouth, difficulty in swallowing, bloated stomach, excessive swallowing of air, belching and flatulence.

General and psychiatric symptoms: chronic and easy fatigability, weakness, irritability, poor concentration and performance of tasks, exhaustion, sleep disturbances and nightmares, anxiety, tension, apprehension, depersonalization, feeling of unreality, phobic states and panic attacks.

The five most common symptoms of Hyperventilation syndrome according to Wheeler (18) are 1) Palpitations. 2) Breathlessness. 3) Tires easily. 4) Nervousness. 5) Chest pains.

The following points about Hyperventilation syndrome have also been raised by Hardonk and Beumer (13) and Cohen and White (12): No definite relationship was found between psychiatric disturbances and Hyperventilation syndrome, because at rest, or not having an attack, patients were indistinguishable in a clinical sense from 'normals'. The first clear cut symptoms rarely appear before 18 and after 35 years of age, the mean age of onset being about 25 years, twice as many women than men suffering from it. The actual cause of this disorder is unknown, but physiological changes consist of a higher pulse rate and elevated lactic acid concentration after muscular exercise. It is thought to be a fairly common disorder, and it may also be hereditary, as it has been found that when one parent was affected there could be a 37.7% chance that a child will also be affected. And if both parents were affected the chance of a child being affected rises to 61.9%. It can be also a very persistent disorder, because according to Herman *et al.* (19) 40% of 34 hyperventilating children were still hyperventilating twenty-five years later. In one study it was found that out of 861 psychiatric patients 27% were found to be hyperventilators.

Now, if we were to put our faith in these studies, a great chunk of the world's population are panting away in excess to their detriment, males through a sheer effort and females because they are neurotic.

When we have now sorted out these hyperventilating anxiety neurotics, I would like to put this ailment, known today as Agoraphobia, under the microscope.

The term Agoraphobia is derived from two Greek words. Agora, meaning a place of assembly and Phobos, meaning of fear. It was coined by Westphal (20) in 1872, who published a monograph *Die Agoraphobie* in which three male patients were described with the following symptoms: Impossibility of walking through certain streets or squares, or possibility of doing so only with resultant dread or anxiety. The patient experienced great comfort from companionship of men, or even inanimate objects such as a vehicle or a cane. The use of beer or wine also allowed the patient to pass through a feared locality with comparative comfort. One man sought, without immoral motives, the companionship of a prostitute as far as his own door. Some localities seemed to be more difficult to access than others, the patient walking far in order not to traverse them. One patient had also a dislike of crossing a certain bridge. He feared that he would fall in the water. This patient had also an apprehension of impending insanity.

Two years before Westphal, in 1870, Benedict (31) had created for the same syndrome the name *Platzschwindel*, which could be translated 'dizziness in public places'. Westphal won the day, however, and the term Agoraphobia was universally adopted. A pretty bad start for all today's agoraphobics, as anyone who is familiar with Agoraphobia knows, that agoraphobics are not frightened of a market, or assembly place *per se*, but only scared stiff of that *platzschwindel*-feeling, which could arise whilst standing in any of them. More confusing still is the fact that two out of three of Westphal's patients were also said to be epileptics, so this little-read, but much quoted paper was really devoted to a discussion of epilepsy and its link to neurotic symptoms . . .

Literally hundreds of research studies and books have been published on Agoraphobia in recent years and some more useful than others. This quaint little sample is definitely one of the others: 'The anxiety attacks of a female patient with agoraphobia and crowd phobia had the unconscious and definite purpose of making her appear weak and helpless to all passers-by. Analysis showed that the unconscious motive of her exhibitionism was a deep hostility originally directed towards her mother, then reflected onto herself: "Everybody look . . . " her anxiety seemed to proclaim, "My mother let me come into the world in this helpless condition, without a penis".' (22)

Goldstein and Chambless (23) divide Agoraphobia into two separate categories: a) Complex Agoraphobia, where 'fear of fear' is the most central element, often combined with low levels of self-sufficiency, whether due to anxiety, lack of skills or a combination of both. b) Simple Agoraphobia, where symptoms are precipitated by panic attacks due to some endocrine fluctuation, the pharmacological effects of drugs or a physical condition such as Hypoglycaemia.

Agoraphobia begins normally between the ages of 18 and 35. The mean age of onset is about 28 years of age and approximately 88% of agoraphobics are female. (24) We received similar results when in 1982 Dr Rippere and I conducted a postal survey amongst 240 agoraphobic sufferers with the help of The Mental Health Foundation's grant. Dr Rippere's questionnaire was designed to establish whether there could be a connection between Agoraphobia, Hypoglycaemia, an excessive caffeine consumption and food/chemical allergies. When I was planning my part of the questionnaire, I was still obsessed by this Hyperventilation syndrome, but can you blame me, as both symptoms of Agoraphobia and Hyperventilation syndrome seem to be the same. In addition, because 'agoraphobic avoidance behaviour' can be so erratic, as the sufferer can often visit one shop without any particular difficulty, but when he enters another, he is soon overwhelmed with a full-blown panic. Furthermore, when an agoraphobic is accompanied during his excursions by a relative or a friend, he may feel reasonably calm, but if he has to go out on his own, he may literally go to pieces. In short, as I reckoned that we carry our breaths around everywhere we go, it just might then be the governing factor as to whether we experience a panic attack or not. For all these reasons when I was planning my questionnaire for agoraphobic sufferers, besides asking a lot of 'hyperventilating questions', I also included with it a long list of symptoms which were said to be directly caused by Hyperventilation syndrome. Dr Rippere compiled her own separate questionnaire, which was planned to be sent out with mine using the same envelope. When she had finished her questionnaires and I had collected them from the Institute of Psychiatry, you could have blown me down with a feather, when I noticed that her symptom list was nearly identical to mine. This jolting discovery made me pull my socks up good and proper, and from then on every molecule of me was frantically engaged in trying to unravel this wonder of medical mystery.

Now a few words about epilepsy, which can be divided into two basic types: A major fit or 'grand mal' epilepsy and a minor fit or 'petit mal' epilepsy, the former being a syndrome and the latter only a symptom, which can be found in both Hypoglycaemia and Allergies and which is also sometimes known as non-convulsive, or temporal lobe epilepsy.

Harper and Roth (14) compared 30 patients suffering from temporal lobe epilepsy with 30 patients suffering from phobic anxiety-depersonalization syndrome and came to the conclusion that both in phobic states and temporal lobe epileptic states the verbal description of the actual 'attack' can be so varied that on description alone, it seems to be almost impossible to distinguish who is suffering from what. So how do doctors then decide who is epileptic and who is not? I don't like to be the bearer of bad news, but the diagnosis seems to hang merely on this woolly statement 'clinical experience'. So it seems that if you carry your complaints to 'an epileptic oriented doctor' you may leave his surgery as an epileptic, but if your doctor seems to be more keen on 'phobic anxiety-depersonalization syndrome' you might leave his surgery as an agoraphobic.

Now a few words about a condition known as Schizophrenia, which yet again is only a symptom, not a disease and which presently is thought to affect around one person in a hundred in the world. It affects women and men equally of all races and walks of life, and usually begins in early adult life. (25) The symptoms include false beliefs, such as thinking that people talk about him or are against him, when they are not. The sufferer may be hearing voices that nobody else can hear. He may see, taste, smell and feel textures that are not real. The sufferer may think that events, objects or people can control his thoughts, actions and his life. He may think that he is somebody else, maybe some famous person. His thinking may be confused and muddled and his speech may be hard to follow. He may show a complete lack of feeling or indifference towards other people. He may show a general lack of interest towards the outside world, causing him sometimes to withdraw from society entirely. These symptoms can occur in widely different combinations and with varying intensity. Schizophrenias, or these disperceptions of unknown cause have also been divided into so called 'positive' and 'negative' schizophrenic symptoms. The 'negative symptoms' are said to include all the dull and quiet bits like inactivity, flatness of emotions, apathy, withdrawal, listlessness and general withdrawal of human contact. The 'positive symptoms' on the other hand include all the noisy and riotous bits like hallucinations, delusions of grandeur and both disturbing and disturbed behaviour. Many schizophrenic sufferers deny that they are ill. At present there are no laboratory examinations that could 'diagnose' schizophrenia. So whether one acquires the label or not seems to hang again primarily on the doctor concerned, whether he 'favours' the diagnosis or not.

Now a valid point of debate could be, whether a certain 'abnormal behaviour' really qualifies for the diagnosis of schizophrenia, and furthermore, should a doctor insist on treating a patient for schizophrenia, who thinks that he isn't schizophrenic and who has not even asked for help. The National Schizophrenic Fellowship write in their leaflet that schizophrenia is not being stupid, weak, lazy or violent. Only a few people who tend to make headlines may be violent because of their illness, but most people with schizophrenia are shy and retiring. Now, at least in my opinion, any shy and retiring schizophrenic who denies being a schizophrenic and who doesn't run amok physically harming people or himself, should be left alone and not be made even more shy and retiring by the use of major tranqillisers, known in the trade as 'a chemical straight jacket' or a 'liquid cosh'. Naturally whether the alleged sufferer could be left drugless, primarily depends on the ability or willingness of those closest to him to be able to tolerate his 'strange behaviour', which may be often quite impossible.

Finally a few words about alcoholics, or fully qualified drunks as they are known in some circles, who are said to be people who pursue ways of behaving which include excessive continuous, or excessive recurrent drinking of alcohol. Both the behaviour and the drink may cause both physical damage and emotional distress to the alcoholic and other people around him. In spite of this he just continues his undesirable behaviour, nobody understanding why.

3

ON BEING SANE IN INSANE PLACES

I sometimes wonder what would have happened to me all those years ago in Sweden if I had agreed to enter the psychiatric ward for 'observation purposes'. However, as I am still lacking that experience, I will review here an interesting, but quite disturbing study by Rosenhan. (26)

Dr Rosenhan and his colleagues wanted to find out what could happen to so called 'sane people', or people who had never suffered symptoms of any serious psychiatric illness, during and after gaining admission to psychiatric hospitals in the United States. The group of pseudopatients consisted of three females and five males. The youngest of the group was a student of psychology, and the remaining seven consisted of three psychiatrists, a painter, a paediatric doctor and a housewife. The hospital settings were similarly varied as they selected twelve psychiatric hospitals from five different states on the East and West coasts of the United States. Some hospitals were old and shabby, some were quite modern. Some had good staff-patient ratios, some were quite understaffed. Some were research orientated, some were not. Only one of the selected psychiatric hospitals was in private hands. All in all, these hospitals presented a good cross section of psychiatric establishments. All admissions were done secretly i.e. the hospitals concerned were not informed about the experiment. It was also agreed beforehand that each pseudopatient would have to get out by his own devices, that is, to be able to convince the hospital staff that he was sane. In order to be admitted all pseudopatients decided to complain of the same symptoms, which was to tell the psychiatrist, that he was hearing 'hollow' or 'empty' voices. Also during admission, the only details the pseudopatients decided to change were their names and the nature of their occupation. No other alterations to their personal histories, background or circumstances were made. Everyone selected a different hospital and each of the pseudopatients was admitted in without any difficulty whatsoever.

As soon as the pseudopatient was admitted, he started to behave as he normally behaved, speaking to other patients and staff as he always did. When asked by the staff how he was feeling, he answered back politely that he was now quite well thank you, as the 'hollow' and 'empty' voices had now stopped. However, this bit of good news was completely ignored. Besides talking to other patients the pseudo-patients also spent a lot of time writing down carefully all their observations about the ward, fellow patients and the staff. Initially these notes were taken secretly, as they thought if the hospital staff found their notes, they would surely insist on knowing what they were writing about and realize that they had entered psychiatric hospitals on false pretences. It soon became clear, however, that none of the staff were in the slightest bit concerned about their note-taking, let alone coming over and enquiring what their writing was about. They could even leave their notes quite undisturbed in the day-room as no one seemed to show any interest. The only people who seemed to notice were the fellow patients who frequently remarked in passing: 'You are not crazy. You must be a journalist or a professor who is checking up on the hospital.' The closest any staff member came to questioning the notes was when one pseudopatient asked the doctor what kind of medication he was receiving and began to write down the answer. 'You need not write it down,' he was told gently, 'If you have any trouble remembering it, just ask me again.' After the experiment was over, however, and the pseudopatients were able to check their medical records, three of them showed a regular daily entry: 'Patient engages in writing behaviour.' This seemed to confirm the disturbing fact that once you have been thought of as 'mentally ill', anything you choose to do from then on, seems to be observed through this ridiculous psychiatric jargon. The following story is another sample of the same: A group of patients were sitting and chatting away outside the cafeteria entrance an hour before lunch time. When a psychiatrist saw the patients, he pointed at them explaining to some young medical students who had accompanied him, that such behaviour was characteristic of the 'oral-acquisitive nature of their mental illness.' It never seemed to occur to him that the patients might have been a bit hungry, but furthermore to the point, that there are very few things to look forward to in any psychiatric hospital except meal times.

The length of hospitalization between the eight pseudo-patients ranged from 7 to 52 days, with an average of 19 days, during which time they received altogether 2100 different pills, including Elavil, Stelazine and Thorazine. This medication was not swallowed however, but pocketed and eventually deposited in the lavatory.

Generally the psychiatric staff tried to avoid any continuing contact with any of the patients., By far their most common response seemed to be either a very brief reply to any question asked, and even this was usually done while they were hurriedly on the move. More often than not, most questions were just ignored. An encounter took frequently the following bizarre form: Pseudopatient: 'Pardon me doctor, could you tell me when I would be eligible for grounds privileges?' Doctor: 'Good morning Dave. How are you today?' (Doctor moves off without waiting for reply.)

On the patient's point of view, powerlessness is evident everywhere. The patient is also deprived of many of his legal rights by dint of his psychiatric label. His freedom of movement is restricted. He cannot initiate contact with the staff, but is only allowed to respond if staff approach him first. Personal privacy is minimal. The patient's quarters and possessions can be entered and examined by any staff member for whatever reason. His personal file is also available to be read by any member of the staff, including 'helping volunteers', or whoever chooses to read it, regardless of their therapeutic relationship to him. Even the most intimate privacy was lacking, as bathrooms or lavatories may have no doors.

At times depersonalization reached such proportions that pseudopatients had the sense that they were completely invisible, or at least unworthy of account. For example a nurse would unbutton her uniform in order to adjust her bra in the presence of an entire ward of viewing men, not trying to be seductive, but simply because she didn't seem to notice them. Members of staff also frequently stood in front of a patient, pointing directly at him and loudly discussing him as if he did not exist. Two of the pseudo-patients on admission even had their physical examination in a semi-public room, while staff members went about their business as if nothing was happening. On the wards attendants delivered verbal and even sometimes physical abuse to a patient in the presence of other patients, while a pseudopatient was busily writing everything down. This abusive behaviour terminated immediately however, when another staff member was known to be coming, as staff are credible witnesses, but patients are not.

Despite the fact that immediately after admission all pseudopatients behaved in the psychiatric ward quite 'normally' or just as they would behave in their everyday lives nobody, except other patients doubted their insanity. However, when the pseudopatients finally managed to get themselves discharged, every one of them was discharged with a diagnosis 'schizophrenia in remission', which means that the person is still considered as being a schizophrenic, but only behaving 'normally' for the time being.

After completing the first part of their research, Dr Rosenhan and his team decided to conduct another experiment: the staff of a psychiatric teaching hospital was told that at some time during the following three months one or more pseudopatients would attempt to be admitted into the hospital. That in mind, each staff member was asked to rate very carefully every single patient who presented himself for admission, according to the likeli-hood that the patient may be a pseudopatient. During the three month period 193 patients were admitted, out of which 41 patients were alleged with confidence to be pseudopatients by at least one of the staff members, 23 patients were considered to be suspect by at least one psychiatrist and finally 19 of the patients were considered to be pseudopatients by one psychiatrist and at least one of the members of staff. During this experiment, however, the truth was that all patients were in fact 'real' and none of Dr Rosenhan's team had tried to gain admission.

These experiments show clearly that it seems to be extremely difficult to distinguish between so-called 'sanity' and 'insanity'. Furthermore, nobody is 'sane' all the time. We all lose our tempers sometimes 'for no good reason'. Likewise we all occasionally get depressed or anxious for no reason we can really specify. Similarly according to Dr Rosenhan and his team, the so called 'insane' were not always 'insane', as the 'bizarre behaviour', for which reason the fellow patients had been admitted into the psychiatric wards in the first place, seemed to constitute only a small fraction of their total behaviour pattern. In fact most of the patients behaved quite sanely the majority of the time, even sometimes more so than the staff, as they were at least able to recognize pseudopatients as 'normals', whereas the staff didn't even have a clue.

The results of these experiments make one think how many 'sane people', but not recognized as such, are at the moment lingering in our psychiatric institutions, and furthermore, how many sane people are presently walking around who have been stigmatized for life by well-intentioned, but nevertheless erroneous psychiatric diagnoses, such as 'schizophrenia in remission', 'psychopathic personality', or some such thing. Whether we like it or not, the disturbing truth is that a broken leg is something one recovers from, but so called 'mental illness' allegedly endures for ever and also carries with it an unpleasant personal, legal and social stigma, leaving the poor individual to remain as a second class citizen for the rest of his life. As Dr Rosenhan puts it: 'The mentally ill are society's lepers . . . ' This being the case I have never really been able to understand why individuals enter psychiatric institutions in the first place. It has just got to be one of the following two reasons: Either the mental symptoms a person experiences bother him so much that he enters voluntarily to a psychiatric hospital in the hope of being 'cured', or alternatively, the mental symptoms a person experiences bother other people so much that he is sent to a psychiatric institution whether he likes it or not.

Now let's see what could really be the matter with the poor blighters. Marshall (27) studied case records of 175 patients admitted to a psychiatric hospital and found out that 44% of the patients had a physical condition in need of attention, 22% suffered from a physical condition which was a direct cause of their 'mental illness', 6% resulted from it, and in a further 15% of the patients a physical and psychiatric disorder occurred together but were not seemingly related.

Herridge (28) studied physical disorders in 209 patients in a psychiatric hospital and found out that 5% suffered on admission from a major physical illness. In 21% a physical illness was a direct cause for their 'mental illness', 8% resulted from it and in a further 16% physical and psychiatric illness occurred together but were not related.

Maguire *et al.* (29) investigated 200 patients admitted to a psychiatric hospital and discovered that a physical illness was present in 33.5% of the patients. For example one male and one female patient, both treated for depression were found to be suffering from severe rheumatoid arthritis. One schizophrenic female patient was found to be suffering from severe iron deficiency anaemia. One female patient who was treated for an anxiety state, was found to be suffering from epilepsy. Two female and one male patient, all of whom were in the psychiatric hospital because of personality disorder, were found to be suffering from diabetes, severe acne and severe glaucoma respectively. By the way, this rating 'severe' was made when it was thought that the physical illness was at least comparable in importance to the psychiatric illness . . . At least sanity prevails somewhere, because couldn't it just be conceivable that a severely arthritic person would also be depressed? And as far as the severely anaemic schizophrenic was concerned, the poor blighter just might not be able to think straight because her brain's blood was so badly defective. Furthermore, I can also imagine an anxious epileptic. However, my heart bled particularly for those folks who had been shut into a psychiatric institution for the treatment of their 'personality disorder', because of their severe acne, diabetes or glaucoma. Let's face it, if my own face was covered with unsightly pimples, or my eyesight failing because of severe glaucoma, or even if I were a diabetic, the last thing I would need treatment for would be my personality.

Comroe (30) made a follow-up study of 100 patients diagnosed as suffering from neurosis. This study showed that 24% of the patients presented a definite evidence of physical illness, which, in most cases had already been present during the original admission to the psychiatric hospital. Comroe felt that this diagnosis 'neurosis' is becoming now too common, not only among very busy general practitioners, but also in the hospital wards and out-patient departments, as it seems to be popular malpractice to relegate all patients with somewhat bizarre symptoms complexes, without significant evidence of any organic disease, into the category of 'neurotics'. Furthermore he felt that the 'neurotic' is apt to be regarded by the general practitioner as a nuisance, rather than as a sick man which he may indeed be, as his study showed that some of the 'neurotic patients' were in fact suffering from such physical disorders as pellagra, diabetes, gall bladder disease, ulcers, chronic appendicitis etc. He concluded his study by stating that if a diagnosis of 'neurosis' is made, a careful periodic physical check-up should be performed to make sure that the possible presence of a physical disease is excluded.

Hall *et al.* (31) gave a thorough physical examination to 100 patients admitted to a psychiatric hospital in order to find out if a physical cause could be found as the reason for their mental illness. Out of 100 patients 80% were found to have a previously undetected physical illness requiring medical treatment. In 46% of these the physical illness was thought to be causative, or at least contributory to their psychiatric symptoms, 61% of these showed an immediate clearing of their psychiatric symptoms as soon as their underlying physical disorder was treated. Here are some examples: 'Schizophrenia' was found to be directly caused by such underlying physical disorders as folic acid deficiency, hypothyroidism, hyperthyroidism, severe anaemia, diabetes, malnutrition and hypoglycaemia. Some of the schizophrenics were also found to be suffering from allergic conditions and candida albicans i.e. yeast infection. Depressive disorders were found to be caused by diabetes, hypothryroidism, hyperthyroidism, hypoglycaemia, anaemia, and porphyria, the latter leading to low zinc levels. Personality disorders and hysterical personalities were found to be caused by diabetes and hypothyroidism. Candida albicans was also found to be present. Acute psychotic reactions were caused by hypothyroidism, severe anaemia, diabetes etc. In this group multiple allergies and candida albicans was also found to be present. Organic brain syndrome was found to be caused by chronic lead poisoning, malnutrition etc. Food allergies were also found to be present. Acute anxiety neurosis was directly caused by hypoglycaemia. 13% of the patients were found to be substantially malnourished and had evidence of vitamin and other dietary deficiencies. 8% of these patients got well by eating a proper diet with added nutritional supplementation alone, while the remaining 5% required additional treatment.

These studies indicate clearly that at least one quarter of patients lingering presently in psychiatric wards are not even mentally ill, but suffer from a physical illness which causes them various 'mental symptoms'. In my opinion however, the percentage is much higher, as I firmly believe that the majority of mental problems are often only chemical problems, and once the brain's chemistry has been corrected, the 'mental illness' is corrected as well. But more about that later.

4

FROM RESPIRATORY ALKALOSIS TO METABOLIC ACIDOSIS

I have to warn you that this chapter may be particularly boring, but I feel I have to write it because both Hyperventilation syndrome (Respiratory Alkalosis) and excessive lactic acid accumulation (Metabolic Acidosis) have been frequently suggested in current medical literature as being some of the major physiological causes for various anxiety related disorders (11, 12, 15, 32, 33, 34, 35, 36, 37, 38, 39) Anybody who finds the following tedious should skip this chapter and move swiftly to the next.

In order to clarify a bit how my mind works, I would like to tell you a little story: This happened many years ago when I was first taught to drive a car. After some necessary preliminaries my driving instructor led me to the driver's seat and started, at least in my opinion, an enormously boring and complicated chin-wag, while pointing at the gadgets and knobs on the dashboard. When he had finished, he asked me promptly to start the engine. Instead of doing as he asked, I just sat there, utterly puzzled, just staring at the knobs and dials which, at least as far as I was concerned, didn't seem to make any sense whatsoever. As I just sat there fidgeting and sighing with my eyebrows knitting furiously through sheer frustration, the instructor naturally wanted to know what on earth was the matter. Feeling a bit sheepish I had to tell him the honest truth, that as far as I could see, there was no conceivable way in which I could ever learn to use all those umpteen knobs and gadgets before I was told clearly how they all related to the mighty engine itself. My instructor gave me a very bored sideways glance, but nevertheless heaved his posterior out of the car, opened the bonnet and beckoned me to join him.

The following hour was spent in an animated conversation about the fascinating mysteries of a car engine and its mechanics in relation to those bits and knobs on the dashboard and on the floor.

This little tale describes well where, at least in my opinion, current medical thinking, as well as this diagnosis of 'hyperventilation syndrome' has gone somewhat wrong, as this hyperventilation syndrome is just a mere 'knob on the dashboard' directly connected to the 'engine' itself, which in this context is the whole human body and its biochemistry. Therefore in simple terms: If the engine is playing up, it is a complete waste of time just to fiddle with the knobs. In order for me to arrive at such a simple explanation, I can thank only various books on biochemistry, literally hundreds of different research studies, which were kindly supplied to me by the BMA library, several scientifically minded doctors, my own ferret-like mind, not forgetting TBE and his continuous encouragement by telling me to stop whining and get on with it. To cap it all, I thoroughly enjoyed my scientific journey, as I found human biochemistry one of the most fascinating subjects I have ever encountered. Just finding out that we are nothing much else but an immensely complicated bag of salty water, cells, enzymes, hormones etc. zapping around in a leathery skin, supported by a skeleton and a tube running from mouth to anus, was a revelation not to be sniffed at. All my friends who, at the best of times, had frequent doubts as to whether everything was as it should be between my earlobes, were now convinced that I had finally flipped. Wherever I went, I had a sort of tightly concentrated faraway look on my face, broken occasionally by little yelps of 'I think I've got it', 'I can't believe it' or 'Quite incredible.' I can only describe this time as experiencing frequent scientific orgasms which I found really enjoyable . . . However, to come down to earth again.

Breathing has the following basic functions: to charge haemoglobin with oxygen and to get rid of excess carbon dioxide. However, carbon dioxide is not only a waste gas, but an important substance for the body mechanism, because when it is mixed with body fluids it produces carbonic acid. This carbonic acid with bicarbonate has a vital function in preserving the correct internal acid-base balance in the body fluids which is known as hydrogen ion concentration or pH for short. Our body is a very demanding piece of machinery and in order for it to work properly, besides needing food, water, oxygen and a correct temperature, it is also very keen to keep a correct acid-base balance. This balance, or pH is maintained at its normal value of 7.4 by buffer systems of which the balance of bicarbonate (base or alkaline) with carbonic acid (acid) is quantatively the most important. (40) Besides keeping a correct acid-base balance, carbon dioxide also influences the transmission of nerve impulses and regulates breathing by direct action on the respiratory centre in the brain stem. It also controls the blood flow to the brain, as a low level of arterial carbon dioxide may cause constriction of blood vessels which in turn can reduce oxygen availability. Reduced carbon dioxide may also decrease the amount of oxygen available from haemoglobin and slow down its release. Hence the net result on the brain could be less blood delivering less oxygen and delivering it more slowly, which in turn may cause feelings of dizziness, faintness and visual disturbances. As Dr Lum (36) describes it: The cerebral effects of low carbon dioxide level is at least as serious as the effects of Hypoglycaemia (Low blood sugar) which in many respects it resembles.

Now if you off-load an excessive amount of carbon dioxide by overbreathing, the plasma pH rises, leading to a condition known as Respiratory Alkalosis (Hyperventilation syndrome). If this continues, in a matter of some days, sometimes even hours, this excessive carbon dioxide loss is followed by renal excretion of bicarbonate in order to restore this disturbed pH balance to its normal value of 7.4. This condition where the pH is back to its normal value, but where now both carbonic acid and bicarbonate are low, is known as a Compensated Respiratory Alkalosis, which is usually found in people living in high altitudes. (41) This condition however, doesn't necessarily cause any symptoms, because people have adapted to it, but this acclimatization will usually take a fair amount of time. Now these folks who are said to be suffering from Hyperventilation syndrome are believed somehow to acquire a habit of breathing in such a way that their arterial day-to-day level of carbon dioxide is persistently low, or alternatively their breathing response to any kind of stimuli is exaggerated, so that they are constantly on the threshold of chronic 'hyperventilating symptoms', which I have already been talking about in the previous chapter. The diagnosis for this Respiratory Alkalosis or Hyperventilation syndrome is the so-called 'Overbreathing Provocation Test', where the patient is asked to pant vigorously about 40–60 breaths per minute, for about three minutes. If symptoms develop, which the patient recognizes as similar to his original symptoms, he is said to be suffering from a Hyperventilation syndrome. If during the test the symptoms become very severe, the patient is instructed to breath through a paper bag for a while, which means placing a paper bag firmly over one's nose and mouth and continuing to breathe into it until the symptoms disappear. The aim of this bag-rebreathing method is to try to retain some of the carbon dioxide which was initially lost by overbreathing. The treatment for chronic Hyperventilation syndrome is to teach the patient slow abdominal breathing with very little upper chest movement. The rate of breathing aimed for at rest is about 8–12 average breaths a minute. This new breathing pattern is then thought to allow the respiratory centre to readjust to a higher level of carbon dioxide, when symptoms should also diminish. However, one thing which should be always remembered is that low blood sugar or Hypoglycaemia augments the effects of overbreathing, therefore no diagnostic significance should be attached to this Hyperventilation Provocation Test if the patient's blood sugar is lower than 120mgm%. Furthermore, low blood sugar retards the response to breathing re-training and the patient will only respond if he is first asked to modify his diet in order to combat the hypoglycaemic tendency. (42) One more fact which I find very interesting, is that in order to diagnose Hypoglycaemia by using the six hour Glucose Tolerance Test, the patient is also asked to hyperventilate, or alternatively exercise, which will always bring on symptoms which otherwise might remain hidden . . . Now there is food for thought, because at least as long as I have been involved with people diagnosed as suffering from Hyperventilation syndrome, none of them have had their blood sugar monitored at any time, let alone during the overbreathing provocation test. Therefore could it be just conceivable that the horrendous symptoms which were experienced during the provocation test, were not experienced because the patient was suffering from Hyperventilation syndrome, but because he was in fact Hypoglycaemic? But more about that later . . . .

Another thing which makes me feel not at all at ease with this Hyperventilating syndrome, particularly concerning the treatment i.e. this breathing re-training, is the fact, that even if we can indeed learn to control both the frequency and depth of our breathing to some extent voluntarily, our respiratory centre, which is controlled by so many different factors, seems to possess a rhythmic activity of its own. There is now quite enough evidence that the breathing centre which is sensitive to carbon dioxide is quite separate from the centre which is responsible for the reflex adjustment of breathing. For example, a release of neurotransmitters such as adrenaline and noradrenaline will stimulate breathing immediately. A rise in blood pressure tends to depress breathing and a fall in blood pressure tends to stimulate it. Our breathing can also be controlled by various drugs, both prescribed and non-prescribed, such as tranquillisers, nicotine, caffeine etc. (43) In fact I have talked to quite a few patients who are on various medications including tranquillisers, and who, at the same time, have been attending breathing re-training classes, sometimes for years, without any success whatsoever. Some of them were getting pretty fed up to say the least, which I can well appreciate, because personally I can think of nothing more tiresome than to keep counting one's breath from one minute to the next, hour after hour, day after day, for months or years on end, and not getting any better as the result . . . . Therefore my suggestion would be that you breathe as you please. Now having said that, at least try not to pant vigorously, as besides that you might be Hypoglycaemic and panting brings on the attack, you will also lose that precious carbon dioxide, which in turn makes you lose that precious bicarbonate, and before you know where you are, you may not suffer from Hyperventilation syndrome or

Respiratory Alkalosis any more, but Metabolic Acidosis due to an excessive lactic acid accumulation . . . . This comes about because the lost serum bicarbonate is soon replaced by lactic acid, which has been found to happen in some human subjects only after a few minutes of hyperventilation. (44) Therefore it could be said that the terminal stage of Hyperventilation syndrome or Respiratory Alkalosis is Metabolic Acidosis. (41, 45) However, in order to prevent Respiratory Alkalosis from becoming Metabolic Acidosis, all one has to do, is to replace the lost carbon dioxide by, for example, using the 'paper-bag method' (46) or alternatively, replace the lost bicarbonate by some alkaline forming substance such as sodium bicarbonate. (41, 45) Now you might remember I was discussing this Overbreathing Provocation Test in order to diagnose Hyperventilation syndrome. If during the test symptoms become very severe the patient is asked to breathe through a paper bag for a while to abolish them. The mind boggles, but I would put my money on it, that it is not so much the Hyperventilation syndrome or Anxiety Neurosis, Soldier's Heart, Effort syndrome etc, which causes the dreaded symptoms, but this lactic acid accumulation or Metabolic Acidosis. Somebody kindly correct me if I am wrong . . . Now if I am indeed right, we might as well look more into this Metabolic Acidosis business.

Roberts *et al.* (41) writes: 'The condition which is most often confused with Respiratory Alkalosis, and has most often resulted in mistaken diagnosis, is Metabolic Acidosis, as in both of these conditions there is a decrease in carbon dioxide and the patient may show some degree of hyperventilation. The differentiation of Respiratory Alkalosis and Metabolic Acidosis may be resolved by measuring the pH and carbon dioxide concentration of the blood and by calculating PCO_2 (carbon dioxide partial pressure). However, since the pH determinations may be difficult to obtain, this is often impossible, and unless the measurement is carried out meticulously by a highly skilled technician, the pH may be dangerously misleading.'

So it looks now that we hyperventilate because our body is in an acidic state, which happens for example during an allergic reaction, of which I will be talking about later. We also seem to hyperventilate when our blood pressure falls, or during the release of such neurotransmitters like adrenaline and noradrenaline, the former being released in abundance during a hypoglycaemic episode, of which I will also be talking later. We also either hyperventilate or hypoventilate when we have a cigarette, a cup of coffee or have swallowed our tranquillisers, or any other pills and potions our doctor has decided to prescribe to us. All in all, we either overbreathe or underbreathe merrily away for all sorts of reasons. And to cap it all, while we are at it and haven't got a meticulous highly skilled technician handy to measure our pH, carbon dioxide and PC02 precisely at that time, we would be surely at a loss as to whether we were hyperventilating because we are suffering from Respiratory Alkalosis or Metabolic Acidosis. I must say that it is just as well that our body chemistry is in charge of that breathing business, as it would surely be pretty nerve racking to leave it entirely to our own conscious command. As it just might happen that one particular day we might be so busy with shopping, paying bills, shouting at the kids and so forth, that we might simply forget to breathe altogether.

You might remember that I mentioned at the beginning of this chapter, that not only Hyperventilation syndrome or Respiratory Alkalosis, but also Metabolic Acidosis, particularly excessive lactic acid accumulation has been put forward as a reason for various anxiety related disorders. (38, 39)

Now that we have examined Hyperventilation syndrome near to perfection and how Respiratory Alkalosis can lead to Metabolic Acidosis and furthermore, that it is somewhat doubtful, at least to me, that this Respiratory Alkalosis is particularly responsible for the symptoms production, the culprit being instead Metabolic Acidosis, primarily an excessive lactic acid accumulation . . . . Now that we have sorted this one out, it may be pertinent to have a brief look at whether other physiological conditions, besides over-breathing, can lead to Metabolic Acidosis and to an excesive accumulation of lactic acid.

Because I don't want to become more boring than I am already, I have decided to write this next bit using only very brief statements. The reference section of this book is then for those heavy intellectuals who wish to delve very deeply into the mysteries of our cellular constituents.

Lactic acidosis is considered to be one of the most common causes of Metabolic Acidosis. (47) It could be said that an excessive lactic acid accumulation is simply related to the factors which will stimulate the production of lactate to the levels the body is comparatively incapable of removing. The following factors are capable of stimulating lactic acid production: First of all overbreathing, which we have already discussed at length, and infusion of pyruvate, which is the only known precursor of lactate. Also infusion of glucose, insulin, adrenaline and, naturally, muscular exercise. (44, 48, 49) In fact lactate levels in human subjects are known to rise already in anticipation, before the actual beginning of muscle movement. Similarly it falls after a resting period of about one hour or so. (46) Some toxic substances, particularly alcohol, which is known chemically as ethanol or ethyl alcohol, can be the cause of excessive accumulation of lactic acid. The same goes for an excessive ingestion of fructose or fruit sugar. Dr Randolph (50) and Dr Philpott (51) in turn have found that an excessive cellular acidosis can be caused during a maladaptive reaction to any foods or chemicals a person is allergic. A suggested treatment to this reaction consists of an alkaline forming drink of a mixture of sodium and potassium bicarbonate (2:1), stirred in an 8-ounce glass of water.

Both lactic and pyruvic acids are directly connected with the body's carbohydrate metabolism, therefore any condition which hinders the body's ability to metabolize carbohydrates properly can also lead to an excess of lactic acid.

In our body's carbohydrate metabolism two energy cycles interact: one is NAD, or that of hydrogen transfer, and the other is ATP, or phosphate transfer, both of which need to work properly an adequate supply of vitamins and minerals, particularly B-group vitamins must be present. Therefore it is also possible that an excessive lactic acid accumulation is caused by a lack of these essential nutrients. (52)

I must stress here, however, that this lactic acid isn't just a mere nuisance to be got rid of at any cost, as when it is produced in our body in correct quantities, it is an important substance for the whole of our muscular physiology. When a sufficient amount of oxygen and proper amounts of essential nutrients are available, it can easily be converted back to pyruvic acid and that way re-entered back to cell energy metabolism. An adequate oxygen supply will be affected if a person is anaemic, and also during allergic episodes, which are known to cause local swelling in parts of the body affected, and which can lead to a reduction of oxygen supply to the tissues involved. However, I will be talking about both of these conditions in later chapters.

In my opinion Hyperventilation syndrome as a diagnostic or clinical entity may not exist at all, but all these distressing symptoms which are said to be caused by overbreathing, may be directly caused by a rapid fall of blood sugar or Reactive Hypoglycaemia, which in turn can lead to Metabolic Acidosis due to its adrenaline releasing effect. However, having said that, breathing does matter a lot, particularly during an anxiety attack which, in my opinion, is directly caused by a rapid fall in blood sugar or a hypoglycaemic episode, which always leads to a massive release of adrenaline in order to release stored glycogen from the liver to correct this hypoglycaemic state . . . . Now you might remember that adrenaline is one of the substances which leads automatically to an increase in breathing which, at this specific time would be a silly thing to do, because if you overbreathe during a low blood sugar episode, you will feel worse. Therefore, just as one feels a panic attack looming ahead, or during an attack, while one is usually only concentrating on not dying, which by the way will never happen, one must also remember the following: Stop breathing immediately and keep on holding your breath as long as you comfortably can and not until you are blue in the face. When you feel that you have had enough of that breath-holding then start to release air out of your lungs very slowly and evenly until you feel that there isn't a breath of air left in you. When you are ready to breathe in again, don't make this in-breath deep, long or anything extravagant, just let it pop into your lungs as naturally and effortlessly as you can, followed again by a very even, long, slow out-breath. What is important to remember, is that it is just this long out-breath which helps you feel relaxed and calm. (53) If your panic attack happens outside, or somewhere you can't just flop into a chair or lie down, do not panic, if you excuse the pun, but keep calm and concentrate on your breathing. While you are at it, just remind yourself that this is just a low blood sugar attack and what this present mental and physical mayhem is all about, is that your whole being is temporarily lacking a sufficient amount of glucose, or blood sugar, for its proper function, and once it gets this temporary hiccough sorted out properly, you will be as good as new. While your body is trying to sort itself out, you can help it by being a good sport and by not panting vigorously, but breathing slowly and evenly as I have already described. When the worst is over and you have been able to pull yourself together to some extent, you should offer your body 'a hypoglycaemic snack', of which I will be talking more later, followed by more slow and even out-breathing. This slow out-breathing is best done just by humming any old tune quietly to yourself, whilst letting your shoulders drop and relax and generally thinking nice and pleasant thoughts . . . . In my opinion nothing more is needed to conquer a 'hyperventilating-hypoglycaemic panic attack'. However, some of the so called 'hyperventilation syndrome experts' tend to come forward with all sorts of daft suggestions, such as that 'paper-bag' method. It may be all right in theory, but it certainly is pretty silly in practice, as what on earth would passers-by think seeing you staggering about with a brown paper bag half covering your face. In my opinion going through a full-blown panic attack is a bad enough experience without being escorted to the nearest nick for alleged glue sniffing as well.

5

PSYCHOLOGICAL OR PHYSIOLOGICAL?

In order to throw some light on this much disputed subject, I would like to discuss here four different medical approaches by four doctors of four different medical disciplines to patients suffering from the same symptoms. First of all I would like to talk about a psychiatrist's point of view. For this purpose I would like to have a look at Dr Lloyd's review of literature *Medicine without Signs*. (54) The study is well researched, consisting of a good reference section of over eighty references, so I would think that it summarizes fairly well most of the current trends of psychiatric thinking.

Dr Lloyd points out that about 28% of all patients attending general medical practices have been diagnosed as suffering from a psychiatric illness. So also have 20% of patients attending gastro-intestinal clinics and 25% of patients attending neurology clinics.

A wide variety of symptoms localized in a part of the body may herald psychiatric illness, but certain patterns predominate:

Neurological symptoms, such as headache and dizziness are the commonest symptoms encountered in psychiatric practice. Insomnia, fatigue and irritability are often also present.

Pain is a common complaint in psychiatric illness, being present in half psychiatric in-patients and over half a sample of patients in general practice with certain emotional disorders. In depressive illness the preoccupation with pain may dominate the clinical picture so completely that the patient may not appear depressed and does not even admit feeling depressed. (I really have a difficulty in understanding this type of reasoning, as it indicates that if you are aching all over and no physical cause is found, a psychiatrist will diagnose you as suffering from depressive illness, even if you are not depressed at all. Mind you, if I were aching all over, I would surely get a trifle down in the mouth.)

Hysterical symptoms are said to be rare, but certain forms of hysteria continue to pose diagnostic problems, particularly in the differentiation between hysterical and epileptic seizures. However, patients with hysterical seizures may usually be distinguished from epileptics by their high rate of personal and family history of psychiatric illness, previous suicide attempts, sexual maladjustment and current affective disorders. (So I reckon if I feel dizzy and pass out, I can't be suffering from epilepsy if I can prove that I have a family of nutters at home, have attempted suicide or my sex life is maladjusted.)

Cardiovascular symptoms in psychiatry consist primarily of palpitations and chest pains, both of which are usually caused by Effort syndrome and Neurocirculatory Asthenia. (Or Soldier's Heart, Anxiety Neurosis, Hyperventilation syndrome etc.)

Respiratory symptoms of a psychological origin are primarily abnormalities of the rate and rhythm of breathing due to hyperventilation (Or Soldier's Heart, Anxiety Neurosis, Hyperventilation syndrome etc.)

Genito-urinary symptoms are frequent. It has been established that up to 30% of patients now seen in genito-urinary clinics have menstrual irregularities and sexual problems of a psychological origin, as no evidence of infection or any other physical cause can be found.

Dermatological symptoms are found to play a part in widespread psychological disturbances, including toxic psychoses, schizophrenia, depressive psychosis, personality disorders and social difficulties.

Gastro-intestinal symptoms in psychiatry consist of anorexia, weight loss, vomiting, abdominal pain and bowel disturbances. At least 20% of gastro-intestinal patients were shown to have a psychiatric illness without an organic disease. These patients were characterized by obsessional traits, previous psychological symptoms and an early parental loss. (I have got to admit that I have great difficulty in believing that previous obsessional traits, psychological symptoms, especially early parental loss can make you have the jitters, constipation or a tummy ache, but there we are.)

Disturbances in body image are also a part of psychiatric symptoms, where the patient complains of ugliness or deformity of one part of the body, which to the observer appears quite normal or only minimally disfigured. The nose, chin, ears and breasts are the commonest sources of complaint in this condition. A diagnosis should be then based on the associated psychopathology, whether this will then be a depressive illness, psychosis or more often a disturbed personality. (So it now looks as if anyone who dares to detest the shape or the size of their features wouldn't have enough to put up with already, the sufferer might also be tagged with such additional burdens as a disturbed personality or even psychosis. Depressive illness is a possibility however, because if I had the misfortune to look like something the cat brought in, I am convinced that I would feel occasionally a bit depressed, which is only fair.) However, some follow-up studies have shown that patients with minor deformities may derive considerable psychological benefits from surgery. (Well, well, I said to myself, at least some sanity prevails, but my feeling of contentment was short-lived.) A more recent study however, has reported a higher rate of severe neurosis and schizophrenia in patients who had a rhinoplasty ('a nose job') for cosmetic reasons, than on those operated on for disease or trauma. (It now looks as if one just can't win in this psychological merry-go-round, because if you dare to complain to your shrink about the shape or the size of your hooter, you might easily be told that it is not your nose which needs shaping but your psychotic or disturbed personality. But if you just mind your own business and get your nose sorted out to your liking, you may soon find a neurotic or schizophrenic label tagged on to your case notes.)

The study concludes that doctors should educate their patients to recognize the emotional origin of their symptoms so that mental illness could then be identified with mental symptoms rather than distinguished by an ailment of the body. It was also thought that some of the reason why

patients seem to prefer to present psychiatric illness as
bodily complaints, could be because of the inevitable
'stigma' which seems to be attached to psychiatric diagnoses, as well as the belief that doctors would be more
helpful and interested in physical rather than emotional
complaints . . . . In my opinion however, a great number of
doctors already educate their patients in the emotional
origin of their symptoms, because diagnoses such as
'psychosomatic' or 'it is all in your mind' seem to be in
pretty frequent use in today's medical vocabulary.

Secondly I would like to talk about the physician's point
of view. For this purpose I would like to review Dr
Gottlieb's paper *Non-organic Disease in Medical Outpatients.*
(55)

In the first place Dr Gottlieb examined all case records of
the 329 patients seen by him between January and June
1952. He found out that 128 of these patients, which is 39%,
had belonged to this so called 'non-organic group'. This
non-organic in medical jargon means patients to which all
available medical examinations give negative results.

In 1963 he again examined case records of 204 new
patients seen by him between January and June, when he
found that on this occasion the non-organic group
amounted to 82 patients, which was a staggering 40.2% of
the total admissions. The following symptoms were found
to be present:

Gastro-intestinal symptoms including nausea, vomiting,
abdominal pain and distension, loss of appetite, diarrhoea,
constipation, flatulence, burping and difficulty in swallowing . . . . All medical examinations gave negative results.

Cardiovascular symptoms including precordial pain or discomfort, palpitations and 'missed heartbeats' . . . . All
medical examinations were found to be normal.

Respiratory symptoms included breathing difficulties and
coughing . . . . All medical tests were normal.

Musculoskeletal symptoms included weak and painful limbs
and vague pains . . . . All tests gave negative results.

Neurological symptoms consisted of giddiness, feeling of
faintness, twitching eyelids, double vision and headache . . . .
All examinations gave normal results.

General symptoms were found to be weakness, fatigue and

lack of energy, which in some patients had existed for 20–30 years, or most of their adult lives. Because of this, some patients had been treated for anaemia for several years. Also depression, irritability, a feeling of tenseness, trembling, shaking, insomnia, as well as gaining and losing weight were found to be present . . . . All medical examinations however gave negative results.

Miscellaneous symptoms included excessive perspiration, a feeling of slight fever, swelling and puffiness of legs, ankles, eyes and the neck . . . No obvious organic illness was found and all medical investigations were entirely negative.

Dr Gottlieb also stated that whatever the non-organic symptoms, basically all the patients examined by him were found to be mentally relatively stable individuals in contradiction to patients attending psychiatric departments, as only two of his 82 patients had been treated previously for depression or anxiety. Nearly all his patients however did suffer from some form of anxiety state, with such objective findings as tremors of the fingers and excessive perspiration. Insomnia and an element of depression were also found in most patients, which was only admitted by direct questioning. It was thought that the patients prone to anxiety were simply over-sensitive to environmental stresses, which in turn led the patient to experience these various non-organic symptoms. The conclusion was that as these patients had gone to see a doctor complaining of symptoms referable to specific sites of the body, it would be better for the doctor to reassure them, and when necessary to prescribe anti-depressant or tranquillising medication. It was also thought that for this non-organic group of patients the help of a psychiatrist would rarely be necessary.

Thirdly I would like to have a look at Dr Melvin Ramsay's book *Postviral Fatigue Syndrome, The Saga of Royal Free Disease* (56).

Postviral Fatigue Syndrome is also known by other names such as Iceland Disease, Epidemic Neuromyasthenia, Chronic Fatigue and Immune Dysfunction Syndrome, Chronic Epstein-Barr Virus Syndrome, Yuppie Flu, Myalgic Encephalomyelitis etc., but known as ME for short. Postviral illness is probably responsible for more chronic ill-health than has yet been recognized. This 'post viral debility' conveniently covers the ill-defined states of malaise which may follow any virus infection, particularly if the patient's immune system is defective in the first place. It may start suddenly with an alarming attack of giddiness, but usually it takes the form of an influenza-like illness with headache, pains in the limbs and joints, loss of appetite and sometimes nausea and vomiting. Instead of normal recovery, the patient develops a condition characterised by prolonged fatigue and muscle weakness, particularly after exercise or after emotional or mental strain. This illness occurs mainly in young and middle-aged women. The main symptoms are:

Neurological symptoms: giddiness, vertigo, blurred or double vision, photophobia, tinnitus, sensitivity to noise or difficulty in hearing, coldness of hands and feet, hot and cold flushes, general malaise, night-sweats and headaches.

Respiratory symptoms: breathing difficulties and sometimes mild sore throat.

Cardiovascular symptoms: palpitations

Gastro-intestinal symptoms: nausea, vomiting and diarrhoea.

Musculo-sceletal symptoms: generalised muscle weakness, easy muscle fatigability, muscle tenderness, muscle aches and pains, a stiff and painful neck, pins and needles and numbness in various parts of the body.

Genito-urinary symptoms: frequency and difficulty in urination.

General and Psychiatric symptoms: emotional lability, impaired memory, inability to concentrate, depression, irritability, feeling of confusion, mixing, or not finding the right words for things, clumsiness, lapses of memory, fatigue, exhaustion, nightmares, crying spells, facial pallor, low grade fever, a general sense of feeling awful, anxiety, panic attacks and phobias.

ME Association leaflet *Guidelines for Sufferers* reads: 'ME may suddenly commence with an alarming attack of giddiness but it usually takes the form of an influenza-like illness with headache, pains in the limbs and joints, loss of appetite and sometimes nausea and vomiting. Instead of normal recovery the patient develops a condition characterized by profound fatigue and muscle weakness. In addition some muscles may be acutely painful . . . . The face may show a "ghastly pallor" and this may be observed by relatives even half an hour before the patient complains of feeling ill. The patient now complains of "feeling awful" and even the smallest household "chore" becomes a mammoth task. He or she may now find that their memory is uncertain and that they are unable to concentrate for any length of time; some have difficulty in finding the right word to say, or may start a sentence and be unable to complete it. Sleep rhythm is often disturbed . . . . The symptoms may vary from day to day, or from one time of day to another.'

ME Association leaflet *Psychological and Psychiatric Problems arising from Post Viral Syndrome* reads: 'Phobic symptoms tend to be phobic panic attacks and social phobias. These panic attacks appear to be caused by an unreasonable response to certain environmental stimuli or situations for no obvious reason, usually occurring when one is outside one's well-known territorial or environmental bounds, faced with something different, usually something uncertain. In these situations the sufferer may experience palpitations, hot and cold sweats, anxiety and nervousness combined with an overwhelming flood of adrenaline-type response, causing the person to escape from that situation by heading for home or to another place of safety. The social phobias consist of unwillingness to go somewhere which has presented problems before, such as lifts, large crowds, stores, open spaces, pubs etc. Again, accompanied with a feeling and wish to withdraw and to go home or to somewhere where the person feels safe. Anxiety, which is part of the Post Viral Syndrome consists of a constant feeling of being on edge, nervous, a feeling of agitation combined with a pounding heart, sweats, dry mouth and general feeling of tension. These symptoms are all part and parcel of the actual disease process. Part of these are caused by the virus infection on the neurones within the brain and the central nervous system, part of them are caused by being ill in the first place. In other words, as the result of the patient's illness the patient feels agitated, anxious and depressed. Anxious about the outcome of Post Viral Syndrome, and depressed because he is ill and not knowing what is going to happen in the future . . . . '

Routine physical examinations and ordinary laboratory investigations usually prove negative, so that the patients are usually referred to a psychiatrist. This seldom proves beneficial, and may even be harmful, because then the patient may acquire a label such as 'depressive illness', 'neurosis' or even a 'personality disorder'.

The basic essential treatment is to obtain a correct diagnosis, which can be done by the exclusion of other diseases, as the patient can be helped very much by the knowledge alone, that his persistent vague complaints could have on organic basis.

Dr Behan and his team (57) found abnormal T-helper/T-suppressor cell ratios in some people suffering from Post Viral Syndrome. This finding leads now to a simple question; whether Post Viral Syndrome is really a result of a persistent virus infection, or whether its basic cause may be a defective immune system function?

Abnormal intracellular acidosis has also been found, which was particularly noticeable after exercise. This finding was interpreted as being consistent with an increased lactic acid formation. (58) Attacks of faintness and giddiness are also a common feature in Post Viral Syndrome. These can be usually relieved by a small snack, which is suggestive of Hypoglycaemia. (59) Allergies are also a frequent complicating factor in Post Viral Syndrome. (56).

There is no known cure for Post Viral Syndrome with the exception of sufficient rest, which normally brings some improvement. According to the leaflet *Psychological and Psychiatric Problems arising from Post Viral Syndrome*, besides adequate rest, the illness can only be alleviated symptomatically. The psychological symptoms of panic, anxiety and depression respond to medication, psychotherapy and understanding counselling. Medications of psychotropic nature consist of tricyclic and quadrocyclic antidepressants and monoamine oxidase inhibitors. The use of minor tranquillisers should be avoided, as they are extremely prone to dependency and even addiction.

Nothing more to be said, except that how on earth the medical profession is able to differentiate between Post

Viral Syndrome sufferers, in whom no presence of a virus have been found and of folks who are said to be suffering from Agoraphobia, Soldier's Heart, Anxiety Neurosis, Hyperventilation syndrome and so on and so forth?

Fourthly, I would like to do a very quick summary of two books. One is Dr Theron Randolph's *Allergies, your Hidden Enemy* (50) and the other is by Dr Richard Mackarness *Not all in the Mind*. (60)

Doctors are taught in medical schools that the more symptoms a patient has, the less credence should be given to any of them, since it is assumed that many such patients are hypochondriacs or have imagined their symptoms. Dr Randolph taught opposite, the more symptoms a patient has, the more likely he is to be suffering from an environmental induced disease ie. food and/or chemical allergies.

Dr Mackarness writes (60) 'Like most general practitioners I had several patients crippled by illnesses for whose symptoms I was unable to find a cause. In the old days it was common practice to tell these people to pull themselves together and hope for the best. Nowadays these illnesses are more often labelled psychosomatic and the patient is offered psychiatric help, although this may amount eventually to being told to get on with it, in the nicest possible way of course, and with the prescription of tranquillising drugs .... Because food and chemical allergy is not yet recognized for what it is, no statistical studies have been made, so we can only estimate the incidence. I should now tentatively put the incidence of this type of illness as follows: 30% of people attending doctors' surgeries have symptoms exclusively traceable to food and chemical allergy, 30% have symptoms partially traceable to food and chemical allergy, and the remaining 40% have symptoms which are unrelated to allergy.'

The following general symptoms are of particular importance in allergy and these symptoms always fluctuate:

1) Persistent fatigue not helped by rest.
2) Over- or underweight, or a history of fluctuating weight.
3) Occasional puffiness of the face, hands, abdomen and ankles.
4) Palpitations particularly after food.

5) Excessive sweating unrelated to exercise.

At least one of these symptoms is invariably present in all patients with allergic illness. In addition, one or more of the chronic symptoms will be present, depending on the part of the body involved in the specific allergic reaction:

Neurological symptoms: Dizziness, a feeling of faintness, blurring or dimness of vision, photophobia, itchy or watery eyes, itchy ears, recurrent ear infections, tinnitus, headache, migraine and 'grey-outs'.

Respiratory symptoms: Runny or stuffed-up nose, breathing difficulties, excessive clearing of the throat, hoarseness, chronic cough, mild sore throat, asthma, bronchitis, recurrent sinusitis.

Cardiovascular symptoms: Rapid, irregular heartbeat, 'angina-like' pain, rapid and/or slow pulse rhythm.

Gastro-intestinal symptoms: Bloated stomach, constipation, diarrhoea, belching, flatulence, abdominal pains and cramps, nausea, vomiting, colitis, ileitis.

Genito-urinary symptoms: Urgency or frequency of urination.

Dermatological symptoms: Itching, eczema, dermatitis, hives, facial pallor.

Musculoseletal symptoms: Aching muscles, swollen and painful joints, arthritic pains, weakness of limbs, backache, stiff and painful neck, numbness and pins and needles in various parts of the body, excessive swelling of fingers, hands and feet.

General and Psychiatric symptoms: Alternating dullness and irritability, mental lethargy, confusion, restlessness, hyperactivity, lack of confidence, mental exhaustion, stuttering, inability to find words for things, lack of comprehension, impaired attention, crying for no reason, aggressive behaviour, unresponsiveness, inability to concentrate, lack of energy, extreme fatigue, general weakness, drowsiness, depression, insomnia, nightmares, anxiety neurosis, panic attacks, flu-like symptoms, dopey and drowsy feeling, 'brain-fag', feeling of being totally drained and exhausted.

There is a widespread agreement that allergies tend to run in families. It is thought that if a person has two allergic parents he has got a 65–75% chance of developing allergies at some time of his life, and a 35–50% chance of doing so if only one parent is allergic. (61)

Females seem to be more prone to develop severe allergies than males. Action Against Allergy produced statistics which showed that out of 251 severe allergics 88% were females. (62)

Fabienne Smith (63) has been able to show abnormal T-helper/T-suppressor cell ratios in people suffering from severe allergies. This same finding has also been established by various clinical ecologists in the United States. It has been also found that virus infections frequently seem to precipitate maladaptive allergic responses. (50, 64) Allergic reactions lead frequently to a local reduction in oxygen supply in the tissues involved, causing Metabolic Acidosis. And finally, hypoglycaemic episodes can be evoked in a person who has ingested any food or come into contact with any chemical to which he is allergic. (51)

6

TOOLS OF THE MEDICAL TRADE

Alexandra Wyke wrote an interesting article in *The Economist* about pharmaceuticals: (65) 'The drugs industry is a remarkably successful mix of hard science and hard sell. At one end of it are the organic chemists, biochemists, biophycisists and pharmacologists deploying all the paraphernalia of science to develop and test new chemical compounds. At the other are the salesmen, bombarding doctors with anything from ballpens to computers, organizing all-expense-paid "Symposia" in colourful locations and even offering cash inducements to conduct bogus trials. But the salesmen are selling a little harder these days, it is partly because the other end of the industry, the respectable end, has not come up with the goods. The glossy, high-technology image of the drug industry hides an uncomfortably antique range of products. The patents on many of these products are running out, and there is little at the moment to replace them. From 1945 when penicillin was first developed as an antibiotic, to 1960, when the tranquilliser Librium was launched, drug discoveries came thick and fast, antibiotics to fight bacteria and medicines to treat asthma, arthritis, cancer, heart disease and mental illness, as well as contraceptives and vaccines. Since then nearly all the new drugs have simply been safer or more effective versions of products already on the market. For this reason they are often disparagingly known as me-toos . . . After the thalidomide disaster the public began to look more carefully at the drugs they were prescribed and discovered that many of them carried risks as well as benefits. The most notorious example of an abused and misused product was Hoffmann-La Roche's mild benzodiazepine tranquilliser, Valium, dished out throughout the western world to relieve the 'stress' caused by a driving test, a dental operation, an examination, or life itself. A survey conducted by Dr Mitchell Balter of America's National Institutes of Health in the late 1970s estimated that about 3.5 million Americans had been taking benzodiazepines for more than a year. This sort of prescribing did wonders for Valium sales. Ten years ago it was the world's top-selling drug and about 90 million prescriptions a year for it were written in the United States. But the drug's effects on its users were widely criticized. Allegations that it was addictive gained wide currency and led doctors to consider the prescription of such 'mild' drugs much more carefully.'

Catalan *et al.* (66) writes in the British Medical Journal: 'Without a doubt doctors are worried about the scale on which benzodiazepines has been prescribed in general practice. Precise data cannot be cited since official statistics do not list benzodiazepines separately. Nevertheless, in England annual prescriptions for tranquillizers and sedatives (including benzodiazepines) in the NHS amounted to about 21 million in the late 1970s and about 18 million in the early 1980s. In these same two periods prescriptions for hypnotics (mostly benzodiazepines) ran steadily at about about 14 million a year. These prescriptions were largely issued in general practice. A recent survey in five group practices showed that diazepam was the most frequently prescribed of all drugs. During one year sedative or hypnotic drugs were prescribed at least once to 16% of women and 7% of men registered in five practices: in women aged over 45 the figure was above 25%. These drugs are prescribed mainly to patients with minor affective disorders which make up a large part of a general practitioner's case load and commonly presents with symptoms of anxiety, depressed mood or insomnia.'

Tuula Tuormaa writes: One of the most distressing iatrogenic illnesses of modern time is chronic benzodiazepine addiction and withdrawal. This condition has been described by many authors. (67, 68, 69, 70a, 71, 72, 73, 74) It has been estimated that about one third of patients taking benzodiazepines for six months or more become dependent, some do so after only a few weeks of treatment. (75) It has been found that desmethyldiazepam, a breakdown substance of benzodiazepine is known to continue to act in the body for about 100 hours. (69) Because of this slow elimination, cumulation can occur on repeated therapeutic dosage which can lead eventually to an excessive sedation causing chronic symptoms including the following: general weakness, dry mouth, lack of co-ordination, double or dimmed vision, muscle weakness, giddiness, loss of concentration and memory, impaired speech, mental confusion, sleepiness, emotional anaesthesia, agitation, low grade fever, low blood pressure, allergic reactions, panic attacks and agoraphobia. These symptoms develop insidiously whilst the patient continues to take therapeutic doses and they increase in dosage reduction and withdrawal.

The early appearance of benzodiazepine withdrawal is characterized by acute anxiety and psychotic symptoms lasting for several weeks, followed by a prolonged period of distressing mixed psychological and somatic symptoms. The average withdrawal period has been estimated at approximately six weeks for every year one has been on the drug. However, Tranx, or The National Tranquilliser Advice Centre has established that the withdrawal period can take an average of up to two years before the sufferer can be completely free of symptoms, even for those individuals who have been on these drugs for only a relatively short time. (70b) The symptoms of withdrawal are numerous and the majority of patients experience most of them: (67, 68, 69, 70, 74)

Neurological symptoms include: weakness, lack of co-ordination, trembling, numbness, blurred or double vision, giddiness, severe insomnia, tinnitus, headache, sensitivity to sound, light, taste and smell, a tingling feeling or pins and needles in various parts of the body.

Cardiovascular symptoms include: palpitations, flushing, chest pains and hyperventilation.

Gastro-intestinal symptoms include: nausea, dry mouth, vomiting, constipation, diarrhoea, abdominal pain, difficulty in swallowing and gaseous distention.

Musculosceletal symptoms include: muscle pain and stiffness, severe neck pain and stiffness.

General and Psychiatric symptoms include: acute anxiety, depression, hyperactivity, panic attacks, agoraphobia and other phobias, perceptual distortion, hallucinations, agitation, feelings of depersonalization and unreality, lack of confidence, tension, paranoid feelings, irritability, aggression, speech difficulties and stuttering, lack of concentration and memory and being unable to think straight. Also, particularly in the elderly both benzodiazepine addiction and withdrawal have been confused as early senile dementia. Benzodiazepines can also cause aggression and hostile behaviour in some individuals, particularly when an element of frustration is introduced into the situation. (76a) Brain scan abnormalities have also been detected in some long term benzodiazepine users compared to controls. (71)

Danish doctors Jensen and Poulsen studied the amnesic effect of diazepam (Valium) and found that what patients have learned while on the tranquillizing medication, can be forgotten when they stop taking the drug. (69) This amnesic effect may not trouble every one who has been on these drugs, but it certainly affected me. As it happened, I first became interested in human biochemistry whilst I was still on Valium. I read and studied a great deal of the subject and also remember learning a lot. But lo and behold, after my dreaded drug withdrawal period was finally over, all my acquired knowledge just seemed to drain away from my brain cells. This sensation was most weird. After my withdrawal was completed I had to start again from the beginning. When I studied and re-read all the books and notes I had sweated over before, I did recognize all my books, my underlinings as well as my notes as my own, but that was as far as it went. It was as if I had been two separate people, the Valium addict who had just gone away with all her knowledge and the other me left behind to start all over again. While withdrawing from that dreaded drug I also developed a slight stammer-like speech defect which is with me even today and which I find extremely frustrating.

The following information I have collected from a leaflet published by MIND called *Minor tranquillisers: Hard Facts, Hard Choices*: Although Valium is perhaps the most well known brand name of all the benzodiazepine group of drugs, there are many others. They are all chemically related and some of them are prescribed as tranquillisers and others as sleeping pills. Here follows a list of the most familiar ones. I will mention the brand name first and the medical name will follow in brackets: Librium Libritas, Tropium (Chlordiazepoxide), Frisium (Clobazam), Tranxene (Clorazepate), Alupram, Atensine, Diazemuls, Evacalm, Sedapum, Solis, Tensulm, Valium, Valrelease (Diazepam), Anxon (Ketazolam), Ativan (Lorazepam), Nobrium (Medazepam), Serax, Serenid D, Serenid Forte (Oxazepam). The following tranquillisers are usually described as sleeping pills: Rohypnol (Flunitrazepam), Dalmane (Flurazepam), Noctamid (Lormetazepam), Mogadon, Nitrados, Remnos, Somnite, Surem (Nitrazepam), Euhypnos, Normison (Temazepam) Halcion (Triazolam)

The following are a few samples of letters written by people who were trying to withdraw from their tranquillizing medication. These letters were published in a book called *'That's Life' Survey on Tranquillisers*. (77)

Paulette from Mevagissey: 'I would feel violently giddy and even after three years I still do. I felt so terribly ill that I would cry in desperation. And for a spell I felt violent. My family has suffered also. My doctor has said that there is nothing he can do. Many times I would feel committing suicide was the only way to stop it. I had palpitations, insomnia and aches and pains. I was very tense and anxious and was unable to talk to people. I felt as if I was drunk. Because I felt so ill, I felt as though I was going to die and never recover.'

Anne from Gravesend: 'I cut down very gradually but after four months I have all the major withdrawal symptoms. I feel completely exhausted. I went back to my doctor last week only to be told that I probably need to take more tranquillizers to stop the symptoms. Or I can try to cope. At the moment I am shaking all over, feel tension in my face (the last time this happened my jaw locked and I couldn't move my jaw for a few days. I have become hysterical with fear). I have bad twitches in my eyes and I am frightened of going out alone. I have not increased the tablets so far but I now fear that I may have to – to help me cope with myself again. I feel that I am crying out for help but no one wants to know.'

Mary from Brighton: 'It's hard to describe just how ill I was. My head did not belong to me. I shook. My legs were like jelly. I felt like a walking zombie. I felt sick, I cried a lot. I felt terrible. It was hard facing every day.'

Gabriel from Twickenham: 'I felt depressed, lonely, confused, forgetful, things were generally dreadful. I couldn't remember what day it was. My head felt as though it was bursting. I had terrible stomach pains and problems passing water. I was given pain killers by my doctor for the pain and was admitted to hospital. It was a very upsetting time. I was insulted because I wouldn't eat. While in hospital I cut out taking tranquillisers altogether. I had terrible, terrifying stomach cramps. Altogether I had 20 months of hell.'

Annabel from Stoke-on-Trent: 'I felt like death warmed up. My legs were like jelly. I was tearful. I had a bad head and was very shaky and unstable. I was frightened to go out of doors. It was a very troublesome time both emotionally and physically and my husband was very disturbed to see me in such a state. Because of my run-down state I couldn't stand bright sunlight and my vision was very poor. My eyes hurt and itched.'

Ellen from Colchester: 'I have total absolute panic where fear sweeps over me to the extent that I pace about, lie down, rush outdoors, then indoors. I can't stay still, need to hold on to someone yet want to feel free. I feel that my whole body up to my head is going to burst and I can do nothing.'

Christianne from Kirkby: 'I couldn't be bothered to go out, and found that I couldn't answer the telephone. I used to watch the phone when it rang. I broke out in perspiration and just couldn't answer it. When I did meet people they seemed to drain all my energy. I had to ask my only relative to ring twice first and then I would answer knowing who it was.'

Shirley from Rugby: 'My symptoms became very bad. I became hyperactive. I would suffer terrible tension attacks. My limbs would tingle and I would feel as though I was in a dream. I had agoraphobia in the sense that I became frightened to venture too far from home in case I got ill. I was afraid of being left on my own. I had panicky pressure across my head. I felt a lack of confidence and I put on three stone in weight over a very short time. With all these symptoms I became bed-ridden. I felt myself to be a real addict. My doctor and I then made a decision to go back on tranquillisers and I felt very disappointed. Within a day all my symptoms disappeared but my confidence was totally shattered.'

Tuula from Jyväskylä: The less said the better. Even after all these years just thinking how eerie and agoraphobic I felt while on Valium, let alone during the dreaded with-drawal period, which in my case lasted nearly three years, makes me quite cheesed off. The mere thought that drug companies as well as doctors as their dispensing tools, can just shrug their shoulders and scuttle away from the scene without even an apology, leaving in their trail this devastat-ing mass of human misery, has made me lose the appropri-ate respect to some aspects of humanity. Let's face it, other drug pushers are punished at least with lengthy jail sentences.

Now a few more words about this condition known as agoraphobia. In my opinion agoraphobia can indeed be divided into two main categories: A simple agoraphobia, which is directly caused by repeated hypoglycaemic episo-des, and a complex agoraphobia, which is caused by a tranquillizing medication, which could in turn lead to a chronic hypoglycaemic state. The reason which has led me to consider this possibility is simple: The basic day to day control of our blood sugar levels depends primarily on a close co-operation between insulin and growth hormone. In short, hypoglycaemia stimulates growth hormone release and a chronic growth hormone deficiency increases the blood sugar's sensitivity to insulin. (78) Tranquillizers are potent growth hormone activators, thus helping the blood sugar to rise. Apparently, after long term therapy, tolerance will develop to this growth hormone releasing effect. Lader (72) studied patients on benzodiazepines and control subjects and found out that an injection of diazepam released growth hormone into the plasma in control subjets, whereas patients on long term tranquillizing medication showed almost total tolerance. After a period of withdrawal, however, the growth hormone reappeared. These findings could suggest that the first therapeutic action of benzodiazepines may just be their blood sugar increasing potential, which, after a long term therapy will depress growth hormone release, which in turn could lead to a chronic hypoglycaemic state. The fact, which could also support my hypothesis, is that symptoms of both hypoglycaemia and tranquillizer addiction/withdrawal are rather similar.

Evelyn from Ipswich: 'When I was on Valium, three

tablets a day, I thought the side effects I was having were all due to my anxiety and depression. I felt as if I was dying, shortness of breath, panic attacks, feeling sick, bad headaches, dizziness, drowsiness. I felt wobbly and unbalanced and had pains in the chest and stomach. Before taking Valium I did not feel like this. I could go out anywhere. On Valium I could not face people and was frightened to go outside the house.'

Dr Ashton writes: (67) 'Eleven out of twelve patients developed agoraphobia whilst taking benzodiazepines. Six were completely unable to go out of the house alone and others had to overcome feelings of panic to do so and were not always successful. Sometimes they would "freeze" with panic while out. Five patients had had unsuccessful psychiatric treatment for agoraphobia with drugs, psychotherapy or behaviour therapy. This symptom improved remarkably however, with no other treatment but benzodiazepine withdrawal.' In my own survey amongst 240 agoraphobic sufferers, 121 were on various benzodiazepines, out of which 71 were on Valium.

Mental illness is remarkably resistant to investigations by conventional biological methods; drugs are still the major research tools. In psychopharmacological studies using animals, the most popular are so called 'conflict' tests. In a classical conflict test hungry rats are trained to press a lever for food, or thirsty rats are taught to approach a water spout. In order to create a 'conflict' these rats are first trained, then punished with an electric shock each time they approach to eat or drink. Now the conflict rises for the animal: should he accept an electric shock or remain hungry or thirsty? In such experiments behaviour can be completely suppressed, so that the rat stops eating and drinking altogether until he is given benzodiazepines. From then on the poor little blighter doesn't seem to care a damn any more how many electric shocks he gets, but scurries bravely forth in order to satisfy his hunger and thirst. (79) Need I say more?

Now when we have sorted out the very basic background of these so called 'minor tranquillizers', it is time to find out more about so-called 'major tranquillizers'. I have collected most of the following information from a leaflet published by MIND, called *Major Tranquillisers: The Price of Tranquillity*.

Major tranquillizers are a group of drugs which are designed to control symptoms of more 'serious' mental disorders, such as schizophrenia. These drugs are also known as neuroleptics or anti-psychotic agents. They never 'cure' schizophrenia in the real sense of the word, but can be helpful in controlling the 'schizophrenic symptoms' to some extent. Here follows a list of the most familiar ones. I will mention the brand name first and the medical name will follow in brackets: Largactil (Chlorpromazine), Moditen (Fluphenazine hydrochloride), Stelazine (Trifluoperazine), Neulactil (Pericyazine), Melleril (Thioridazine), Serenace (Haloperidol), Droleptan (Droperidol), Redeptin (Fluspirilene), Orap (Pimozide), Taractan (Chlorprothixene), Clopixol (Clopenthixol decanoate), Depixol (Flupenthixol decanoate), Modecate (Fluphenazine decanoate).

The most usual side-effects associated with the major tranquillizers are as follows: sedation, apathy, trembling hands, dry mouth, blurred vision, sensitivity to light, stiffening of muscles, drowsiness, reduced blood pressure. Impotence may also occur. However, the side effects of major tranquillizers which cause the greatest concern are Pseudo-Parkinsonism and tardive dyskinesia.

Pseudo-Parkinsonism is the most common side-effect of major tranquillizers and can be extremely unpleasant. When the patient is suffering from Pseudo-Parkinsonism his muscles stiffen and weaken, which gives the face of the sufferer a mask-like appearance. The mouth tends to hang open and an excess of saliva may be produced. His hands start to shake and his fingers move around as though he is rolling something between his fingers. When walking, he seems to lean forward shuffling along using short steps. These symptoms vary from person to person and are more likely to cause problems if high dosage has been prescribed. If the symptoms become too distressing, they can be treated with following drugs: Artane (Benzhexol), Cogentin (Benztropine), Disipal (Orphenadrine), Kemadrin (Procyclidine). These drugs have side-effects of their own, which can be uncomfortable and sometimes upsetting. The most commonly reported side-effects are: dry mouth, which can make eating difficult, upset stomach, constipation, dizziness and blurred vision. Changes in heart rhythm, feeling 'nervy' or on edge and increased sensitivity to light, noise and sound may also appear.

When major tranquillizers are used for prolonged periods of months or years, there is a danger that the patient's central nervous system will be permanently damaged resulting in tardive dyskinesia. The literal translation of this term is 'late onset of difficulty of movements', where the person develops involuntary or uncontrollable movements of his face, body and limbs. No one really knows how common it is, but The American Psychiatric Association suggests that up to 20% or one in five patients who use major tranquillizers for a period of years will develop tardive dyskinesia, but there are no hard figures to back up this claim. The best estimates indicate however, that at least 10-20 per cent of patients in mental hospitals, and at least 40 per cent of elderly people who have been on major tranquillizers for many years, will experience some degree of tardive dyskinesia if they are treated with these drugs for prolonged periods. The early signs of tardive dyskinesia are blinking, slight movements of the tongue, and tic-like twitches of the lips or face. As the condition processes these facial movements and grimaces become more exaggerated and the limbs and body also may develop involuntary movements. Hands twist and fidget, feet tap, legs are crossed and uncrossed. The body may rock to and fro and the shoulders shrug. Breathing is often irregular and sometimes accompanied by grunting noises. These symptoms usually clear of their own accord within months after the medication is stopped, but for some individuals this condition appears to be permanent and irreversible.

Now some words about depression and treatment. I have collected most of the following information from a leaflet published by MIND, called *Anti-depressants: First Choice or Last Resort?*

The majority of people suffering from depression will be treated by their GP, although people in very serious distress may be referred to a psychiatric hospital. Whatever the setting, the most commonly used treatment for depression is antidepressant drugs, of which 7.5 million are prescribed yearly in the UK, as well as electro-convulsive therapy or

ECT, which are often the only help on offer for the treatment of depression in the National Health Service.

Monoamine-oxidase inhibitors or MAOIs were the first anti-depressants to be introduced, but the combination of the side effects and dangerous interaction with certain foods such as cheese, Marmite, pickled herrings etc. has resulted in them being prescribed less often than before. Taking the wrong food and drink in combination with MAOIs usually results in a rapid rise in blood pressure and/or temperature and a very severe headache. The most well known MAOI anti-depressants used are: Brand name Nardil (medical name Phenelzine), Marsilid (Iproniazid), Marplan (Isocarboxazid) and Parnate (Tranylcypromine). Side effects are dizziness, low blood pressure, disturbed sleep, weakness in muscles, dry mouth, agitation, headache, constipation and passing water less often. Rashes, hallucinations, inflammation of the blood vessels, anaemia, kidney disease and liver damage could also occur. At the present time, because of MAOI's dangerous interactions with certain foods, another type of antidepressant, known as tricyclic anti-depressant are usually the first ones to be prescribed for someone diagnosed as depressed. The tricyclics were introduced in the 1960s along with the tetracyclic and bicyclic anti-depressants, which belong to the same 'family' of drugs. They all work acting on chemical processes in the brain, but although we know what they are supposed to do, we still don't fully understand how they do it. The overall effect is however, to change a person's sensitivity to emotions. The most usual anti-depressants which are prescribed nowadays are: Amitriptyline, Domical, Elavil, Lentizol, Saroten, Tryptizol which all are brand names. (Amitriptyline Hydrochloride, a medical name), Evadyne (Butriptyline), Anafranil (Clomipramine Hydrochloride), Pertofran (Desipramine Hydrochloride), Prothiaden (Dothiepin Hydrochloride), Sinequan (Doxepin), Tofranil (Imipramine Hydrochloride), Prondol (Iprindole), Gamanil (Lofepramine), Ludiomil (Maprotiline Hydrochloride), Bolvidon, Norval (Mianserin Hydrochloride), Allegron, Aventyl (Nortriptyline), Concordin (Protriptyline Hydrochloride), Molipaxin (Trazodone Hydrochloride), Surmontil, (Trimipramine), Vivalan

(Viloxazine Hydrochloride). The most usual side effects of these drugs are: dry mouth, a feeling of sedation, blurred vision, constipation, feeling sick, passing water less often, low blood pressure, changes in heart rhythm, sweating, rashes, disturbed behaviour (particularly in children), confusion (particularly in elderly people) reduced sexual arousal, a fainting feeling, sleep disturbances and insomnia, feeling anxious and tense, numbness and tingling of fingers and toes, and headaches. Less common side effects are serious blood disorders, arthritis, fits, heart disease, bruising, jaundice and black tongue. These anti-depressant drugs don't 'cure' depression as such and furthermore they seem to 'work' only for two depressed people in three, when they can provide some relief for a while, until the depression lifts of its own accord, or the sufferer's personal circumstances improve. All anti-depressants now available have side effects which may be particularly troublesome in the early stages of treatment, which can be a serious problem as these drugs can take up to four weeks before they start relieving symptoms. They may also be toxic or poisonous for some people. The combination of delayed action, side effects and toxicity may well explain why each year in Britain some 400 people use anti-depressants as a means to end their lives. There is no doubt now that many people experience withdrawal symptoms when they stop taking anti-depressants and the physical and mental problems caused by withdrawal are often mistaken for a re-emergence of the mental distress which led to the drugs being prescribed in the first place. Studies have shown that withdrawal symptoms are most common and severe in people who have been on these drugs for longer than two months and who stop taking them suddenly. The following symptoms appear when a person is withdrawing from anti-depressants: stomach cramps, vomiting, diarrhoea and a loss of body fluids (these symptoms can be especially severe in children and elderly people) difficulty in getting to sleep, followed by very vivid dreams early in the night, restlessness, agitation and uncontrollable movements of the limbs. Severe mental problems such as very serious depression may also occur. Also people who do not have a previous history of serious mental ill-health problems may develop a disturbed and extremely excitable behaviour. People withdrawing from MAOI anti-depressants may experience headaches, shivering and shaking, numbness and tingling affecting any part of the body, severe nightmares, feeling sick, sweating and panic attacks. A few people experience hallucinations and/or delusions.

Now that we have got all this drugging and pill popping out of the way, it is time to take a brief look at the mind-bending procedure of electro-convulsive therapy or ECT for short. I have collected most of the following information from MIND factsheet *Electro-Convulsive Therapy*.

Electro-convulsive therapy involves passing an electric current through the brain to produce a convulsion or a 'fit'. Convulsions were first used as a form of treatment in 1933 by Dr Von Meduna, a Hungarian psychiatrist who noticed that schizophrenic patients rarely suffered from epileptic fits while people with epilepsy were free from schizophrenia. This observation led him to believe that it was impossible for schizophrenia and epilepsy to occur in the same patient, and he reasoned that an artificially produced epileptic fit could cure schizophrenia. This was soon found to be untrue, but it was noted that the depressive element in the condition of some people with schizophrenia responded favourably to the convulsion. In the early days the convulsion was produced by injection. Electricity was first used in Italy in 1938, which is now the standard practice with an anaesthetic and muscle relaxant administered to modify the convulsion. Two forms of ECT are used today: bilateral and unilateral. In bilateral ECT the electrodes which pass the electricity through the brain, are placed one on either side of the head. With unilateral ECT both electrodes are applied to the same side (usually the right side of the head for the right-handed person and vice versa). The advantage of unilateral ECT is that it significantly reduces distressing side-effects which can occur immediately after the administration of the electric shock, particularly memory disturbance and confusion, although a 1980 research study found that unilateral ECT was rarely or never used in four out of five clinics.

The actual ECT procedure happens as follows: The patient removes false teeth, sharp jewellery and shoes, loosens tight clothing and lies on a padded table or couch. S/he is then injected with a short-acting general anaesthetic, followed by a muscle-relaxing drug. The relaxant paralyses the muscles and ensures that the patient doesn't hurt himself during the convulsion. The general anaesthetic is given mainly because it is very unpleasant to be paralysed while you are fully conscious. As soon as these injections take hold, an anaesthetist inflates the patient's lungs with oxygen during the brief non-breathing period, which results from the action of the muscle relaxant. A gag is placed in the patient's mouth so that he doesn't bite his tongue or damage his teeth, and the electric shock is then administered.

Although ECT has been established as a standard psychiatric treatment for nearly forty years, there is now considerable doubt and debate whether it actually works, nevertheless there are still around 160,000 sessions of ECT administered in the UK each year.

The most common side effects of ECT are drowsiness, confusion, dizziness, weakness, nausea, vomiting, palpitations, problems with eyesight and muscle aches and pains. The most worrying side-effect of ECT however, is undoubtedly loss or disturbance of memory. Some of the research studies which have looked at that aspect of ECT administration suggest that these memory disturbances are short-lived and that memory soon returns to normal. Other studies indicate that there is indeed a link between memory loss and ECT, especially if ECT is administered badly . . . . Never mind, if an allegedly civilized human being can subject his fellow man to such inhuman practices as ECT, memory loss could only be a blessing in disguise.

Now a few words about hospitals and if they are indeed as good for a patient's health as is believed.

Hospital food, school meals and other institutional catering unfortunately share a reputation for predictive awfulness. Modernization of facilities has in some instances led to improvements, which have tended to concentrate more on palatability and variety of the menu, rather than on the nutritional content. We are still reading reports such as that of long-term patients with psychiatric illness in a London hospital, who had nutritional deficiencies of vitamin C, vitamin D and folic acid, though without the appearance of clinical signs. The patients most likely to become malnourished, not surprisingly, are those who are most ill. An additional problem may be the side effects of treatment with drugs. Thus illness, drug treatment, poor appetite and the possibility of monotonous menus and unattractive food, may all help to explain a report from the United States that half of all hospital patients are suffering from some degree of malnutrition, and that between 5–10% literally die of starvation. (80, 81, 82) Some hospitals manage to kill their patients through food poisoning. Very recently my morning paper informed me that rotting scraps of food and dead flies were found in water containers in one hospital kitchen, whilst cockroaches roamed about the foodstores, and eggs were left in corridors that were so hot the eggs almost boiled. In another hospital kitchen insects were found in the chicken stew, but patients were told that they wouldn't harm them as they had been well cooked. In one hospital, flakes of asbestos were discovered in food samples.

A recent report by doctors found that one in ten patients pick up infection while in hospital, which costs the National Health Service an extra £111 million a year. MPs have suggested that patients should be warned about the risks of entering a hospital, although doctors argue that if they realized the dangers they might suffer heart attacks!

After reading all this I am simply amazed that the great majority of people still can't wait to be 'under a doctor' or 'under a hospital' in order to be able to keep on 'taking their tablets' or have their brains re-arranged with ECT. I find this particularly disturbing where mental health issues are concerned. Let's never forget that we all possess only one brain and if its delicate balance gets all mucked up with the dreaded drugs, poisonous potions, electric shocks etc, including their side effects, there is no way of telling that we might not eventually end up mentally much worse off than we were at the start of this drug-oriented régime. However, there is now quite enough evidence to show that one doesn't necessarily have to join this dubious drug march, as there is an alternative, but more about that later.

7

TIME FOR DECISION

What has baffled me more than anything else after all these years of reading and concentrating on various research studies, is the uncanny similarity between the basic symptomatology of Anxiety neurosis, Hyperventilation syndrome, Agoraphobia, 'psychiatric symptoms', Non-organic disease, Post Viral Fatigue syndrome, Hypoglycaemia and Food/chemical allergies. When I have approached the medical profession to clarify how they can tell the difference i.e. who is suffering from what, I have been invariably offered that woolly medical explanation: 'Clinical experience', which, at least in my opinion, is not accurate enough. That being the case, until someone comes to me with a good scientific explanation for differentiation, I will just have to believe that the only reason why the symptoms tally is that we are dealing here only with one condition; a Food/chemical Allergy combined with Reactive Hypoglycaemia, and the rest of the diagnoses are just the same old medical jargon which has baffled patients, as well as some doctors for a very long time.

The reason I prefer to choose Food/chemical Allergy/Hypoglycaemia as the forerunner out of this battery of names is that it is the only condition which can be effectively diagnosed and treated using current knowledge of Clinical Ecology and Nutritional Medicine. The rest of these ailments, in my opinion, are not so much diagnoses but rather admissions of defeat. All they can tell us is that the medical profession is baffled. In my opinion there is no such thing as Anxiety neurosis, Agoraphobia, Non-organic disease etc, there are only patients whose ailments resist diagnoses by traditional laboratory techniques. In other words, after giving a battery of laboratory tests and getting no indication of physical malfunctioning, illness is then labelled psychosomatic, psychological, neurotic, agoraphobic or other meaningless jargon. Throwing about all these fancy names might make the doctor feel educated and medically sophisticated, but it simply isn't quite good enough. The patient also needs some consideration. Fair enough, besides these vague diagnoses, the medical profession do have on their side the mighty drug industry, which at least as far as the mental health field is concerned, can be simply lethal. Some doctors also occasionally use various forms of 'talking therapies', which can be quite helpful. Furthermore they also have that magical 'doctor's reassurance', which always has been a bit of a mystery to me, as at least in my case, doctors have reassured and re-reassured me over and over again that there was nothing whatsoever wrong with me, but regardless I didn't seem to get any better as the result.

The following points are some of the bases of my argument that we are dealing here with only one illness, not several, as the differential diagnoses would suggest.

First of all I would like to look at how all these conditions relate to one another. The main and most noticeable factor is of course that they all share the same symptoms. Furthermore the five most common symptoms of both Hyperventilation syndrome and Allergies are pretty nearly the same. Hereditary precentages of both Hyperventilation syndrome and Allergies are also pretty close. Severe symptoms of both Hyperventilation syndrome and Allergies can be alleviated by an alkaline forming substance such as bicarbonate. Metabolic acidosis or lactic acid accumulation seem to play a part in Hyperventilation syndrome, Allergies and Post-Viral syndrome. Allergies play a part in Post-Viral syndrome. Hypoglycaemia plays part in Post-Viral syndrome. Hypoglycaemia plays a part in Allergies. Hyperventilation is used in order to confirm a diagnosis of Hypoglycaemia. The mean ages of onset of Anxiety neurosis, Hyperventilation syndrome and Agoraphobia are the same. Of both agoraphobics and severe allergics, 88% are females. Furthermore, Hyperventilation syndrome, Anxiety neurosis and Post-Viral syndrome seem to have similar high female prevelance. Abnornal T-helper/T-suppressor cell ratios have been found in both Post-Viral syndrome and Allergies. Virus infection can cause both Allergies and Post-Viral syndrome and so on and so forth. And secondly; according to research studies, it has been found that about 28% of all patients attending a general medical practice have been found suffering from a psychiatric illness (54), about 40% seem to be suffering from non-organic disease (55) and a further 30% have symptoms exclusively traceable to food/chemical allergies. (60) Now, if I am able to add up correctly, nearly 100% of all patients visiting their doctor have either a psychiatric illness, non-organic disease, or allergies. Or alternatively, psychiatric illness, non-organic disease and allergies may be the same. I prefer the latter explanation rather than the former, as otherwise the headshrinkers and allergists would be the only medics needed to treat the whole nation.

If I were able to organize a little get-together between one typical anxiety neurotic, one hyperventilator, one agoraphobic, one person suffering from non-organic disease, an allergic and a person who has been diagnozed as suffering from Post-Viral syndrome, I wouldn't be a bit surprised if the latter would feel a bit out of place. The reason being, because he is the only one who has got a proper virus to fall back on, which makes him medically just a bit special. However, he might not be so special after all. The reason is explained clearly in a letter which was sent to me by the chairman of Action Against Allergy, Mrs Amelia Nathan-Hill: 'I am delighted to inform you that you have won the first prize in our 1987 International Clinical Ecology Competition with your paper: "A Brief Review of the Immune System and its Function in Relation to: Post-Viral Syndrome, Non-Antibody Mediated Allergy, Auto-immunity and Immune Deficiency", which is very relevant at the moment when so many allergics seem to be suffering from Post-Viral syndrome.'

I don't mind telling you that I find this Post-Viral business or ME a bit frustrating, mainly for the following reasons: First of all, I have always been a bit baffled by the fact that the presence of a virus, or an enterovirus, any of which are thought to be one of the possible causes of the symptoms of ME, can often also be detected in perfectly healthy individuals. (83) This being the case, I find this crazy obsession with trying to detect the presence of a virus in an ME sufferer rather a waste of time. Secondly: in cases where ME symptoms have started with an acute attack of giddiness and the presence of a virus has not been detected, I would like to suggest that in those people the ME symptoms are not caused by a virus at all, but by Reactive Hypoglycaemia, of which I will be talking more in later chapters. Each time, however, when I have tried to put these points forward to 'ME experts', I have usually been met either with a stony silence, or alternatively an impatient grunt indicating that as we doctors are very busy people, we certainly don't have time to enter into detailed discussion with anyone who doesn't possess medical qualifications; which in turn leaves me more frustrated than ever.

Harry Benjamin writes about germs and viruses in 1936: (84) 'One has only to pay a flying visit to any hospital or busy panel doctor's waiting room, or to watch the stream of cars continually rolling up to the various doors in Harley Street, or read the patent medicine advertisements in the newspapers, to realize that the world's disease problem is still waiting to be solved at medical hands. Indeed, it appears to be growing more and more insoluble every day. Why? Because Medical Science has always looked to externals for the cause of disease, instead of to factors at work within the body of the individual concerned. Consequently, despite its skill and honesty of purpose, the medical profession continues to add error to error, and pile up enormity upon enormity, in attempting to "cure" disease by means of administration of poisonous drugs and vaccines, and the very drastic employment of the surgeon's knife, without having the faintest idea that what it is inevitably doing is really adding to the disease bill of the nation, rather than subtracting from it . . . . When Pasteur elaborated his celebrated germ theory of disease, the whole medical world enthusiastically and unhesitatingly accepted it, in full belief that there at last was the conclusive solution to the vexed problem of disease, the solution they had long been waiting for. At last the dread cause of disease was fully established. It was germs! Disease was due to germ infection. All one had to do was to kill the germs, and the disease would disappear. But after fifty years of adherence to the germ theory and despite literally astonishing feats of bacteriological science, disease exerts as firm a hold upon humanity as heretofore. The germs appear to thrive better than their victims . . . . Pasteur, because of the superficial plausibility of his germ theory, has set the whole medical fraternity on a wild-goose chase which is leading them nearer and nearer to the brink of futility in the effective understanding and treatment of disease . . . . But Medical Science still holds public sway, and society's complete sanction for what it does, because the vast majority of people are still completely unaware of the underlying futility of orthodox medical methods of treatment. On the surface these methods appear to be doing something, the cutting and slashing and dosing and doping appear to achieve results, so that even the medical profession itself is hoodwinked into genuinely believing that it is actually overcoming disease . . . . until the yearly statistics are looked at . . . . The medical profession, thanks to its hidebound and obsolete attitude to disease, is a menace. The sooner people begin to realize this no doubt startling fact, the better. No one who has not tried can understand the almost utter hopelessness of attempting to convey these simple truths to the conventional-minded people of today, steeped as they are in implicit belief as to the wonder-working powers of "the doctor": accepting everything as he says with childish faith and obedience, as coming from one who surely knows all there is to know about disease, its causes and cure, absolutely convinced as to the efficiency and healing value of the vari-coloured medicines they trustingly carry home with them after a visit to the surgery, speaking with bated breath of "great specialists" and miraculous eleventh-hour operations performed at a moment's notice which have saved the lives of near and dear ones, fully satisfied that the ills they suffer from are nothing whatever to do with their habits of living or the food they eat, but are due to nasty pernicious little germs, sent by a perverse Providence to harass them, or "the weather". No one, I repeat, who has not tried can understand the hopelessness of trying to convince people such as these (and they make

up fully ninety-nine percent of the population of all
civilized countries) that medical practice – based as it is
upon a completely erroneous philosophy of disease, despite
all its skill, knowledge, position, prestige, power, authority
and so called "achievements" in alleviating the suffering of
humanity, is really and truly a menace, and most insidious
menace, be noted, to the health and welfare of society, by
actually intensifying disease instead of overcoming it.'

Pretty strong stuff, you have got to admit, but Harry
Benjamin makes it absolutely clear that it is certainly not
the medical profession he is criticizing, but only their views
of the cause and treatment of diseases. He is a naturopath
by profession and he believes in the biological concept of
medicine, which is based on the fact that the primary cause
of a disease is not a bacterium, a bug, a germ or a virus, but
the body's own weakened resistance brought about by
man's own health destroying living habits, such as faulty
nutrition leading to nutritional deficiencies, exogenous
poisons from polluted food, air, water and environment, the
use of toxic drugs, both prescribed and non-prescribed, a
lack of sufficient exercise, rest and relaxation, combined
with an excessive physical or mental stress.

Another interesting man Dr Orr lectured to the British
Medical Association on 11 March 1931. (85) 'In the last
twenty years there have been rapid developments in our
knowledge of animal nutrition. This knowledge continues
to accumulate at an increasing rate. It has such a direct
bearing on the prevention or cure of disease, that nutrition
may now be regarded as a new branch of medical science. In
experimental studies with animals it has been observed that
there are all stages of malnutrition, ranging from what we
regard as normal health, to that in which the gross and
terminal symptoms appear. In early stages of all deficiency
disease there is generally found indications of lowered
vitality. Young animals have a slower than normal rate of
growth, the reproductive powers of adults are defective, the
coat is dull and lustreless, appetite is decreased, and the
animals show, instead of the *joie de vivre* of the perfectly
healthy animal, lethargy and other signs of premature
senility. It has been noted by many workers that susceptibility to certain infectious diseases is definitely greater in

groups of animals of deficient diets than in comparable animals on complete well-balanced diets. It has been repeatedly noted that animals on diets deficient in fat-soluble vitamins for example, have a higher proportion of deaths from respiratory and alimentary infections. It is also believed that with deficiency of calcium and iron there is increased susceptibility to pulmonary infections. *In animals suffering from even minor degrees of deficiency, resistance to organisms normally present in the body may be reduced, and hence bacteria, which, in an animal on perfect diet might remain non-pathogenic, find in the abnormal tissues and fluids of the host, a favourable medium in which their activities can give rise to the specific infection.'*

You might remember Sir Almroth Wright's words on how a new idea of medicine has to pass three different stages: 1) When it is regarded as ridiculous. 2) When doctors say, OK, it is possible, but where is the proof? 3) Everyone dismisses it as obvious. It is now 59 years since Dr Orr talked about nutrition as a new brand of medical science, which already then had a previous twenty years of development. This adds up to a grand total of 79 years. To date doctors have had 79 years to consider nutrition as treatment for both physical and mental ill-health as either ridiculous, or at best bordering on 'OK, it is possible, but where is the proof?' I am quite aware that we patients have got to learn to be patient, but this is really more than ridiculous.

Vets and farmers always look at the diet when an animal is off-colour and so should doctors when their patients are off-colour. Just because we are smart enough to build computers, travel to the moon and do brain surgery unfortunately doesn't make us on a cellular level much smarter than an ordinary mouse. All us complex warm-blooded mammals are only a collection of cells interlocking with each other. In order to keep going each cell needs water, oxygen, natural daylight, a correct temperature, protein, carbohydrates and fats. During ingestion these nutrients are then broken down further to amino acids, vitamins, minerals and essential fatty acids which keeps our cellular mechanism in good working order. All these nutritional substances are needed in the right individual proportions for good physical and mental health. Note, that

I said individual, because our personal nutritional needs
are as different as our fingerprints. Dr Roger Williams (86)
a famous chemist, who has done a great deal of research on
the subject, calls it Biochemical Individuality. No nutrient
does anything by itself. They always work as a team and in
that way they act constructively as the building blocks of
life. Unfortunately most people eat so carelessly that their
cells rarely ever get a 'square meal' and as the result their
poor little cells limp along as best they can in a pitiful
malnourished state. This semi-cellular illness can become a
serious disease, particuarly when it affects the mind.
Philosophers did a great disservice when they suggested
that head and body are some sort of separate phenomena.
This bizarre concept has been largely responsible for the
idea that mental illness was somewhat different from
physical illness. I believe this just isn't true. Our brain cells
are also a collection of cells and a part of our living
organism, and when its metabolism becomes disordered
due to a lack of proper nourishment, excess toxic-produc-
cing substances, hypoglycaemia, allergic stresses etc, our
behaviour, memory, perception, thinking and feeling also
become disordered. In short: a well-nourished and non-
toxic brain thinks normally and a malnourished and toxic
brain thinks abnormally.

The human brain and nervous system are almost totally
dependent on glucose or blood sugar for normal functioning, so amongst the first things that happen if sufficient
blood sugar is not available to the brain is a lack of normal
emotional control. This fact that brain cells are more
sensitive to blood sugar changes than other cells in the
body has led researchers to believe that it may also be more
sensitive to other nutritional deficiencies. It has been
indeed established that the very first signs of sub-clinical
vitamin deficiencies lead to a marked change in emotional
state.

We look to our doctors to guide our health and if our
doctor doesn't mention diet, we seem to assume that
nutrition as a prevention and treatment, for both physical
and mental illnesses, just can't be important and it doesn't
matter a damn what we eat as long as our bellies are full.
This kind of thinking is simply disastrous. We seem to

forget that the study of medicine is just that, and that in medical schools doctors study diseases, not health. Any teaching of the subject of nutrition is primarily limited to the recognition and treatment of so-called nutritional deficiency diseases, such as scurvy, pellagra, rickets and beri-beri, all of which are the final collapse of vitamin deficiency states. However, before this final collapse occurs, there is a vast 'grey area' of vitamin and mineral deficiency states which lead to varied malfunctions in our emotional health. We call these sub-clinical vitamin/mineral deficiency states, with which the majority of doctors are not familiar.

Our brain cells ultimately receive from our blood only those nutritional elements which are furnished in the food we eat, and if we eat carelessly our brains become malnourished leading to all sorts of mental disturbances. This malnutrition of affluence is rife amongst our western civilization, as there certainly is more than enough food for calories available, but the food is often nutritionally of such poor quality that malnutrition easily occurs. This term of malnutrition is applied to any individual who, due to careless eating habits and food selection, suffers from inadequate provision of essential nutrients such as vitamins, minerals and essential amino- and fatty-acids. Starvation on the other hand, which is unfortunately found frequently amongst the population of poor countries, means that the individual is suffering from a general shortage of food.

Our food furnishes all the vital raw material required for the synthesis of the most essential chemical substances, such as enzymes, hormones, co-factors etc., which are indispensable to our body's health maintenance and repair. In fact there is no body activity in which nutrition is not involved and with the exception of stress, nutrition is the only factor that can be controlled in most diseases, therefore it certainly should be the number one target in all treatments. Particularly when we are confronted with any disorder of so called 'unknown cause', whether mental or physical, we must consider diet as a factor.

Sub-clinical vitamin/mineral deficiency, allergies and hypoglycaemia should be routinely suspected in any patient with multiple physical and psychological symptoms, as the massive suffering doctors now inflict on their patients by the use of tranquillizing drug prescriptions, is really a terrifying price to pay for their failure even to consider the possibility. Thankfully all is not quite lost yet, as amongst this drug-oriented madness, there works a tiny nucleus of medical men, known as Clinical Ecologists or doctors interested in Nutritional Medicine, who believe like naturopaths, that the primary cause of most human ills is not some awful microbe, pernicious virus or a prowling germ which float around all over the place just waiting to bounce indiscriminately on poor unsuspecting victims. They believe that the majority of human ill health, both mental and physical, is primarily caused by man's own health-destroying living habits, leading to a weakened constitution and a weakened immune system function, which in turn makes him vulnerable to all sorts of mental and physical disorders. The basic treatment idea of these medical men is not to try to suppress or stimulate indiscriminately isolated bits of the patient's biochemistry by poisonous drugs, but to find out and advise their patients how best to strengthen their own biological body constitution to deal most effectively with a prowling germ or nasty virus, which never stop harassing us, as they are as much a part of the living universe as life itself.

Let's not forget what Dr Orr lectured to the British Medical Association in 1931, when he told them that animals suffering even a minor degree of nutritional deficiency, bacteria, which in animals on a perfect diet might remain non-pathogenic, find in the malnourished tissue fluids of the host a favourable medium in which their activities can give rise to specific signs of infection.

Let's not forget Harry Benjamin's words either, when he wrote in 1936 that besides astonishing feats in bacteriological science, diseases seem to exert as firm a hold on people as before, as the germs appear to thrive better than their victims. I can't but agree with them both.

So it looks now as if all sorts of bugs, viruses or germs don't necessarily cause symptoms in a healthy body, whether animal or man, but start playing havoc in an individual who allows his biological defence mechanism to

be weakened by the following factors:
1) Wrong food selection and careless nutritional habits which lead to sub-clinical vitamin/mineral deficiencies.
2) Excessive use and accumulation of toxic substances, which include the following: a) All non-prescribed drugs such as tobacco, alcohol, caffeine etc. b) Drugs prescribed by a doctor. c) Environmental pollutants such as food additives, agricultural pesticides, unclean water, air etc. d) Electro-pollution. e) Toxic metals such as lead, cadmium, aluminium and mercury.
3) Various addictions, whether to drugs, chemicals or to foods, which can cause addictive/allergic stresses and hypoglycoemia.
4) Lack of sufficient exercise, rest and relaxation.
5) Excessive physical and mental stress.
Naturally if you have been fortunate as to have inherited from your parents a strong biological constitution, your body system and mind can take more environmental insults than if you have the misfortune to be born of feeble stock. However, even if the latter is your case, you can always improve your lot by proper nutrition and a maximum avoidance of toxic pollution.

All these above-mentioned points formulate the basic structure of Naturopathy, Clinical Ecology, Environmental Therapy, Orthomolecular Medicine, Nutritional Medicine and Nutrition.

Since I now firmly believe that most conditions of ill health, both mental and physical, have the same underlying cause, the basic treatment principle for all disorders will be likewise the same, an approach which I will be starting to unravel in my next chapter.

8

THE ALLERGIC MARCH

Ever since the term allergy was invented it has been a subject of controversy amongst the medical profession as to how the term allergy should be defined. The majority of doctors still believe that the term allergy should be limited to those conditions which can be demonstrated by presently available immunologic laboratory techniques, including skin tests. The minority agree with the majority, but also include in this allergy category a hidden, masked or unsuspected food allergy, which can't be demonstrated in laboratories, which, in the majority's point of view should be called food intolerance.

Dr Clemens von Pirquet (87), who invented the word allergy, writes in his original paper: 'For this general concept of a changed reactivity I propose the term Allergy. *Allos* implies deviation from the original state. . . . A foreign substance which by one or more applications stimulates the organism to a change in reaction is an Allergen. This term traces its origin to the word Antigen, which implies a substance capable of giving rise to the production of Antibody. The term Allergen is more far-reaching. The Allergen compromises besides the antigen proper, the many protein substances which lead to no production of Antibodies, but to *supersensitivity.*'

Von Pirquet didn't say anything in his paper that an Allergy diagnosis must include positive skin tests or anything of that sort, therefore, as I see it, Allergy really is Allergy, not Food Intolerance.

The Royal College of Physcians and British Nutrition Foundation published a joint report in 1984 called *Food Intolerance and Food Aversion* (88) The following statement is found under the heading 'Conclusions': 'Reactions of food

94

intolerance have gained increasing recognition in recent years, but the lack of adequate scientifically based research and the lack of medical interest has led to the proliferation of organizations, centres and individuals offering advice which has little scientific basis.'

The following words are found under the heading 'Targets of Research': 'While some advances have been made in the understanding of food intolerance and food aversion in the last ten or twenty years, our knowledge of the aetiology of these conditions, of reliable diagnostic methods, and satisfactory forms of treatment, is inadequate. It would be impossible to describe all the gaps in our knowledge, but research into various areas enumerated below appears to be particularly urgent and timely: (Here are three of their six points.)

1) To define the mechanism, immunological or non-immunological, by which foods and food additives cause reactions in susceptible individuals and to assess the prevalence and relative frequency of the different sub-categories of food intolerance and food adversion.

2) To determine the similarities and differences in symptomatology between patients with food intolerance and various psychiatric conditions, particularly depression, personality disorder and eating disorders.

3) To examine the influence of the maternal diet during pregnancy and lactation and the effect of post-natal environmental influences on the immune responses of the infant and the development of food intolerance.'

Fair enough. While the allergy sufferers and people suffering from depression as well as those people suffering from personality disorders can fully sympathize with the medical profession's fervent desire to find out how allergy 'works', they are not any more willing to continue suffering from straight forward neglect just because of it. Furthermore, the longer this neglect continues, the medical profession can be assured that in time, more and more organizations, centres and individuals will come forward offering advice to other sufferers which have 'little scientific basis'. On the other hand these 'non-scientific organizations' are not after all such a dreaded curse as doctors like to think. Dr Vicky Rippere (89) conducted a research study on various self-help organizations concerned with allergies and found out that a considerable greater benefit and less adverse reactions occurred in people undergoing self-treatment than amongst the same sufferers undergoing medical treatment. One obvious reason was the avoidance of adverse side effects resulting from medical drugs. The most damning thing which was found to happen following self-treatment was that the sufferer didn't get any better as a result. All in all, it now appears that allergic sufferers prefer to get better, or at worst remain the same on unscientific grounds, than to get worse on scientific ones.

Allergies can be divided into two basic categories: First, a fixed allergy, when you always know that you have it, because as soon as you eat the offending food or are in contact with your allergy producing substance such as pollen, animal dander etc., you get a reaction. Most doctors when they talk about allergy, talk about these fixed allergies where the patient breaks out in a rash as soon as s/he eats shellfish or starts to wheeze because of pollen. These patients produce anbormally large amounts of antibodies, usually indicated by an abnormally high immunoglobulin E (IgE) level, which can be demonstrated in the laboratory, including skin tests. These patients are called atopic and usually suffer from such everyday allergies as asthma, hayfever etc.

Second is an unsuspected, hidden or masked allergy, which can not yet be demonstrated in laboratories and which the majority of doctors prefer to call food intolerance. However, a minority of doctors do prefer to call them allergies as Dr Von Pirquet first intended and which is also good enough for me.

This chapter deals only with the latter allergy or with this unsuspected, hidden or masked allergy. Because so many excellent books have been written about the subject already, I will outline here only the very basic points. Most of the following information I have collected from books by Dr Randolph (50), Dr Mackarness (10, 60), Dr Crook (90), Dr Forman (61), Dr Philpott (51), Dr Mumby (91), Dr Smith (92) Dr Mandell (93) and Amelia Nathan-Hill (94)

In order to get this allergy ball rolling, let's look first at what kind of symptoms you could experience if you have the misfortune to suffer from hidden or masked allergy.

Skin symptoms: Allergy can cause all sorts of rashes, which may appear as welts or hives. Your skin may appear scaly, dry or thickened and it may itch and tingle all over, or alternatively feel numb. You may have a very pale and sallow complexion even though you are not anaemic. You may also sweat excessively.

Nose and throat symptoms: Allergy can make your nose itch intensively, run or stuff up. When it runs, the discharge is usually clear. Allergy can make you sneeze excessively. It can also cause mucus drip down your throat so that you need to clear your throat a lot. Allergy can cause sinus trouble, nose polyps, frequent 'head colds', mild sore throat, bronchitis and asthma. Allergy may force you to breathe most of the time through your mouth, because of your blocked nose and sinuses. Allergy can make your voice become hoarse and sometimes even lose your voice periodically. Allergy may constrict your throat so that you have difficulty in swallowing.

Ear symptoms: Allergy can make your ears itch, buzz or hurt. You may suffer from repeated ear infections. Your ears may accumulate excessive wax which interferes with your hearing. You may even experience Ménière's syndrome with buzzing and deafness in one ear accompanied by vertigo and dizziness. Even brief fainting spells could occur.

Eye symptoms: Your eyes may itch, burn or water excessively. They may appear red or 'blood shot'. Your eyelids may become puffy and you may develop bags or dark circles under your eyes. Your vision may start to dim and blur. You may suffer from photophobia.

Chest symptoms: Your chest may feel tight and you may suffer from a cough, various chest pains, wheeze or rattle. You may bring up phlegm. You may suffer from a rapid and/or irregular heart beat and pulse rhythm. You may suffer from all sorts of breathing difficulties and a shortness of breath. Allergies may also lead to high blood pressure.

Digestive symptoms: Your stomach can become quite bloated and may hurt so much that you think you have an ulcer. You could suffer from constipation, diarrhoea, indigestion, belching and flatulence. You may feel nauseous and even vomit occasionally. You may suffer what

some doctors call 'an irritable bowel syndrome' or from
ileitis or colitis.

Circulatory symptoms: Allergy can make you flush or turn
pale. It can cause you to suffer from bad circulation causing
cold hands and feet.

Genito-urinary symptoms: Allergy can irritate your bladder
so that you may need to pass water more often than usual.
You may experience burning during urination. Allergy can
also cause itching and extra secretion of mucus from the
vagina. Allergy can cause also bed-wetting.

Musculosceletal symptoms: Allergy can make your whole
body ache and your joints become stiff and painful. It can
make you have 'arthritic pains' all over. Allergy can make
you suffer from painful muscle spasms, tightness and
stiffness in any muscle group in your body which is
particularly noticeable in the neck and shoulder area.
Allergy can cause excessive swelling in any part of the body,
neck, face, fingers, feet etc.

Psychological and general symptoms: Allergy can make you
irritable, overactive and restless, but more often it causes
you to feel tired, lethargic, sluggish and drowsy. It can cause
you to suffer from 'brain fag', when you have great trouble
in concentrating and remembering things. It can make you
so confused that you will have difficulty in finding the
correct words for things, or alternatively words may come
out in the wrong order, making your speech very difficult to
follow. Allergy can make you suffer from an extreme feeling
of fatigue, low grade fever, lack of energy and general
weakness. You may have trouble in sleeping or if you
manage to sleep, your sleep is restless with nightmares.
Allergy can cause you extreme depression. Allergy can
make you feel totally drained and exhausted. Allergy can
also lead to a low blood sugar or hypoglycaemia with its
accompanying anxiety and panic attacks.

Dr Randolph was the first one to use this word 'brain fag'
to describe the most characteristic form of an advanced
form of food/chemical allergy. Brain fag is difficult to
describe to those who have not seen it close up. It is a form
of mental fatigue, a much more serious and debilitating
symptom than physical tiredness. It is characterized by
mental confusion, slowness of thought, depression, feeling

of sadness, irritability, impaired memory, lack of comprehension, minimal brain dysfunction, indecisiveness, mental lapses and aphasia (speech difficulties). Patients are often called 'phobic' as they often feel too dizzy to walk, cannot get out of bed, cannot express their thoughts or remember what they are told. They seem to have lost their desire for life, and sometimes even call themselves 'the living dead'. Such patients are almost never properly diagnosed. They have 'graduated' to this condition through a number of previous levels of physical and mental distress. They therefore often have thick medical files, filled with long lists of complaints, many of them seemingly of mental origin. In truth, their mental problems are basically physical problems as they are directly caused by food/chemical allergy. Such patients are among the prime recipients of mood-altering drugs, electric shock therapy and psychotherapy and are constantly hounded by the 'pull-yourself-together-brigade'. However, none of this does much good, and as time goes by, they tend to get progressively worse, as the general course of an untreated allergic illness is usually downward.

When I first studied this mighty long list of seemingly unrelated allergic symptoms, my very first reaction was simple disbelief, as all I saw staring back at me from the print was 'a dashboard littered with knobs and gadgets not connected in any way to the engine itself', which, at least in my book, could not be right. However, after getting more acquainted with the subject I realized that it is quite possible after all, because these allergic reactions seem to have a combination of the following factors in common: Small blood vessels become porous causing leakage of fluids, including histamine, to the tissues involved, muscles of various parts of the body tighten or go into spasms and mucous membranes of the body become irritated causing an excessive mucous secretion. All these facts in turn can lead to a lack of oxygen supply to the tissues involved and also to a diminished pancreatic function, leading to metabolic acidosis.

We know that different people respond differently to allergy in different parts of their bodies. For example, if your small blood vessels become porous leading to leakage of fluids you will develop welts, hives, puffiness and swelling etc. If your muscles tighten up and go into spasms this can cause stiff joints, joint and neck pains, dimness and blurring of vision etc. If your mucous membranes become irritated, your nose, throat, bronchial tubes, intestinal tract etc. become irritated. Doctors usually name your illness according to the tissues involved in the allergic reaction. Therefore if your skin is affected, you may be diagnosed as suffering from eczema, urticaria or any other skin disease. If your muscles are affected, you may be diagnosed as suffering from myalgia, arthritis etc. If your mucous membranes are affected, you may be diagnosed as suffering from bronchitis, asthma, colitis or 'irritable bowel syndrome' etc. Now given that practically any part of the body can be affected by allergy, it would be mighty strange if the brain were not affected by allergy in susceptible individuals. In fact brain allergies or cerebral allergies exist, and most patients suffering from them seem to belong to the following diagnostic categories: hypochondriasis, organic brain syndrome, anxiety neurosis, phobias, transient confusion, agoraphobia, temporal lobe epilepsy, depression, personality disorder, ME etc. or at best, just a nuisance.

Dr Randolph writes: (50) 'During my forty years as an allergist I have treated 20,000 people for food allergies and related problems and have dealt with virtually every kind of chronic illness on allergic bases. About 7000 of these 20,000 patients were primarily suffering from so-called mental problems.' As I see it, not news to be dismissed slightly.

Now when we have got this basic background and symptomatology out of the way, it may be now appropriate to join 'the allergic march'.

Allergies usually run in families, or more precisely, you inherit your predisposition to your allergies from your parents. Therefore more often than not, if you are allergic, you will usually find some kind of allergy-related illness either in one or both of your parents or nearest relatives, such as asthma, bronchitis, eczema, dermatitis, hayfever, migraine, depression, anxiety neurosis, alcoholism, obesity, personality disorder, agoraphobia, hypoglycaemia, hyperglycaemia etc.

In the majority of the allergic individuals their 'allergic

march' started straight from the cradle, in others the allergy band only starts playing full blast after some 'trigger incident', or more likely, 'trigger incidents', of which I will be talking in the next chapter.

Now if your allergies started from the cradle, your physical and mental history could look something like this: First of all you might not have been breast-fed at all, but bottle fed from birth. You might have suffered from nappy rash or eczema. You might have been difficult to feed, you cried a lot and were often ill with colic. You could have been very late in learning to sit unsupported or to stand and walk, or alternatively you learned to walk very early, without even crawling first. You might have been prone to purposeless movements such as cot-rocking, head banging etc. You didn't seem to know how to smile at all, so you went about your business looking sad and gloomy most of the time. You hated to be picked up and cuddled. You seemed to suffer from a fair share of all sorts of illnesses, such as coughs, sinus problems, eye infections, stomach aches, colds etc. Your nose might have been almost always swollen and stuffed up, so you were prone to mouth breathing. You were a very bad sleeper, waking up in the early hours and refusing to go back to sleep again. You might have suffered from headaches, ear aches, 'growing pains', 'arthritic pains', as well as swollen and painful joints, which made you very irritable and depressed. You might have been a late bed-wetter. You might have been late in learning to talk, and when you finally did, you used to prefer to say 'no' to everything. You might have been a finicky eater, hating to eat anything which needed to be chewed, preferring to eat sweets, biscuits and other sugary foods. You might have suffered from a poor hand/eye co-ordination and/or right/left difficulties, which caused you to be clumsy and accident prone. Because of your co-ordination problems you might have had difficulties with such tasks as dressing yourself, buttoning garments, tying shoe laces etc. You might have been frequently thirsty, demanding squash, pop, milk etc. You might have looked very pale and anaemic with dark circles, bags or excessive wrinkles under your eyes. You might have been repeatedly on courses of antibiotics in order to treat your recurrent

infections. You might even have had your tonsils removed
at an early age in a desperate attempt to tackle your ailing
health . . . . At school you might have been diagnosed as
dyslexic because you had difficulties in learning to read or
to write. You seemed to be always a bit poorly, suffering
from all sorts of infections such as 'colds', sore throats,
headaches, stomach aches, muscle pains, runny nose etc.
You also seemed to be almost always tired and might have
had difficulties in staying awake during the day. You were
generally irritable and had difficulties in waking up in the
mornings. You even might have suffered from school
phobia. Your overall school performance might have been
bad, even though your IQ was normal or above normal. You
might have had difficulties in sporting activities because of
your poor co-ordination skills. You might have suffered
even from occasional 'giddy spells' or fainting fits. You
looked pale and anaemic and might have been treated for
'anaemia' without making any progress whatsoever. You
might have also suffered from 'proper allergies' such as skin
disorders, hayfever or asthma.

  Children with allergies can deviate behaviourally in three
ways. They can be either withdrawn or underactive,
abnormally outgoing or overactive or a combination of
both, which means that these extreme behaviours alternate.
The first types are called 'withdrawers' and the second type
'approachers'. The 'withdrawers' don't usually tend to
attract much attention in medical circles, except in extreme
cases of pathological withdrawal. 'Approachers' on the
other hand stand out in a crowd like a sore thumb and are
soon diagnosed as suffering from Minimal Brain Dysfunction, Hyperkinetic Syndrome, Special Learning Disorders
and Hyperactivity, to name but a few. 'Withdrawers' are
children who seem to be painfully shy, submissive and often
quite fearful. Such a child might be easily frightened by
sudden noises or movements and usually clings to mother
in panic when confronted with strangers or any new
situations. He dislikes to join any group activities, as he
seems to become easily confused when there are many
people about. He generally feels much happier and more
comfortable in a one-to-one relationship. He is often a
loner, may lack friends and seem to prefer animals to

people.

The 'approacher' or hyperactive child on the other hand can be a moving disaster. He dashes headlong into everything being quite unaware of danger or dangerous situations. The word 'no' has no meaning to him whatsoever. He seems to have a very short attention span and gets very easily frustrated. He seems to have little interest in toys or books except a wish to break them or tear them apart. He cruises around the house with a glassy look in his eyes, frantically touching, hitting, pulling or biting everything or everyone. He tears off his clothing, ignoring hooks or buttons. He can't stand to be picked up or cuddled. He seems to race purposelessly around whining or shouting with red patches on his cheeks, earlobes and nosetip glowing, making a thorough nuisance of himself. When he is given a pencil, he usually holds it very tight in his fist, furiously scribbling down any old line over and over again. He may suffer from unpredictable temper tantrums and aggressive behaviour . . . . When he goes to school, he is generally very disruptive, unco-operative, defiant and disobedient. He may also be very bossy, selfish, stubborn and impudent, which causes him to have difficulty in making friends. Teachers and other pupils may start to pick on him to which he responds either with tears or fighting.

Most parents and doctors seem to have a mistaken idea that allergic babies and children will 'grow out' of their allergies, as the 'proper allergy symptoms' such as eczema often seem to disappear around four or five years of age. This is not so, as the baby who reacted to milk for example, usually becomes a child, teenager or adult who suffers from other allergies in different ways. Because childhood hyperactivity has been recognized as a medical problem only very recently, there are not many follow-up studies around which could enlighten us as to how hyperactive children fare as adults.

Weiss *et al.* (256) have done some studies on the subject. For example their five year follow-up study indicated that the prognosis of hyperactive children as they matured into adolescence was relatively poor. They found out that despite a decreased rating of hyperactive behaviour itself over a period of five years, as adolescents, they continue to be distractible, emotionally immature and unable to maintain goals, causing them often to develop a poor self-image. The school records of hyperactive adolescents showed a greater incidence of failed school grades and lower rating in all subjects of their school reports compared to matched control children in the same school. The hyperactive children continued to use impulsive rather than reflective approaches to cognitive tasks, and over a five year period they showed no improvement on tests of intelligence, visual tasks or performance of motor skills. About 25% of a group of 64 engaged in delinquent behaviour, which was a far higher percentage than matched controls. Most hyperactive children become more 'normal' in their teens, but their initial problem such as distractibility and excitability were still troublesome. In addition they had often become disobedient and rebellious at home and were having serious difficulties with their school work. A significant minority, maybe one in four, were involved in enough antisocial behaviour to make their peers pessimistic about their future.

Now that we have established what hyperactivity is, we might as well try to find out some sort of 'connection' between allergies and hyperactive behaviour.

Weiss *et al.* (96) published a report in 1971 of children who were suffering from hyperactivity and who also had a family history of allergies and/or carbohydrate-related metabolic disorders such as hypoglycaemia or diabetes. They found out that many of these hyperactive children had also physical symptoms including atopic dermatitis, abdominal pains, rhinitis, sinusitis, ear infections, headaches, joint and muscle pains, wheezing and a number of other physical signs. They concluded that an allergic component could indeed be involved in hyperactive behaviour, but not 'the usual kind of allergy', because most results of the skin tests showed negative results to the incriminating foods.

Egger *et al.* (97) conducted a controlled trial using a simple dietary modification (oligoantigenic diet) on 76 hyperactive children. The research results were published in *The Lancet* in 1985. They found that out of these 76 hyperactive children 62 improved, and a normal range of behaviour was achieved in 21 of them. In addition to hyperactivity, other 'side symptoms' such as headaches, abdominal pains and fits also improved. They established that food colourants, especially tartrazine and preservatives, especially benzoates were the commonest substances which produced abnormal behaviour, although no child in this study reacted to them alone. Cow's milk, chocolate, wheat, oranges and eggs were also high on the list. 32 out of these 76 children were found to be atopic, or suffering from either eczema, asthma or hayfever. 52 children had a first-degree relative who was atopic, and furthermore 24 children had a history of hyperactivity in their first-degree relatives. They concluded their study by pointing out that the suggestion that diet may contribute to behaviour disorders must now be taken seriously.

A couple of years previously Egger et al. (98) conducted another double-blind controlled trial using an oligoantigenic diet on 88 children suffering from migraine headaches. The result of this study was published in *The Lancet* in 1983. This trial consisted of 40 boys and 48 girls aged between 3 and 16 years. 48 of these children had a history of atopic disease and 65 had a first-degree relative who either suffered from migraine and/or atopic disease. After dietary manipulation 93% of these children recovered from their migraine attacks. However, the good news doesn't end there, as it was also discovered that the diet modification didn't only cure their migraine, but also their 'associated symptoms', such as abdominal pain, diarrhoea, aches in limbs, fits, rhinitis, recurrent mouth ulcers, asthma, eczema and their behavioural disorders. It was in fact established that almost all of these children tested suffered some sort of behavioural disturbances during their migraine attacks. Furthermore 41 of these children showed hyperactive behaviour at other times. When their diet was corrected, besides curing their migraine, the hyperactive behaviour also ceased in a majority of cases. Epilepsy improved also, and all anti-epileptic drugs were discontinued from the children who became fit-free. These children also remained fit-free unless they broke their diet. Most of these children reacted to several foods and more often than not they seemed to crave the offending foods, and they usually ate or drank the offending food or drink in large quantities when

they had the chance. In this particular study the mos
allergy producing substances were found to be: cow's milk
egg, chocolate, orange, wheat and benzoic acid. This
particular study also pointed out the sheer futility in using
skin tests in trying to diagnose masked or hidden allergies
as only three children out of these children tested had
positive skin test results. Similarly it was found that only
28% of 64 children tested had a high serum IgE levels, but
even in these cases IgE antibodies were not helpful in
identifying the troublesome foods. They concluded their
study by pointing out that patients with migraine and
epilepsy, and probably with epileptic headache, are likely to
benefit from this dietary approach, therefore identification
of food allergy is important, which is then in turn easily
treatable and the benefit experienced by the patients was
often very great.

Dr Buisseret (99) studied 79 children aged between
eleven months and seventeen years who were diagnosed as
being allergic to cow's milk. These patients were found to
be suffering in addition to difficulties with infant feeding
and diarrhoea, clinical features such as constipation,
vomiting, intestinal colic, growth retardation, eczema,
asthma and psychological disturbances. In fact 33% of these
children had received medical advice because of psychological disturbances, usually because the child was excessively nervous, timid, 'highly strung', aggressive, withdrawn or
prone to nightmares. All these physical and psychological
symptoms were reversible after milk was withdrawn from
their diet. Children who often complained from abdominal
pain prior to going to school, and after eating milk and
cereal for breakfast, were thought to be malingering. In
most of these children suffering from milk allergy, one or
both parents were found to be atopic and most of these
children were bottle-fed from birth. In this particular
experiment 69% of skin tests gave negative results. Dr
Buisseret concluded his study by stating that a correct
diagnosis of milk and/or other food allergies could spare
the child prolonged medical treatment and could also help
the child to resolve his behavioural or psychological
difficulties.

Dr Crook (100) writes in *The Lancet*: 'In my general paediatric and allergy practice I have found that 75% of my hyperactive patients improve, often dramatically, when their diets are changed. I base this statement on a clinical study of 182 new hyperactive patients who came to me during a five year period. Sugar was identified by the parents as the leading troublemaker, with food dyes (especially red) and additives second. Many children also showed adverse reactions to a wide variety of other foods, including milk, corn, chocolate, wheat, egg and citrus fruits . . . . Naturally it would be helpful if the offending foods could be identified by immunological tests, including prick tests, radio-allergosorbent assays, scratch tests and leucocyte inhibition of histamine. However, the adverse reactions to foods which cause hyperactivity rarely belong to one of the four types of immunological reactions outlined by Gell and Coombs . . . . In about 1745 James Lind observed that putting limes on board British ships prevented scurvy. Yet it was 50 years before supplementation of the diets of British sailors with limes and other fresh fruits and vegetables became a routine practice . . . . and it was not until 1919 that Albert Szent-Györgi isolated vitamin C and provided scientific explanation for the efficiency of limes . . . . Now hundreds of American physicians have found that most irritable, unhappy, hyperactive children can be helped by a carefully designed trial diet in 5-10 days. And after the child's symptoms show a convincing improvement which lasts 48 hours, the food troublemakers can be identified by having the child eat them again, one food a day, over a second 7–10 day period. James Lind would have approved of this approach.'

Before we move from allergic children to allergic adults, I would like to point out some interesting observations: First of all that there seems to be an elevated frequency in left-handed individuals associated with allergies, migraine and developmental learning disorders such as dyslexias and stuttering, also that a great chunk of hyperactive children seem to be blue eyed, blond boys. (101a) Furthermore that children with hyperactivity and learning disorders can go on to achieve great things. For example Thomas Edison was described as ineducable, and Winston Churchill was said to be so difficult to manage as a child that he needed a 'stalwart nanny' to cope with him.

Now a few words about allergic adults: Dr Grant (102) conducted an elimination and challenge diet amongst 60 migraine patients for the purpose of establishing whether food/chemical allergies could be the cause of their migraine attacks. Eight men and fifty-two women took part. Out of these 52 females tested, 87% had been using oral contraceptive steroids (the Pill), tobacco and/or ergotamine, for an average of 3 years, 22 years and 7.4 years respectively. The commonest foods causing migraine in this study were wheat, orange, egg, tea and coffee, chocolate and milk, beef, corn, cane sugar and yeast, in that order. When these foods were avoided, all patients improved and 85% became headache-free. She concluded that both immunological and non-immunological allergies seem to play a part in the provocation of migraine attacks. Furthermore that using oral contraceptive steroids for 3–4 years and/or tobacco smoking over 20 years could lead to a development of migraine allergies. Tobacco smoking because of its toxic compounds, and the Pill, because it is composed of steroids, both of which may interfere directly with the immune mechanism.

Jones et al. (103) studied whether specific food allergies could be a major factor in provoking Irritable Bowel Syndrome (IBS). This IBS is a common gastro-intestinal disorder in which abdominal pain accompanied by diarrhoea or constipation and flatulence occurs without any evidence of organic disease. The cause of this condition is unknown, but it has been suggested to be largely psychological. Treatment may include bran, bulk laxatives, antispasmodics and tranquillizers, but all these treatment approaches have been found to be usually unsatisfactory. This study established that in fourteen of the twenty-one patients tested, the following food stuffs were responsible in provoking their IBS symptoms, some patients being affected by more than one of these items: wheat (9 patients), corn (5), dairy products (4), coffee (4), tea (3) and citrus fruit (2). Their IBS was cleared simply by avoiding offending food(s).

Darlington et al. (104) conducted a placebo-controlled, blind study of dietary manipulation in the treatment of rheumatoid arthritis. The results indicated that dietary changes may be of help at least in some rheumatoid patients.

Finn and Cohen (105) used dietary manipulation on six patients with long-standing physical and mental symptoms, who had not been helped by many years of conventional medical investigations and treatment. They found out that these patients experienced immediate relief of their chronic symptoms when they avoided certain foodstuffs. For example, a patient who was diagnosed first as suffering from pulmonary embolism, later cardiac neurosis and finally agoraphobia, was found to be allergic to tea, coffee and tomatoes when tested in controlled experimental conditions. The patient was cured by simple avoidance of the allergy producing substances. Another patient was cured from panics, depression, faintness and sweating after avoiding all caffeine based substances. The study points out that both an excessive caffeine consumption as well as various foods can indeed contribute to widespread and disabling mental and physical symptoms in people who happen to be sensitive to them.

Dohan and Grasberger (106) studied schizophrenic patients, who on admission to a locked ward were randomly assigned to a cereal, grain-free, milk-free diet. Schizophrenics on a milk and cereal-free diet were able to be discharged from the hospital twice as rapidly as control patients who were consuming a high milk and cereal diet. When wheat gluten was added secretly to the cereal-free diet, it abolished this effect. They concluded that cereal grains may be pathogenic for those individuals hereditarily predisposed to coeliac disease. This study, as well as Dohan's previous findings indicate that cereal grains may be involved in the pathogenesis of some schizophrenias. They felt therefore, that if a simple diet manipulation proves to be an effective long-term therapeutic adjunct in the treatment for schizophrenia, it should be worth trying, as it could save a lot of unnecessary suffering.

Philpott (107) and his team studied a random sample of 53 hospitalized schizophrenic patients and found out that 92% of them were found to be allergic to at least one or more common substances, including wheat, corn, cow's milk, tobacco and petrochemical hydrocarbons.

Kay Hall (108) reviewed 156 research studies concerning the role of allergy in various nervous system diseases. Her findings show that allergy can cause diverse behavioural and neurological disturbances including schizophrenia, depression, learning disabilities, explosive outbursts and erratic and antisocial behaviour. It can also cause a feeling of extreme drowsiness, sometimes with alternating excitability, anxiety, tension, dizziness, irritability, a sensation of imbalance, stiff and painful joints, shoulders and neck, a difficulty of a co-ordination of speech, jumbling of words etc.

These are just a few samples of dietary treatments which have been published in reputable scientific journals. There are hoards of others, but this little book of mine is not geared to deal with them all. However, these few reflect in a 'round-about' way what we have already discussed about allergies causing a myriad of mental and physical ill-health. Now for example, let's take the children's migraine study. The study talked about migraine and 'associated symptoms' of abdominal pain, diarrhoea, aches of limbs, fits, rhinitis, recurrent mouth ulcers, asthma, eczema and behavioural disorders. I personally find this way of looking at an illness like migraine quite strange. But let's face it, maybe this crazy 'piece-meal' approach to an illness is necessary if Clinical Ecologists are to penetrate the current medical way of thinking, as unfortunately nowadays more and more doctors are trained to specialize in ever-decreasing bits and bobs of the human body. There are now heart specialists, nerve specialists, skin specialists, ear, nose and throat specialists, eye specialists, pain specialists, brain specialists and so on and so forth. I suppose while these 'bit-specialists' are in charge of the current medical show, the Clinical Ecologists have no other choice but to dance to the same tune and offer migraine with 'associated symptoms', eczema with 'associated symptoms', aches and pains with 'associated symptoms', fits with 'associated symptoms', behavioural disorders 'with associated symptoms' and so on and so forth. However, whilst this merry-go-round is going on, let's continue to look more closely at allergies and addictions.

9

ARE YOU A FOOD JUNKIE?

It is well known that any man or animal can develop an addiction to any substance in the universe which has been introduced into the body in large enough doses for a sufficient length of time. Bearing that in mind, unsuspected, masked or hidden food allergy is said to differ only in degree from a drug or alcohol addiction. According to Dr Randolph, the most addiction producing substances in order of severity are: heroin plus other opiates and natural drugs, all synthetic drugs as well as chemical exposures, food and drug combinations such as caffeine, cigarettes, alcohol, strong teas etc, and finally foods, ie. sugars, starches, proteins, oils and fats, in that order.

The following studies may throw some light on how so-called food addiction might come about: Zioudrou et al. (109) was able to isolate some purified peptides with opioid-like activity from pepsin digest of wheat gluten and milk casein. They named these peptides exorphins, because of their exogenous origin and morphine-like activity. These exorphins are thought to function like endorphins and enkephalins, which are widely distributed in the human body and which are in turn thought to function like hormones or neurotransmitters. They also seem to have the remarkable property of being able to activate receptors in the brain to which drugs like morphine and other narcotics usually become attached. In order for these exorphins to function like opioid peptides in the body, brain and central nervous system, they have to fulfill the following criteria: First of all they should be produced in the gastro-intestinal tract, secondly they should survive degradation by the intestinal tract and be absorbed into the blood stream, where they should be able to cross the blood-brain barrier, and finally, interact as opiates in brain opiate receptors. Zioudrou and his team were able to demonstrate that some exorphins indeed survived degradation by the intestine and entered the blood stream.

Dr Hemmings (110) studied whether or not some dietary proteins extracted from wheat could cross the blood-brain barrier, when labelled with radio-iodine, and fed by a stomach tube to rats. His findings were positive. He suggested that some dietary proteins may be only in part degraded in the gut to small peptides and amino acids, leaving the rest to be transmitted into the lymph and plasma as a large molecular mass, from where they are able to enter the tissue cells all throughout the body . . . . Now there is food for thought.

Now a few words about the immune system in relation to allergies. Our immune system is involved in allergies in two ways, that is, through circulating antibodies i.e. the humoral system, and through circulating lymphocytes, i.e. the cellular system. Immediate sensitivity, or the fast response of an allergy is primarily mediated through the humoral system, or with the help of B-lymphocytes, and all doctors acknowledge this. The unsuspected, hidden, masked or addictive allergy, or the slow response, of which we are talking here, is mediated through the cellular system and with the help of T-lymphocytes, which only a minority of doctors wish to acknowledge.

The very first task of our immune system is to react against virtually any substance which is recognized by our body as 'foreign'. However, our immune system is more capable of recognizing some substances as 'foreign' than others. Proteins and carbohydrates for example are strong antigens. So are bacteria and viruses since they have protein and carbohydrate exposed at their surfaces. Lipids and nucleic acids, on the other hand, are weak antigens, and most very low molecular compounds, such as natural or synthetic drugs, as well as other toxic chemicals may not be antigenic at all in their own right. But they seem to have the ability to act as haptens in the body, which are then able to combine with large body proteins, forming so called 'haptenated proteins', which are then in turn able to function just like a partial or complete antigen. (111) To put it simply, our immune system is capable of reacting one way or another against every conceivable 'foreign substance' in the universe, including drugs, bugs, food colourings, toxic chemicals, and in susceptible individuals, against various everyday foods themselves.

We have already discussed in the last chapter how the tendency to allergies seems to run in families. However, it is not the 'type' of allergy which is inherited, but the predisposition to allergies, which means that we can inherit from our parents a substandard immune system function, which doesn't seem to be effective enough to deal with an excess of cumulating 'foreign insults', leading eventually to the appearance of our individual allergic symptoms. What I mean by individual allergic symptoms could be seen like this for example: Your mother might be allergic to eggs and when she eats them she seems to develop all sorts of eczematous rashes. Your father might get stiff and painful neck and other joint pains if he smokes excessively. Your brother might develop a congested chest and blocked sinuses soon after consuming dairy products, and you in turn might become weepy, sullen and madly depressed if you are exposed for any length of time to an environment consisting of hydrocarbons such as household gas, burning oil, coal or petrol fumes .... As a general rule, however, most allergics have multiple allergies which affect various parts of their bodies at different times of their lives. In other words, any food or chemical can produce any symptoms at some time in someone who is allergic to them. Furthermore, the same foods can produce different symptoms in different people, as well as different foods producing different symptoms in the same people.

Now that we have established in a round-about way that most human ills are directly caused by defective immunity, it might be worth having a look at how our immunity might become so defective that the poor thing can't even tell the difference between a proper virus and a slice of morning toast.

The following factors have been found to contribute to a defective immune system function:

Hereditary factors which may include: a) Pre-conceptual nutritional deficiencies of one or both of your parents. b)

Your mother's diet may not have been nutritious enough whilst she was expecting you. c) Your mother might have suffered either from a heavy metal toxidity such as lead, cadmium etc. and/or consumed excessive amounts of drugs while pregnant. d) You might have been born prematurely or were a low birth-weight baby. e) You might have been not breast-fed at all, but introduced to foreign proteins, such as cow's milk soon after birth.

These are just some thoughts on how a defective immune system may come about. However, I must stress here that not everyone who might have had a similar background to that mentioned above, is a sickly individual. Now having said that, in my opinion at least, every baby should be given all conceivable help to be born as healthy as possible, therefore if I were you and planning a family, before even thinking about any serious hanky-panky, I would first contact an organization called Foresight, which is an association for the promotion of pre-conceptual care, and I would listen extra carefully to what they have to say. I will be including their address at the end of this book.

Even if you might have been born with a fairly adequate immune system function, the combination of the following factors can be responsible for suppressing its efficiency:

a) An excessive use of antibiotics and other inflammatory drugs.
b) Chemical toxic overload such as polluted food, water and environment.
c) An excessive use of both prescribed and non-prescribed drugs such as tranquillizers, the Pill, nicotine, alcohol, caffeine etc.
d) Food addictions, which differ only in degree and severity from drug or chemical addictions, as everything in this world is really made of chemicals.
e) An overload of other allergic stresses such as pollens, moulds etc.
f) Viral, bacterial and fungal infections.
g) Serious operations, injury and even in some cases, childbirth.
h) Excessive and prolonged physical stresses such as cold, heat, exercise, fatigue etc.

i) Excessive mental stresses. For example Bartrop *et al.* (112) were able to demonstrate a significantly suppressed immune system function after breavement.

j) Not forgetting careless food selection which can lead to overall vitamin and mineral deficiencies, leading to further impairment of immunity.

To sum it up. It could be said that everyone prone to allergies seems to have his own tolerance level at which allergic symptoms will appear, and furthermore this tolerance level depends entirely on the state of his immune system function. In other words, a person will only develop allergic symptoms when his total immuno-suppressive load, some of the factors I mentioned above, builds up and exceeds his own personal resistance level. In short, any potential allergic may be likened to one walking on a knife edge, from which he will easily fall, as any additional immuno-suppressive stress soon paves a way to full-blown allergic symptoms.

Taking this approach to the development of allergies, one could now argue, that an allergy really has many different causes, because your allergic symptoms may not even show until your total stress load overcomes your personal tolerance level. This in mind, at least in my opinion, there should also be many different treatment approaches to allergies, which I will be discussing more fully at the end of this chapter. But before we get there, I would like to explain as best as I can, the so called 'elimination and challenge' approach for the diagnosis and treatment of this mysterious unsuspected, masked or hidden food allergy, which has also been clearly described in the Royal College of Physicians' and the British Nutrition Foundation's joint report under the heading *Diagnosis of Food Intolerance and Allergy*.

The report points out that a diagnosis of food allergies can only be established if the symptoms disappear with the elimination diet and if a controlled challenge leads to a recurrence of symptoms or some other clearly identified change. They write: 'A simple diet can be given over a period of at least two, preferably three weeks, eliminating either individually identified foods, or if these cannot be determined, eliminating all those foods which are most closely associated with adverse reactions. It should be accepted, however, that improvement on an elimination diet may take up to three weeks, and there may even be withdrawal symptoms in the first week. Only if symptoms disappear within the period of the diet, is the possibility of food intolerance worth pursuing by means of food challenge tests, or by challenge with measured amounts of food preservatives or dyes . . . . As with any form of challenge testing, some caution is necessary when tests are carried out in highly sensitive subjects in whom severe reaction may be provoked.' To put it simply: Any substance can be considered being an allergy producing substance for you if:

a) You feel better by avoiding it.
b) You start feeling ill on re-exposure to it.
c) And your doctor has excluded all other possibilities for your present symptoms by thorough physical and laboratory examinations.

This delayed or masked allergy occurs when unsuspected sensitivity has been developed to something eaten or inhaled in frequent intervals. This is often likened to addictions, because usually the poor allergic blighter gets into a rapid cycle of pick-up and hangover symptoms with his addiction, whether it is a food or a chemical. In addition he also seems to crave or to be 'hooked' on the particular food or chemical which makes him feel ill in the first place.

This concept of allergy/addiction was first discovered by Dr Rinkel (113) from his experience with his own allergies. It came about when he had been suffering for a very long time from a chronic runny nose, sore throats and ear infections, so he decided to start to experiment with his own diet to see whether any foods could conceivably be the cause for his annoying chronic symptoms. He decided to give up eggs for a while, which he had been eating literally every day for many years. After a few days without eggs he thought he felt somewhat better. On the fifth day, however, he ate a piece of birthday cake his wife had made him, not realizing that it had eggs in it. Ten minutes later he collapsed in a dead faint on the floor and didn't come around for several minutes. When he was told that the cake was made with eggs, he reasoned that being without eggs for some days previously could have made him become highly sensitive to them, so that even the very small amount of egg found in the cake could cause him to experience an acute allergic reaction. He defined this newly-found allergic phenomenon 'masking', which he describes in the following way: If one uses a food every day or so, one may be allergic to it, but never suspect it as a cause of any chronic symptoms, as it is usually common to feel better after that meal at which the food is used than before the mealtime.

This idea of elimination diet is not a new concept by any means. In fact it was described in medical literature as early as 1928 by Dr Rowe. (114)

Now that we have skated over the very basic background of the unsuspected, masked, hidden or addictive allergies, it seems timely to get on with the actual allergy detection and find out what to eliminate, when to eliminate and how long to eliminate. But before we start, let's stress again that food/chemical allergy may not be the cause or the only cause of your present illness, but it is almost certainly the most unrecognized one by the majority of today's medical profession. So if your doctor has definitely excluded all other possibilities for your present feeling of ill-health by all necessary examinations and found nothing whatsoever to account for your annoying symptoms, you really should suspect that you may be allergic.

As we have already seen, the basic diagnosis of masked allergy can only be confirmed by abstaining from the allergy producing food and/or chemical, until your symptoms subside, which happens often between 4-12 days of avoidance, and then challenging with a dose of that avoided food-chemical and observing results. This 4-12 days' testing period comes about, as it has been established that avoiding a masked allergen for less than 4 days will simply continue the masking process and by avoiding the food for more than 12 days, the sensitivity to it might be temporarily lost . . . . Before we start, please note that this elimination/challenge test should be done under medical supervision, particularly if your symptoms include epileptic fits, diabetes, asthma, schizophrenia and severe depression. Or at the very least you should have always somebody with you who could contact a doctor if necessary.

At the very beginning everything is suspect. This includes all your medications, even your vitamin tablets or your toothpaste. However, you can simplify this elimination process a great deal if you can answer honestly to the following questions: 1) What are your favourite foods and drinks? 2) Which foods or drinks would you hate to give up in order to control your allergies? 3) Which foods/drinks/ drugs do you consume at least once every day, or nearly every day? I don't want to be the bearer of bad news, but your allergy producing substance is almost certainly one or more of the substances you mentioned when you replied to the questions above. Furthermore, I am nearly certain that it is to be found amongst the following items: dairy products such as cow's milk and products made of it, eggs, or cereals, particularly wheat. Foods which contain a lot of additives and refined sugar. Stimulants such as caffeine, strong tea, chocolate, cola drinks, alcohol and tobacco. And finally prescribed drugs, particularly tranquillizers. Now when you look carefully at this list of substances you can see that all of these have been introduced really relatively recently to man's diet, which is only some thousands of years ago. Before this pre-cereal diet, for millenia, Stone Age man was a simple hunter-gatherer, who grazed around all day eating whatever he might find such as berries, roots, nuts, fruit, and if he was lucky, occasionally catching a small mammal or a fish. I mention this, because a basic elimination diet means simply that one should adopt a diet, similar to the Stone Age diet for a period of at least a week, or preferably up to three weeks as the Royal College of Physicians' report suggests. Also do not forget that the report points out that you might suffer from 'withdrawal symptoms' for the first week or so. Naturally it is entirely up to you how long you are willing to stick to your diet. However, if I were one of those folks who had become simply sick and fed up with being sick, regardless of all reassurances, tablets, pills and potions, while being faithfully under a doctor or a hospital, I surely would consider staying on the Stone Age diet for at least three weeks and keep my fingers crossed.

The following foods are allowed on the Stone Age diet:

All kinds of fresh meats, fowl and fish, all kinds of fresh vegetables, fruits, nuts and berries. Freshly ground salt and pepper for seasoning, cold-pressed vegetable oil for cooking and herb teas and bottled water for drinking. The following foods are forbidden: All manufactured, processed, adulterated and colourfully packaged foods, including all sugars, sweets, fizzy drinks, squashes etc. All cereal foods such as bread, breakfast cereals, biscuits, cakes etc. All dairy produce, such as cow's milk and foods containing cow's milk such as cheese, butter, cream, and also eggs. All smoked and tinned meats such as sausages, luncheon meats etc. And finally coffee, tea, chocolate and alcoholic drinks. Tobacco smoking should also be discontinued.

The oligoantigenic diet or 'few foods diet' which Dr Egger and his team used on children suffering from migraine and hyperactivity, is based on the fact that the more limited the range of foods, the greater chance there is of identifying the allergy producing foods. Their 'few foods diet' consisted of one meat (lamb or chicken), one carbohydrate (rice or potato), one fruit (banana or apple), one vegetable (brassica) and spring water, accompanied with vitamin/mineral supplementation.

It looks as if in this 'masked allergy business' there are nowadays as many names and approaches for elimination diets as there are doctors interested in the subject. However, all of them do have one thing in common; all of them are trying to find out which foods and/or chemicals are responsible for your allergy producing symptoms. I personally have always been an individual who dislikes fuss and prefers things as simple as possible, therefore I wouldn't let these different approaches confuse me unduly, so in order to unravel the mysterious substances which may be responsible for my ill-health, I would just avoid for a start all the most well-known allergy producing foods, drinks and chemicals and wait to discover whether I would be feeling better as the result. I would avoid all foods containing sucrose or table sugar, cow's milk and related products, all cereal products, egg products, as well as all manufactured, processed and adulterated foods and stick religiously to all fresh meats, vegetables and fruits. I also would forsake for three weeks or so, my beloved tea, coffee, chocolates and booze and stick to bottled waters and herb teas. As far as cigarette smoking goes, all I can tell you about the subject is that cigarettes have been found to be extremely allergenic for some susceptible individuals. Therefore, if you are a smoker and one of those unfortunate ones, all you have to do to get better, is to quit smoking altogether. You might become as miserable as sin doing all that, but at least you will be both physically and mentally healthy in your misery.

Now if your symptoms don't improve within three weeks on the diet, it is probable that foods are not the cause of your symptoms, or alternatively your elimination diet still contains foods to which you may be intolerant. Alternatively your ill-health is caused by an addiction to any medical drugs you might be on, or possibly indoor or outdoor pollution. In fact when you compare the symptom list of masked allergies and the side effects of tranquillizing medication, take or leave a few points, the list is remarkably similar. Therefore, at least in my opinion, it may be pretty nigh impossible to establish whether you are an allergy sufferer while you are on your tranquillizing medication. So if you happen to be one of those unfortunates who is hooked on tranquillizers, the only thing to get better, is to try to withdraw from the dreaded drug. However, do not try to do it alone. If your doctor is unable to help you, do contact an organization called Tranx, who are experts on the subject and whose address I'll be including at the end of the book.

If your symptoms are caused by indoor/outdoor pollution, or in other words, by some chemical odours or vapours, the basic rule of thumb is that if you feel better away from home, the culprit is most likely found inside your own home, and if you feel worse outside your home, the culprit is very likely outside. The worst offenders are odours of burning coal, oil, gas, petrol, cigarette smoke, cleaning fluids, paraffin, wax polishes, tars, fresh newsprint, disinfectants, bleaches, detergents, rubber, plastics, adhesives, fresh paint, turpentine, formaldehyde, chlorine, moth balls, insecticides, ammonia, pine, perfumes and so on and so forth. In fact it has been said that if you can smell it, you can also be made ill by it. Likewise if you seem to ancy certain smells, particularly if they seem to give you a lift', that substance is particularly suspicious.

You can test your reaction to various chemicals using a so-called 'sniff' or inhalation test. First of all the test is only valid if each substance tested had been eliminated completely from your environment for at least five days. Place a small amount of cotton wool with a few drops of tested chemical in the bottom of a jar, close the jar with an airtight lid and leave it sealed up for five days. For actual testing open the jar in a well-ventilated room, sniff and notice reaction. Do you feel nauseous or faint? Has your pulse rhythm increased? Do you suffer from palpitations? The more strong or unpleasant the reaction, the more poisonous that substance is for you. In order to test natural gas, after five days avoidance just sniff an unlit gas outlet for five seconds or so and see what happens.

Tobacco is close to being an almost universal allergen and about 75% of the world's population are thought to be allergic to it. (51) In order to test whether you are allergic to cigarettes and you are a smoker, just discontinue smoking for five days and in the sixth day smoke continously at least four cigarettes one after the other. If you then experience some of the following range of mental and emotional symptoms, such as mild or severe anxiety, tension, fatigue, dizziness, weakness, perceptual distortions or even hallucinations, cigarettes certainly can't be good for you. Now while we are with this nicotine weed, I find this a good opportunity to try to explain how some addictions manifest themselves.

If you cast your mind back, you might remember how you felt when you were trying to learn to smoke cigarettes, providing of course that you are a smoker, or an ex-smoker. I bet my bottom dollar that it must have been really hard work, because your first nimble steps to nicotine addiction were most certainly paved with all sorts of unpleasant setbacks. Besides possibly feeling guilty, you felt nauseous, dizzy, weak, shaky and generally green around the gills. As with most addictions, a persistent use of the addictive substance, in this case cigarettes, causes these unpleasant symptoms to be delayed in time, and even temporarily or partially relieved by smoking again. This state of dependency is termed addiction.

It has been suggested that the majority of addictions pass through three separate physiological stages: First of all, an alarm stage, where the body, when first subjected to the addictive stress, reacts with a shock horror, just like you with your first cigarette. Secondly, a stage of adaptation, where the body doesn't really like it much, but puts up with it, and even 'craves' the addictive substance for the fear of withdrawal symptoms. And finally, a stage of exhaustion where, regardless of the increasing doses, the withdrawal symptoms start to predominate.

Professor Hans Selye named these three stages General Adaptation Syndrome, but more about him later . . . . Now it is thought that also some people with food addictions experience similar physiological patterns, where the person addicted seems to require ever-increasing 'doses' of his addictive foods to keep 'well'. By keeping 'well' means the maintenance of the 'highs' or the stimulatory effects, and the evasion of the delayed withdrawal symptoms or 'hangovers'. However, this may take several years, depending entirely on individual susceptibility. But it is suggested that sooner or later the majority of people with addictions finally slip into the state where no amount of the formerly addictive substance seems to bring on the good old state of well-being, causing the dreaded 'hangover state' to predominate. This is said to be the start of his present 'illness'.

Now the principle of testing for all addictive substances, whether cigarettes, foods or chemicals, is exactly the same. Avoid the addictive substance until your body is free of it and then challenge it with the addictive substance and notice any reaction. As far as food addictions or masked allergies goes, it takes about four days to empty 'an average bowel', and if the food is eaten more frequently than every four days it will be permanently within the body, hence this magic four day avoidance marker.

The first week or so on this elimination diet you may not feel well at all, because you might experience these so called 'hangover symptoms'. However, from then onwards you should feel like a new man or woman, whatever the case might be. In some cases, particularly where the allergies have been very long-standing, you might need up to three weeks on the elimination diet before feeling any benefit. Now let's assume that you have been on the Stone Age diet up to three weeks and as the result you do not feel any better at all, so what then? Providing that you have already excluded environmental vapours and odours as a possible reason for your symptoms, it is conceivable that your elimination diet might still contain foods to which you are allergic, or alternatively foods may not even be responsible for your present ill-health.

If I were faced with this dilemma, I would still persevere with my diet for a while, and then choose for the elimination purposes all sorts of unusual foods which I don't usually eat, while at the same time invest some of my hard-earned cash on books concerned with allergies, some of which I have mentioned at the beginning of this chapter. I also would join some 'non-scientific' organizations concerned with the plight of allergy sufferers, such as Action Against Allergy, Hyperactive Children's Support Group etc. in order to learn as much as I can what it is all about. Addresses will be found at the end of my book. The only reason why I would carry on, would not be based on any kind of bloody-mindedness, but a fervent desire to get better without the poisonous pills and potions doctors are so ready to prescribe and which often make one more ill than before.

Now back to basics. Let's presume that you have been on your elimination diet long enough to feel like a new woman or man, and presumably you are now more than pleased with the new you. However, scientifically speaking you are a dead loss until you are able to prove which substance made you ill in the first place. In order to find that one out, you should now do a spot of 'challenging'.

I would like to repeat again that some symptoms experienced when challenging with suspected allergy producing foods can be quite severe, therefore ideally of course this food challenging should be done under medical supervision, particularly if your symptoms include epileptic fits, asthma, schizophrenia, severe depression or if you are a diabetic. However, if you are unable to find a sympathetic doctor to help you out, do at least make sure that you have somebody with you while you are at it, who could get appropriate help if you need it.

First of all remember to challenge or to test only one food item in every four to five days whilst sticking strictly on your non-allergenic foods. Consume the test food regularly each day in substantial quantities to see if you get a reaction. If after four days of eating the suspected food, no reaction occurs, the food is not allergenic for you. Now add this 'safe food' to your diet and test the next and so on and so forth. Reactions to foods under test conditions may not be the same as your usual reactions to them, as often moderate food allergies together can potentiate one another.

Now what kind of reactions would the challenging test produce? This is highly variable for different individuals, but watch out for the following: Do you start to sneeze? Is your nose becoming stuffy or runny? Is excessive mucus accumulating in your throat? Is your skin tingling all over or does it feel cold or flushed? Do you feel pins and needles or numbness in your arms and legs? Do you feel sick? Do you start to feel irritable, depressed, nervous or excited? Do you suddenly feel very sleepy? Do you start to sweat? Do you have palpitations? Are you feeling dizzy or shaky? Is your vision becoming dim or blurred? Do you generally feel lousy? In my opinion one of the best indicators in checking how allergenic food or chemical is for you, is to test your writing ability during the reaction. This writing test seems to reflect a whole load of human potentials, such as thinking processes, emotions, perceptions, as well as motor co-ordination. So after you have challenged yourself with the test food or chemical, sit down and do a spot of letter writing and compare the results later on with your normal handwriting. If the two don't seem to bear a great deal of similarity, and particularly if your writing after the test substance looks more like a drunken spider's samba steps, this is usually ample proof to any allergic sufferer that one is in a very sorry state. Most of these symptoms appear fairly soon after challenging, often within an hour or so. However, in some instances the symptoms begin fairly mildly, only reaching the full force about a couple of days later, or so called 'cumulative effect', which can particularly happen when testing wheat products. But regardless of how mild, severe or lengthy the reaction, you must always wait until the reaction clears up completely before proceeding with further tests. In theory a reaction can really last up to four days, or as long as the food is still in the intestine. Recovery can be usually speeded up by emptying the food residues from the bowel using a mild laxative such as Milk of Magnesia or Epsom salts. All in all, it would be most sensible to introduce a new food every fourth day.

Arthur Coca (115) showed in the 1950s that allergic exposure can alter a pulse rate in some individuals. In order to find out if that is the case with you, do the following: First of all, take your resting pulse for 60 seconds after sitting down for a few minutes, by placing the fingers of one hand on the artery in your wrist. Note down this resting pulse. Now after eating your test food, take a repeated pulse count at 10, 20, 40 and 60 minute intervals when sitting down first for a couple of minutes. Either a rise or a fall of more than ten beats per minute is a very strong evidence that you are allergic to that substance being tested. This pulse test is particularly useful when 'sniff testing' chemicals.

If this allergy lark isn't becoming complicated enough already, here are some more points to be taken into consideration: You might be allergic only to a food when cooked, but not when in a raw state or vice versa, as cooking can alter the chemical composition of a food. Likewise with dried products compared to fresh ones. You may also be allergic to commercially grown fruits and vegetables, but not to organic ones, as the former are usually laced with such toxic agricultural chemicals as synthetic fertilizers, insecticides, fungicides, weedkillers etc. It is also possible that if you are allergic to one substance of the grass family for example, such as wheat, you could also be allergic to other substances of the same family such as rye, barley, oats etc. Also a person who is allergic to beet sugar, may also be allergic to beets themselves and those who react to corn sugar such as dextrose, may also react to corn oil or corn syrup and even to vitamin C tablets, which are often manufactured using corn. Furthermore some individuals may be sensitive only to egg white but not to egg yolk. I could go on iffing and butting for some pages more, but what is the point? I can only say that an allergy is a frightully individual business and tracking down individual allergies is a frightful business. That about sums it up.

Dr Randolph discovered that if an unpleasant reaction to foods does develop, it is usually associated with increased body acidity or metabolic acidosis, which can be relieved by a teaspoonful of alkalizing salts such as 2:1 mixture of sodium and potassium bicarbonate mixed in a full glass of water, followed by a glass of plain water. However, you should not use this treatment more often than a couple of times in a day.

Now comes a bit of good news for a change. These masked allergies usually die down with avoidance, as opposed to fixed allergies which don't. The length of time one should avoid the allergy producing substance until the sensitivity is lost, seems to depend entirely on your biochemical individuality and the severity of your symptoms, as the more severe the symptoms, usually the longer it takes. More often than not, after six months of avoidance the food is usually safe, in many instances two to three months could be enough and from twelve days onwards it is a miracle. Of course it is entirely up to you when you feel you are ready to start to re-introduce your allergy producing foods back to your diet. However, do not forget that anyone with an allergic background is potentially allergic to anything he consumes, or is in contact with often enough. Therefore if you have become allergic once to one food or chemical, you can as easily become allergic to another and this should be remembered particularly when re-introducing your old troublemakers back to your diet. It seems to be that the more frequently you consume any foods or chemicals, the more chances there are that you end up in becoming allergic to them. So in order to prevent new food allergies developing in susceptible individuals, it would be wise to rotate all your foods on a four day basis i.e. you don't consume any one food more often than once every four days. Also it is good to remember that it is always the frequency with which food is eaten that is allergy promoting, than the amount of any food eaten at one time. Or in other words: substantial quantities of any food eaten every four days are much less likely to become troublesome than small amounts eaten every day.

I am the first one to agree that this withdrawal and challenge testing for allergies is a real bore, to say the least, but unfortunately no other allergy tests at present seem to be reliable enough in detecting masked or hidden allergies, as Fabienne Smith (116) points out:

Hospital Blood Tests: These include RAST, PRIST and ELISA. They work for antibody mediated allergies, and not even a great range of those, and they have a poor reliability rate. RAST, the usual one, has high positive and negative failure rates.

Intradermal Skin Tests have a reasonably good reliability rate, but are slow as they involve separate injections for each food. If the injection liquid has a chemical base, especially if it is phenol, it can further damage the immune system and make bad allergics even worse. Saline is the safest base.

Skin-prick or Scratch Tests are worthless for foods, less reliable than tossing a coin.

Sublingual Tests, that is drops under the tongue, work the same way as intradermal testing by getting a food challenge into the blood stream. This is less invasive than injections, but the results are less clearcut and so less useful. These tests seem to work less in older patients.

Cytoxic Tests, when in qualified medical hands, have an 80% reliability rate for foods, though they are less good for inhalants. This makes them a helpful guide for multiple food allergics, especially as the worse the case, the better the reliability seems to be. A great many foods can be tested from one blood sample, and nothing can harm you by getting into your blood stream. As I see it, the choice now seems to be between this extremely tiresome, but accurate 'withdrawal and challenge' and the snappy cytoxic blood test with its 80% reliability rate. The choice is naturally yours. I will include a couple of names of reputable laboratories for cytoxic tests at the end of this book.

We have discussed now *ad nauseam* these so-called food addictions, so it might be now timely to take a quick peep at addictions in general including a few words about alcoholism.

Wherever we look it is not hard to find a human being

busily and seriously engaged in trying to alter his state of consciousness, either by stimulating or by sedating his central nervous system and brain as best he can. If he is not engaged in drinking himself half-cut with alcohol, snorting speed, smoking pot, opium or nicotine, popping tranquillizing drugs or mainlining heroin, you can almost always find him hankering after his daily 'cuppa' whether it be made with caffeine or theopromine. This makes me think that addiction of one sort or another seems to be an integral part of human existence and should not therefore be really condemned. However, addictions only seem to become troublesome if they either make me sick or you unacceptable.

When Dr Randolph studied his patients with various food addictions, he noticed that many of them seemed to react particularly badly to spirits distilled from those food stuffs they were allergic to in the first place. This finding made him think that a great number of folks who seem to drink far too much alcohol for their own and other people's good, may not be addicted to alcohol at all, but crave mainly those substances their favourite tipple is made from. You see, most alcoholic beverages are prepared by yeast fermentation of such cereals as corn, wheat, rye, rice and barley, or alternatively from fruits such as grapes. So if you happen to be one of those dipsomaniacs who doesn't seem to get any kick whatsoever out of a gallon drum of ethyl alcohol, but could give half an arm and a leg for a pint of beer, it just might be that you aren't a dipsomaniac at all, but hopelessly hooked on barley, hops or yeast. So if you don't want to get hopelessly hooked on any tipple, don't drink alcohol oftener than once in every four days. However, if you are already hooked on a particular drink but wish to stay sober one night, don't order your favourite drink, but something which you like the least, as that might be the drink to which you are neither allergic nor addicted. In short, you may be a beer-alcoholic but not a wine-alcoholic.

Since most allergic addictions tend to reinforce each other, a great many people subconsciously develop their whole lifestyles around their addictions. For example anyone who smokes and drinks, seems to smoke more when he is drinking or vice versa. Others seem to smoke more when they are having their cup of tea or coffee. This seems to happen because these people seem to get a much greater kick when these two addictive substances are taken together than when they are taken separately . . . . Such are the wonders of addicted life. However, do not kid yourself, even if all this mind-bending and mind-blowing makes you feel on top of the world and mighty pleased with yourself, you can be assured that while your mind is tripping into great heights under all these toxic and addictive bombardments, your little body organs feel at the same time stressed as hell, which is a bit of a drag.

Now whether one is comfortable in comparing masked allergies with addictions or not, one thing in my opinion is certain, that all allergies, whether antibody-mediated or non-antibody-mediated are directly caused by defective immune system function. We have already discussed at the beginning of this chapter how weak immunity is often inherited and how stresses of all kinds can further suppress immunity and lead to the development of full-blown allergic symptoms. This being the case, let's look more closely at stress.

Professor Hans Selye (117, 118) studied stress response on laboratory rats and found that all of them went through the following three stages: First of all, alarm and distress, secondly resistance and adaptation, and finally illness and exhaustion. When he cut the exhausted rats open at *post mortem*, he found out that amongst other things, the poor blighter's adrenal glands, which usually produce adrenaline, cortisone and other adaptive hormones, were all shrivelled to near nothing and ceased to function. He named these three stages 'General Adaptation Syndrome'. He also went on to study adaptation to various harmful agents in humans and found out that they too seemed to go through the same three stages, except when the human volunteers reached the third, or the illness stage, they were treated one way or another before complete exhaustion, death or a *post mortem* was called for. Now that stress has been shown to affect adversely adrenal glands, it would be a miracle if it didn't also adversely affect the immune system function, which in fact it does. So what is meant with this word 'stress'? In scientific terms stress could be defined as being any wear and tear induced in the body by the adaptive day-to-day struggle of an organism to remain normal in the face of potentially harmful agents. Furthermore, stress is an individual concept, or to put it another way, a fact which I might find stressful, might give you pleasure. However, the following factors almost universally contribute to stress, and avoiding them as much as possible can help to strengthen immunity, which in turn will help you to overcome your allergies, as well as other nuisances which may bother you, such as bacterial or viral infections.

1) Avoid poisoning your body excessively with both prescribed or non-prescribed drugs such as nicotine, alcohol, caffeine, tranquillizers or any other addictive substances.

2) Avoid polluted food, water and environment as much as you are able.

3) Avoid excessive and prolonged physical stresses such as cold, heat, exercise, fatigue etc.

4) Avoid prolonged mental stresses. So if you have emotional problems which bother you or make you distressed and unhappy, don't bottle them up but get them sorted out as soon as you can. If you don't have a good friend to talk to, don't hesitate to seek professional help and find yourself an understanding counsellor or psychotherapist. Again, you will find addresses at the end of my book.

5) And finally, do make sure that you get enough nourishing food for your personal nutritional requirements to help you to strengthen your immune system function. I would also take 'for insurance purposes' one good vitamin/ mineral and essential fatty-acid supplement daily. Also do not forget the importance of sufficient exercise, natural daylight and the art of a proper relaxation.

Finally, a few words about a possible connection between allergies and a condition known as Reactive Hypoglycaemia, to which I will be devoting the whole of my next chapter.

Dr Dunne (119) writes: 'The incidence of allergies goes hand in hand with techno-chemical progress and is today at a higher level than at any other time in the history of human development. But as solutions evolve, our research for more complicated methods of diagnosis and treatment must not blind us to other concomitant factors involved in the allergic syndrome. . . . The commonest of these is hypoglycaemia, a low blood sugar, which is fundamentally a stress condition. Some believe it is a direct response to allergens, others affirm it precedes the onset of allergy. This chicken and egg argument is largely academic for all agree it is a basic cause of severe mental and physical exhaustion.' Dr Cheraskin (120) in turn points out that some allergic reactions are either caused or intensified by hypoglycaemia, as little or no allergic reaction may be found to an offending food or chemical when the blood sugar is normal, but the same substance will produce a strong allergic response during a low blood sugar or hypoglycaemic episode.

10

HYPOGLYCAEMIA – THE DISEASE YOUR DOCTOR WON'T TREAT

Hypoglycaemia translated into lay terms means low blood sugar. Diabetes is the opposite i.e. high blood sugar or hyperglycaemia. These conditions, although diametrically opposed, are closely related, as both are caused by the body's inability to use sugar effectively. This is of course an over-simplification, as in reality hypoglycaemia can be quite a diverse and complex condition, because its symptoms as well as its underlying causes seem to vary from one individual to another. I would like to divide hypoglycaemia further into two separate categories: Fasting or Organic Hypoglycaemia and Reactive Hypoglycaemia. This Fasting or Organic Hypoglycaemia is a condition where the lowest blood sugar level is found after the longest period of fasting and can be caused by pancreatic tumours or hepatic disease. This type of hypoglycaemia is a fairly serious blood sugar disorder, with which we are not concerned here. The low blood sugar condition, which we will be discussing in this chapter is called Reactive Hypoglycaemia, where the fasting blood sugar level is almost invariably normal and is not even abnormally depressed by prolonged fasting, but only falls to abnormal levels in susceptible individuals due to one, or more likely by a combination of the following:

1) Over-consumption of refined carbohydrates. (119, 121, 122, 123, 124)
2) Excessive use of stimulants such as caffeine, strong teas, cola drinks etc. (121, 122, 123, 124)
3) Consumption of specific foods or inhaling specific chemicals to which a person is allergic. (50, 51, 60)
4) Excessive alcohol consumption. (123)
5) Tobacco smoking in susceptible individuals. (123, 125)

6) An excessive physical (123, 126, 127, 128) or mental (123, 129) stress.
7) The stress of pregnancy and childbirth may precipitate hypoglycaemia in women susceptible to it, resulting in a long term period of *post-partum* difficulties. (123)
8) Stressful events such as serious operations etc. (123)
9) A long term use of tranquillizing medication, diuretics, the Pill or high doses of oestrogen. (123)
10) Infections. (123)

Not forgetting careless food selection and cooking methods which can contribute to the development of hypoglycaemia, particularly as all B-complex vitamins, which are essential for a proper carbohydrate metabolism have been refined during the manufacturing process of table sugar. Furthermore, B-group vitamins are also easily lost during cooking because they are water soluble and so are usually thrown out with the cooking water into the sink. The lack of essential trace minerals particularly chromium which is always milled out during the refining process of table sugar and white flour, has also been linked with the current epidemic of various sugar regulatory disorders such as hypoglycaemia and diabetes. (130)

The development of hypoglycaemia is associated with heredity, as it is more likely to be found in persons with a family history of different sugar regulatory disorders such as diabetes, alcoholism, obesity and 'mental illnesses' such as anxiety or phobias. However, its actual onset is usually precipitated by lack of proper breakfasts and generally poor and inadequate diet, particularly when combined with prolonged stresses, whether mental or physical. Reactive hypoglycaemia affects more women than men and the age of onset is usually between ages thirty and forty. (123)

Reactive Hypoglycaemia was first described by Dr Seale Harris (131) in 1924, who twenty-five years later was awarded the Distinguished Service Medal from the American Medical Association.

Reactive Hypoglycaemia has been referred to during these past years by many different names: Functional Hypoglycaemia (123), Neurogenic Hypoglycaemia (132), Relative Hypoglycaemia (124), Hypoglycaemic Syndrome (133), Spontaneous Hypoglycaemia (127, 129), Hyperinsulinism (126, 128, 131) and even Idiopathic Postprandial Syndrome (134).

The proper maintenance of constant and adequate glucose (blood sugar) levels in the body is one of the most important functions of our biochemical being. The entire body needs glucose for strength, action and the maintenance of life. However, the brain and central nervous system are particularly affected when blood sugar is low. The simple reason being that glucose is the predominant metabolic fuel utilized by the brain. Even though our brain accounts for 3% or less of our body weight, approximately 60% of our basal glucose is needed for its proper function. (78) It is also thought that when blood sugar is in very short supply, our normal rational thinking-brain may shut off completely, leaving our primitive survival-brain in charge. It is this transaction which is thought to be the major cause of the personality changes from over-emotion to extreme aggression, which are frequently found in some hypoglycaemic sufferers. The normal, quite placid and well-behaved individual seems to change suddenly and become abusive, aggressive and even physically violent. I could bet that the majority of wife/husband and even child battering is often the consequence of this.

In order to illustrate how various individuals can be affected by hypoglycaemia, here are some examples:

Case 1: A married man, aged 31, was admitted to hospital suffering from attacks of weakness accompanied by ataxia, trembling and a state of panic. He was considered to be a case of anxiety neurosis. His present illness had started three years before when he experienced faintness on leaving a cinema with his wife. These attacks of faintness occurred with increasing frequency, and during the past few months he had been afraid to go out at all unless accompanied by his wife. Frequently before the attack, he would be irritable with a tendency to bump into people when walking. He likened this to a mild state of drunkenness. He would feel weak, sweat, experience nausea, drowsiness and feel afraid. He never lost consciousness. Usually, however, the attacks passed off after resting. He noticed that they never came on after meals and most commonly occurred after exertion. If feeling unwell before a meal he would immediately be relieved by taking food. (135)

Case 2: He had had attacks for about six months of dizziness when walking, blurred vision and a feeling that he may fall. This was accompanied by weakness, a pounding heart, perspiration, tremors and apprehension. He was afraid to walk around the block and stopped working because of tremor and nervousness. (125)

Case 3: He had spells of fuzzy headache, weakness and difficulty in concentrating which had lasted about twenty years. At times the symptoms occurred several times a day, at other times he had only two or three attacks a week. The attacks had been increasing in severity in the last four years and were accompanied by perspiration, tremor and a feeling of great uncertainty. (125)

Case 4: A patient, a twenty-eight year old female art teacher was admitted to hospital complaining of recurrent spells of sleepiness and epigastric pain of three years' duration. These were accompanied by sweating, 'inward tremor', weakness and a sense of loss of contact with her surroundings. Palpitations were noted during some episodes, and blurred vision during others. Attacks usually lasted fifteen to twenty minutes and although she had 'almost blacked out' several times, actual loss of consciousness had never occurred. The patient recognized a definite correlation between the frequency of attacks and physical or emotional exhaustion resulting from excessive hours of work. (127)

Case 5: A patient, a 52 year old widow was admitted when she became unable to concentrate, had anorexia, lack of interest, panic about driving a car, forgetfulness, blurred vision, exhaustion, muscular jerking and a feeling of general numbness, particularly in the head. (124)

Case 6: A patient, a 39 year old housewife was seen first when she was complaining of headache, constant buzzing in the head, inward tremulousness, exhaustion, weakness of the lower extremities, palpitations, tension, abdominal bloating, irritability, dizziness, nightsweats and twitching of the facial muscles. (124)

Case 7: A doctor, a surgeon aged 34, had for eight or nine years experienced waves of intense fatigue which came on most frequently in the afternoons. Although hunger was not a prominent symptom he had discovered that eating a candy bar would quickly relieve the attack. In recent years these attacks had also been appearing in the late mornings. They were more likely to appear during a long morning's work in the operating room, when he would suddenly feel extremely weak and shaky, notice a tremor of his hands and be unable to concentrate because he felt 'all in'. On several occasions he was obliged to leave the operating room. (129)

Now that we have discussed the overall physical and mental effect of hypoglycaemia, let's look more closely at the specific symptoms and other aspects of hypoglycaemia. Besides using dozens of medical research studies, I have collected most of the information for this chapter from the works of the following authors: Carl Pfeiffer (123), Carlton Fredericks (136), Nancy Dunne (119), Paavo Airola (121), Martin Budd (122), Barbara Reed (137) and Alexander Schauss (138, 139)

Symptoms of hypoglycaemia include:

Neurological symptoms: blurred vision, internal tremors, cold hands and feet, itching and crawling sensation of the body, sensitivity to noise, sound and light, excessive sweating, feeling of light-headedness, dizziness and vertigo, migraine-type headaches, insomnia, nightmares and night-sweats.

Carsiovascular symptoms: palpitations and low blood pressure.

Musculosceletal symptoms: muscle and joint aches and pains, muscle stiffness, twitching and cramps.

Respiratory system: gasping for breath, smothering spells, sighing and yawning, hypo- and hyperventilation.

Gastro-intestinal symptoms: chronic indigestion and nausea, abdominal spasms, bloating, dry mouth, constipation alternating with diarrhoea, excessive thirst, occasional ravenous hunger and/or craving for sweets, allergies, anorexia, bulimia and obesity.

General and Psychiatric symptoms: chronic and easy fatiguability, difficulty in verbalizing accurately, depression, irritability, crying spells, difficulty in concentration, mental confusion, exhaustion, restlessness, staggering, memory lapses, nervousness, constant worrying, indecisiveness, moodiness, co-ordination difficulties, temper tantrums, unsocial and antisocial behaviour, suicidal tendencies, a feeling of 'going crazy', anxiety and phobias.

Dr Dunne (119) writes about hypoglycaemic sufferers: 'The major complaint is fatigue which waxes and wanes. They wake up tired, have difficulty starting their day, and may stagger getting out of bed, or even black out, and their limbs feel sleepy. They lack stamina, muscles ache with normal exertion, and effort brings on sweating and exhaustion. Some are overweight. Bouts of sleepiness and low spells occur during the day, especially after the mid-day meal. There is dry mouth, indigestion, bloating and nausea relieved by eating, abnormal bowel function (either constipation or constipation alternating with diarrhoea), and they always need fluids, sauces or gravies with meals because of an ever present dry mouth. Appetite is unbalanced, with either anorexia or ravenous hunger. Light and noise sensitivity, spots before the eyes, blurred vision, night sweats, motion sickness, sighing and yawning, air hunger and ringing in the ears are common. They sleep badly, often with nightmares, and their hands and feet become puffy. They catch infections easily. They may experience tingling of the lips or fingers, crawling sensation or numb areas anywhere in the skin surface. They are acutely sensitive to temperature change and cold hands and feet are classical due to a vasoconstrictive adrenal action in reducing blood supply to non-essential areas in order to maintain adequate sugar supply to vital areas. Episodes of pain without definable cause occur across the shoulders, the back of the neck and in the joints, while migraine-type headaches frequently feature. Severe cases suffer blackouts or convulsions which are instantly relieved by intravenous glucose. In appearance they lack colour, though blush easily, look unhealthy, are gloomy and introspective, and have difficulty in verbalizing accurately. They are often preoccupied with bodily malfunctions to the exclusion of normal interests outside themselves .... Co-ordination is poor, movement may be clumsy with occasional bouts of ataxia .... Besides excessive fatigue, in the early stages the hypoglycaemic sufferer will also experience recurrent feelings of light-headedness and faintness, often combined with all sorts of 'mood disturbances', which can appear in the form of groundless anxiety, irritability, impatience, nervousness, despondency etc. Generally speaking natural personality traits seem to become exaggerated: extroverts become domineering bullies, introverts become timid recluses, fears progress to phobias, irritations to inappropriate temper outburst, depression to deep melancholy with suicidal tendencies, the feeling of dizziness and light-headedness to a fear of venturing outdoors i.e. agoraphobia and so on and so forth.'

Gyland and Salzer (121) studied 600 and 300 cases of hypoglycaemic sufferers respectively. The following results consist of a summary of psychiatric symptoms the majority of hypoglycaemic sufferers seem to experience with percentages of patients complaining of them: nervousness 94%, irritability 89%, fatigue/feeling of exhaustion 87%, feeling of faintness and dizziness 86%, depression 77%, drowsiness 72%, mental confusion 67%, anxiety 62%, unsocial and antisocial behaviour 47%, crying spells 46%, lack of concentration 42%, phobias 31%, suicidal intents 20%, nervous breakdown 17%, previous psychosis 12%. The summary of neurological symptoms with percentages of hypoglycaemics suffering from them looks like this: tremors, both inward and external 54%, numbness 51%, headaches 45%, unco-ordination 43%, blurred vision 40%, staggering/difficulty in keeping balance 34%, 'grey-outs' 14% and convulsions 2%. And finally somatic symptoms, which include: gastro-intestinal disturbances 68%, palpitations/tachycardia 54%, muscular and joint pains 53%, excessive sweating 41%, smothering spells/gasping for air/hyperventilation 37%.

As we see from these lists above, the diversity of hypoglycaemic symptoms can be truly varied. I must stress, however, that by no means all these symptoms are experienced by any one individual, although more often that not, the basic pattern of symptomatology in any one person is usually constant, only the severity of attacks may vary from time to time.

Apart from the fact that there are individual differences as to the level of blood sugar at which symptoms appear, the rapidity with which the blood sugar falls is of prime importance: that is, the more rapid the fall, the more severe the symptoms, which are partly caused by a massive increase in adrenaline secretion which helps to release stored glycogen from the liver in order to rectify the hypoglycaemic state. It has been established that during a rapid fall of the blood sugar, plasma urinary levels of adrenaline can increase as much as 10–50 fold depending on the degree and severity of the fall. It has been also found that the greatest variations of the blood sugar level are usually associated with either an excessive anxiety state or a marked depressive state. In short, the majority of the hypoglycaemic symptoms can be explained in terms of the reaction to the following:

1) A rapidly decreasing blood sugar concentration.
2) The final lowered level when the body, including the brain has less fuel to function optimally.
3) The compensatory reaction to the low blood sugar level, especially the secretion of adrenaline and other counter-regulatory hormones, such as glucagon, cortisol and growth hormone. What particularly interests me here is that tranquillizers, such as benzodiazepines seem to be potent growth hormone activators, thus presumably helping a low blood sugar to rise, but apparently after a long term therapy, tolerance seems to develop to this growth hormone releasing effect.

Lader (72) studied patients on long-term benzodiazepine medication and control subjects and found out that an injection of diazepam (Valium) released growth hormone into the plasma in control subjects, but patients on long-term tranquillizing medication showed almost total tolerance. As I mentioned before, this finding may indicate that the first therapeutic action of benzodiazepines may simply be their blood sugar increasing potential, which, after long term therapy, depresses growth hormone release, which could lead to a chronic hypoglycaemic state. The fact supporting my hypothesis being the uncanny similarity between the basic symptomatology of Reactive Hypoglycaemia and addiction/withdrawl of tranquillizing medication.

The diagnosis of hypoglycaemia is possible by means of a careful dietary history, including eating habits and presenting symptoms, but it can generally be confirmed by a 5- or 6-hour Glucose Tolerance Test, or GTT for short. Besides possibly a pale and unhealthy appearance, outward physical signs are practically non-existent; however, in some individuals one could find a tenderness over the tail of the pancreatic area, i.e. in the left upper quadrant of the abdomen. This tenderness could be felt just below the rib, or at times round the side of the rib cage. (122) According to Dr Dunne, a low blood pressure is almost always evident and coarse hand tremor is often present if the stomach is empty. Dr Pfeiffer (123) has also found a significantly lowered blood spermine level in hypoglycaemic patients.

At present the most reliable test for hypoglycaemia is the 5- or 6-hour GTT, which monitors the individual's glucose regulating mechanism following a challenge of oral ingestion of 50-100 gr of glucose after a fasting period of 12–14 hours. The test is usually given in the morning and the patient has been instructed beforehand not to eat anything the night before and in the morning before the test. Immediately on arrival at hospital or the doctor's surgery, a first blood sample is taken to determine the patient's fasting blood sugar level. After he is given a drink of 50–100 gr of glucose, depending on the body weight, mixed in water. From then on seven to ten small blood samples are taken from the veins of the arm for five to six hours, first half-hourly, then at hourly intervals. For the test to be accurate, it has to last a minimum of five hours. Two to three hour tests may be sufficient in diagnosing diabetes, but are absolutely useless in diagnosing Reactive Hypoglycaemia, since the blood sugar 'swings' invariably occur in the fourth, fifth or even in some individuals the sixth hour of the test.

Results may look something like this: Patients with Fasting or Organic Hypoglycaemia show always a low fasting level, which drops even lower in time. As I mentioned before, this is a serious blood sugar disorder, with which we are not concerned here. In normal, healthy individuals the fasting blood sugar level is about 70–100 mg/100 ml of blood. After 50–100 gr of glucose challenge the blood sugar usually rises within the first hour approximately 50% over the fasting level and then starts to peter down gradually back to the original fasting level. At no time during the test does the blood sugar fall much below the basic fasting level.

A fasting blood sugar in excess of 120 mg/100 ml is strongly suggestive of diabetes. In a diabetic condition, after a glucose challenge, the blood sugar level always rises much higher than normal and also stays much higher than normal for a considerable length of time, depending on the severity of the condition ... Some individuals can suffer both from hypoglycaemia and be a 'pre-diabetic' at the same time. These individuals also have a normal fasting blood sugar level. After a glucose challenge, however, there is first a steep rise of the blood sugar up to a diabetic level, which after three hours or so, will be followed by a hypoglycaemic fall. To be ill with both hypo- and hyperglycaemia at the same time is not so difficult to understand when one remembers that both are disorders where the body is unable to utilize sugar effectively. In fact it has been often said that today's hypoglycaemic is tomorrow's diabetic. ... Now patients with Reactive Hypoglycaemia, of which this whole chapter is all about, the fasting blood sugar level is almost invariably normal. After the glucose challenge, the natural rise will be eventually followed by a rapid drop below the normal fasting range. The faster and the lower the drop, the more severe is the hypoglycaemic state. Also the speed at which the glucose level returns back to normal and how long it remains at the low point, are very important factors to consider.

Anyone who is familiar with diabetics knows that they are often prescribed insulin injections in order to keep their high blood sugar down on a normal range. Sometimes diabetics are known to miscalculate their insulin intake, then they experience a so-called 'insulin shock' or 'hypoglycaemia', of which the BMA family doctor's publication *Life with Diabetes* writes: 'When hypoglycaemia occurs, various symptoms appear. There is a feeling of strangeness and that something is wrong. There is usually sweating, difficulty in seeing straight and shakiness. There may be tingling in the lips and a feeling of hunger ... Others may notice that they are behaving strangely, perhaps unusually truculent or beligerent . . . . '

This Diabetic Hypoglycaemia is usually helped by a quick consumption of sugar or glucose, whereas Reactive Hypoglycaemia will be only aggravated by a consumption of concentrated sugars and should be avoided at all costs as it is suggested that one of the main reasons for developing Reactive Hypoglycaemia in the first place is excessive sugar consumption.

How this has been thought to come about is as follows. The pancreas is an organ whose function is to produce insulin, and as we already know, the main function of insulin is to regulate our blood sugar levels. When a person has digested for a long period of time excess sugar and sugary foods, the pancreas needs to produce insulin constantly, eventually becoming so 'trigger-happy' that when any amount of sugar is ingested, insulin simply pours out, lowering the blood sugar immediately, when the person is said to be suffering from hypoglycaemia. If this goes on for years, it is thought that eventually the formerly 'trigger-happy' pancreas will become more tired and slack with its insulin production, leading finally to a mature onset diabetes or hyperglycaemia.

Now that we have got these hypoglycaemic and diabetic differences and similarities out of the way, we might as well return to the 5-6 hour GTT.

Now let's assume that you managed to have your 5–6 hour GTT test done, with a urine specimen to rule out diabetes, or without, let's see what might happen next. A well known nutritionist from US with a very Finnish name Paavo Airola (121) writes about the subject:
'The fact that you were given a 6-hour GTT test and that your doctor pronounced his verdict, is no guarantee that the diagnosis is correct. It all depends on your doctor's ability to "read the curve". There are so many variances in the curve of actual hypoglycaemics, that unless your doctor has been specifically trained in this field, he may misinterpret the test results. This may happen, and does happen, so often because some doctors regard certain officially set blood sugar levels as "normal", and anything above or below that as "abnormal". For example, some official

sources inform us that levels of blood sugar lower than 60–80 mg are indicative of hypoglycaemia. The truth is that there are no set numbers or points which constitute hypoglycaemia. Medical records show that some patients may experience severe reactions, both physical and/or emotional, although their blood sugar level never dips below 75mg. Some people walk around symptom-free, while others demonstrate neurotic or even psychotic behaviour on virtually identical glucose tolerance test reading . . . . The most important factor to observe when attempting to read the glucose tolerance test chart is not how low the level drops, but how rapid the drop is. The drop from 200 to 100, when it happens in one hour or less, may cause more trouble in some persons susceptible to hypoglycaemia than a slow two to three hour drop from 100 to 50. Also the speed at which the glucose level returns to normal and how long it remains at the low point are extremely important factors to consider . . . . The curve may be pretty low, let's say to 50, but if it recovers quickly and returns to pre-fasting level, it may indicate a very mild case, often without noticeable symptoms. On the other hand, if the lowest point reads 65, but remains there for several hours, such a prolonged low level of blood sugar may result in very severe reactions.'

This is precisely what happened to me in 1983, when I was studying psycho-neuro-immunology in a well-known London teaching hospital under the watchful eye of Dr Nixon. That was the time I became convinced that I must be suffering from Reactive Hypoglycaemia. I had come to that mind-blowing revelation through the simple science of elimination. I had already eliminated from my personal medical file all those silly bits like 'anxiety neurosis', 'agoraphobia', 'temporal lobe epilepsy', 'schizophrenia' and also reluctantly that great favourite of mine 'personality disorder'. Not because I didn't fancy them as such, but because I simply couldn't see them as proper diagnoses, only as the doctors' admission of defeat, telling me that they were baffled. Because of this drastic diagnostic elimination process, I felt at the time that as far as my own illness was concerned, I had now only a couple of aces left to play: Either I must be a 'hyperventilator' or I was suffering from Reactive Hypoglycaemia, or even a bit of both.

In order to establish whether I was suffering from a Hyperventilation syndrome, according to instructions, all had to do was to pant vigorously about 40–60 breaths pe minute, for about three minutes, and if symptoms devel oped which I were to recognize as similar to my origina symptoms, I could consider myself as suffering from Hyperventilation syndrome. So I panted, puffed, snorted wheezed and huffed about, sometimes with the help of a brown paper bag, sometimes without. The end result wa that at times after puffing and huffing vigorously I fel dreadful, and at other times I didn't seem to turn a hair. was truly baffled, to say the least, until one day my eyes fel on the following sentence written by Carlton Frederick (136): 'Useful advances have also been achieved in the techniques of testing for hypoglycaemia. Among these is the observation that stress applied at about the fourth hou of the GTT test, may elicit the full-blown symptoms of low blood sugar in a patient who would otherwise reac normally. The stress may be as minimal as a few minutes of running on a treadmill, or a short period of hyperventila tion.' I don't know about you, but this tiny pearl of wisdom at least in my opinion, seems to open a brand new ball game altogether. That is: if a doctor uses the hyperventilation provocation test for diagnosing Hyperventilation syn drome, and the test happens to be 'positive', how is he going to know for sure, without testing at the same time for hypoglycaemia, whether the poor panting blighter experi enced all the horrid symptoms because he is a hyperventila tor or a hypoglycaemic? Having now realized that hyper ventilation is also used as one of the useful techniques for testing for Reactive Hypoglycaemia, it also dawned on me why sometimes when I was panting vigorously, I felt so grim and at other times I didn't seem very much the worse for wear. The reason must have been that when I was panting after a meal, when usually one's blood sugar is high, I felt all right, but when I puffed and wheezed on an empty stomach, when one's blood sugar is at its lowest, I felt so ill that I was sure I was going to die. From then on, Hyperventilation syndrome as a diagnostic entity started to fade quickly out of grace. Now I had only hypoglycaemia to play with. In order to find out whether even this diagnosis was watertight, I decided on a 6-hour GTT to be performed in the hospital where I was studying, providing my own doctor agreed.

Getting my doctor to agree to the test was an experience in itself. After I had presented my case to him, he seemed to freeze. Followed by a long and prickly silence his face started to shrink and pucker as if he were sucking a sour lemon. This painful expression occupied his features until relieved by a mighty holler: 'I don't believe in hypoglycaemia.' A lesser human being would have given up on the spot, but never a Finn. Having swiftly decided which approach would be most fruitful, I mentally lolled over like a puppy, engaging a soft and silly look on my mush, and started to grovel until he grudgingly relented.

The 6-hour GTT was performed quite informally by one of the young doctors on a hospital ward. The test was not pleasant, because the budding young medic was after my blood most of the time. Generally speaking I didn't seem to feel much worse at any time during the test than I had felt when I was really ill. It was agreed that the test results, when known, would be sent to my own doctor, whom I was to telephone in a few days' time, which I did. I will never forget his voice at the other end of the line. It sounded ecstatic. 'Of course you haven't got hypoglycaemia. I tried to tell you that before, but you just wouldn't listen.' When I asked him if I could see the test results he told me that he hadn't got them, but I might find them at the teaching hospital.

As soon as I had replaced the receiver, I found myself in the London underground, heading straight to the hospital ward and to the young doc who had bled me nearly dry only a few days before. When the young man found out that I was after my test results, his hands started to fumble in his trouser pockets and after a while I was presented with a pile of paper hankies, dirty paper bits and a load of unidentifiable junk. One dirty and crumbled paper bit was my 6-hour GTT result. I thanked him profusely and leapt off the scene. That very same day I sent a photocopy of my test results to Martin Budd, an expert on hypoglycaemia and an author of a book *Low Blood Sugar (Hypoglycaemia) The 20th Century Epidemic* (122). Not long after I received a letter from him indicating that my blood sugar curve confirms a pronounced Reactive Hypoglycaemia, which is now official. Reactive Hypoglycaemia is indicated (91, 140);

1) When the blood sugar in the course of 6-hour GTT fails to rise more than 50 percent above the fasting level.
2) By a glucose curve which falls during the test to 20 percent below the fasting level.
3) By a glucose test in which the blood sugar falls 50 mg percent or more during any one hour of the test.
4) By GTT in which the absolute blood sugar level falls in the range of 50 mg percent or lower. (Anything below 65 mg percent is suspicious.)
5) By clinical symptoms such as dizziness, headache, confusion, palpitations, depression etc. appearing during the course of the GTT, regardless of what the blood sugar readings may be.
6) Also it is significant if blood glucose does not return back to the fasting level after 6 hours.

My own test results scored five out of six. I was positive in all, except number one, which, according to Dr Kingsley is rarely encountered. (91)

Our individual GTT curves differ from one another just like our fingerprints, as do our individual fasting levels, which always must be used as a baseline from which all these other readings are judged. It is essential to remember all this, because as the majority of doctors don't seem to 'believe in hypoglycaemia', it is then left to us to interpret our own test results. I have to admit that I didn't believe in hypoglycaemia either, primarily because I didn't know it existed, but I can assure you that when you happen to suffer from it, you soon become converted.

If done correctly, the 6-hour GTT should always be accompanied with a thorough clinical examination and dietary history. Furthermore, all symptoms arising during the test should be carefully timed and noted. Also during the test, the patient should be encouraged to remain reasonably active, as sitting and lying around will artificially raise the blood sugar level. (121) I find this news particularly interesting in reference to ME, because first of all, the symptoms of ME and Reactive Hypoglycaemia seem to be similar, and secondly, exercise seems to make ME and Reactive Hypoglycaemia worse and rest make them better. With that in mind, don't think that I am completely around the bend if I dare to suggest that those ME sufferers whose stubborn little virus just obstinately remains hidden, may be suffering from Reactive Hypoglycaemia instead. If I am right, other erroneous diagnoses could include: (121, 122, 123, 124, 136, 141) Anxiety Neurosis, Agoraphobia, Panic attacks, Post-natal depression, Parkinson's Syndrome, Rheumatoid arthritis, Chronic bronchial asthma, Allergies, Hyperventilation syndrome, Psycosomatic disorder, Cerebral arteriosclerosis, Ménière's syndrome, Autonomic nervous system disorder, Neurodermatitis, Migraine, Lack of sex drive, Petit-mal epilepsy, Paroxysmal tachycardia, Obesity, Bulimia, Anorexia, Mental retardation, Manic depression, Alcoholism, Drug addiction, Childhood hyperactivity, Juvenile delinquency, Underachievement at school, Hostile and antisocial behaviour, Suicidal tendencies, Manic-depressive psychosis, Psychopathic personality, Second cervical root syndrome, Convulsive disorder, Speech difficulties, Narcolepsy, Ulcers, A proper nut-case, not forgetting my little Personality disorder.

Dr Salzer writes: (124) 'The diagnosis of relative hypoglycaemia may be missed if we think a patient must have an attack of weakness, trembling, tachycardia, sweating and feeling he is going to faint, instead of recognizing that symptoms of relative hypoglycaemia will be those of depression, insomnia, anxiety, irritability, poor concentration, crying spells and phobias. . . . It is therefore essential that every patient coming for psychiatric or neurologic evaluation have a 6-hour GTT as a routine procedure and that we get over the idea that a fasting blood sugar will be of diagnostic help. A two or three hour test is inadequate because in the first few hours the glucose levels may be high, whereas a major drop may occur after this point, and the diagnosis will be missed. It is also extremely important that a complete dietary history will be obtained.'

Landmann and Sutherland (141) conducted a 5-hour GTT on fifty consecutive patients admitted to the Psychosomatic Appraisal Unit of the Winter VA hospital and found out that 44% of them were suffering from reactive hypoglycaemia.

Salzer (124) conducted a 5-hour GTT on 275 consecutive new psychiatric patients seen by him over a period of 15 months and found out that 31% of them were suffering from Reactive Hypoglycaemia with an additional 8% having potential Reactive Hypoglycaemia.

Beebe and Wendel (52) conducted a 5-hour GTT on 133 randomly selected psychiatric patients and found out that 74% of them were suffering from Reactive Hypoglycaemia. They found a large incidence of Reactive Hypoglycaemia and pre-diabetic glucose tolerance curves in patients diagnosed as suffering from a chronic schizophrenia and various forms of psycho-neuroses. In fact patients categorized as chronic schizophrenics, 70% exhibited some form of hypo-glycaemia. . . . This particular finding doesn't surprise me at all, because the typical symptoms of Reactive Hypo-glycaemia such as fatigue, depression, confusion and anxiety are also considered as typical symptoms of schizophrenia.

Kay Hall (142) established through various research studies that Reactive Hypoglycaemia seems to occur in about 30-70 percent of all psychiatric patients and 90% of all alcoholics and alcoholic schizophrenics.

Meiers (143) found an extremely high incidence of Reactive Hypoglycaemia in his patients suffering from peptic ulcer, asthma and alcoholism. His experience is that Reactive Hypoglycaemia occurs in 95% of all alcoholics and up to 70% of all schizophrenics. He also points out that psychiatrists, if they would test for Reactive Hypoglycaemia, would find it in 37–70 percent of all their psychiatric patients of all diagnostic categories.

Langseth and Dowd (144) administered a 5-hour GTT to 261 hyperactive children between ages seven and nine and found out that 74% of the children had abnormal blood sugar curves.

Martin Budd (122) writes: 'Although the medical ortho-dox view holds that Reactive Hypoglycaemia is a rare condition, the evidence points out contrary. I have found that out of 210 patients selected and tested with the 6 hour GTT 92% showed clearly definite Reactive Hypoglycaemia.'

So how about it? How long have we still to wait and how many more millions of innocent people are forced to become addicted to tranquillizing medication before Reactive Hypoglycaemia is finally accepted as a diagnostic entity in orthodox medicine? Already one Finnish female's future plans were screwed up good and proper because doctors 'don't believe in hypoglycaemia'. There are times when I just can't help wondering what might have happened back in 1961, during my fashion studies, when I obviously first experienced my first full-blown hypoglycaemic attack, if I had been diagnosed and treated correctly by simple and straight forward dietary advice, instead of being pompously hauled on board that quacky wagon of drug-oriented psychiatry, and forced into their chemical straight-jacket from which an escape is damned nearly impossible.

Dr Wilder (145) writes: 'Another example of the practical importance of the study of hypoglycaemia is crime. This may sound surprising unless we remember how many psychological features we have found in hypoglycaemia which might result in crimes and transgressions; not only the impairment of judgement and concentration, but also the imperative hunger, the absolute negativism, the irritability, indifference, impairment of moral sense etc. In an article in the Journal of Criminal Psychology we compiled a whole list of cases from the literature and our own experience of crimes committed in the state of spontaneous or induced hypoglycaemia, like disorderly conduct, particularly resistance against police, assault and battery, attempted homicide and suicide, cruelty to children, matrimonial cruelty, various sexual perversions and aggressions, false fire alarm, embezzlement, petty larceny, wilful destruction of property, arson, slander and the frequent violation of traffic regulations. . . . '

Rojas (146) examined the blood sugar in 130 delinquents shortly after their apprehension. In about one third of them the blood sugar was below 75 mg percent; in some cases it was 50 mg and even below 40 mg percent.

Hill and Sargant (147) wrote in *The Lancet* about a law suit of a young man who was accused of stabbing his mother to death, who was not found guilty of murder, but insane because of progressive increasing hypoglycaemia during the time when the murder was committed. Besides the glucose tolerance test, which indicated that he was in fact prone to hypoglycaemia, the argument was based on the accused's story leading to the actual stabbing incidence. There was found to be first a very poor diet for a week, then the usual irritability and an argument in the morning, followed by further poor diet that day, leading up to the actual assault and death, which was followed by six or seven hours of complete amnesia of the event.

Bowill (148) describes an incidence in *The British Journal of Psychiatry* where a doctor's wife, an SRN, killed a cyclist in a hit and run accident. Using material forming the base of the report, the defence counsel was able to show to the court that the defendant suffered from Reactive Hypoglycaemia, and that at the time of the accident she was probably suffering from low blood sugar to the extent that her state of consciousness was seriously altered. The accused pleaded 'guilty', even though she had no memory whatsoever about the accident. A normal fine was imposed, with driving disqualification on the grounds of her hypoglycaemic ill-health.

D'Asaro *et al.* (149) studied the dietary habits of the inmates of Morristown Rehabilitation Centre, New Jersey, and found that most seemed to be straight-forward sugar addicts. They added a lot of sugar to their foods, they drank large volumes of sugar-sweetened coffees and cokes, and between meals they ate numerous candy bars, which of course would be the worst possible thing to do if a person were suffering from hypoglycaemia.

An internationally known criminologist Alexander Schauss (138) writes: 'In countless number of prisons, jails and detention centres I have observed the availability of coffee, sugar, candies and sweet drinks for confinees. In some institutions, the quantities of these substances is limitless. Little or no interest is shown in treating suspected hypoglycaemia. Repeated studies have demonstrated an unusually high rate of hypoglycaemia amongst offenders, averaging 80 to 85 percent, yet most correctional facility medical personnel still treat the problem as non-existent. The usual response is to prescribe medications when the delinquent or prisoner complains about dizziness, cold sweats, nervousness and fatigue, all these being potential signs of Reactive Hypoglycaemia.'

An excellent series of studies about a possible connection between nutrition and behaviour amongst offenders have been conducted by another internationally known criminologist Professor Stephen Schoenthaler.

First Schoenthaler (150, 151) conducted a two year double-blind study amongst 276 juvenile delinquents in one Virginia penal institution only by reducing the consumption of refined sugar. Analysis of 934 infractions committed by these juveniles during the two year period showed that delinquents receiving the lower sugar diet had 82% lower incidence of assault. Theft was lowered 77%, 'horseplay' 65% and refusal-to-obey-an-order 55%.

Next Schoenthaler (152) replicated the Virginia study in Alabama. The first six months of this replication study included a baseline period, followed by a ten month experimental phase, and final six months return to a baseline period. The diet modification in Alabama and Virginia was almost identical. The primary revisions involved only the replacement of soft drinks and junk food snacks with fruit juices and nutritious snacks, and the elimination of high sugar content desserts and cereals. Overall this Alabama study resulted in a 54% increase in the rate of antisocial behaviour in the 104 juveniles who experienced the return to the baseline diet.

Schoenthaler's third study (153) was implemented in the largest correctional system in the world, in Los Angeles County, California. The population of 1382 juveniles who experienced the diet transition showed 44% reduction in the incidence of antisocial behaviour after being placed on a restricted refined sugar diet. . . . This study was particularly significant since the subjects served as their own controls by experiencing both diets, which eliminates the remote possibility that the 1382 juveniles in the experimental group were just 'better kids' since they literally matched themselves.

The fourth study Schoenthaler (154) completed involved the largest group of subjects ever investigated in the area of nutrition and antisocial behaviour. In this study the behaviour of 2005 incarcerated male juveniles was analyzed over a 24 month period. Dietary devisions were limited as in previous experiments to fruit juices replacing sugary soft drinks and nutritious non-refined carbohydrates, such as nuts, fruits or vegetables, as snacks to replace candy and other junk foods. The results showed 25% lower rate of antisocial behaviour in the category of assaults/fights and 42% lower rate in the category of disruptions/horseplay.

At the same time when the Northern California study was being completed Schoenthaler (155) conducted a double-blind study amongst 481 incarcerated juveniles who were simply offered fresh orange juice with breakfast, lunch and dinner as an option to cow's milk and water. Neither the staff nor the juveniles were aware of their participation in this twelve month double-blind study. The incidence of antisocial behaviour in the experimental group receiving orange juice declined by 47%.

Virkkunen (156) studied 23 young male adults with antisocial personality found guilty of violent crimes which included homicides, homicide attempts and rape. All these crimes had been committed while under the influence of alcohol and were usually impulsive. All offenders were tested for Reactive Hypoglycaemia using the GTT, combined with insulin measurements. The results showed both Reactive Hypoglycaemia and an enhanced insulin secretion amongst all these offenders. In order to find out more about the past history of these offenders, both the relatives and the school personnel were sent official questionnaires. The results indicated that all 23 criminals had displayed an attention deficit disorder, usually with hyperactivity in childhood.

Professor Bryce-Smith (157) writes: 'Follow-up studies of children originally diagnosed as hyperactive have shown, in comparison with controls, a higher drop-out and expulsion rate from school, a higher rate of involvement in alcohol and drug abuse and a greater risk of coming before courts. . . . During a (voluntary) visit to a modern UK prison for young male adults convicted of serious crimes, I was informed by the prison psychiatrist that nearly all the inmates were hyperactive as children.'

Now let's go back to Dr Crook's statement in *The Lancet*

(100) 'In my general paediatric and allergy practice I have found that 75% of my hyperactive patients improve, often dramatically, when their diets are changed. . . . Sugar was identified by the parents as the leading troublemaker, with food dyes (especially red) and additives second.'

I don't know about you, but if I had a youngster at home showing an excessive hyperactive behaviour, I wouldn't just sit there tearing my hair out and hoping for the best, or stuff the poor blighter with drugs and talking therapies, but contact Hyperactive Children's Support Group (HAGS) immediately and follow their advice. Because let's face it, a criminal record is no laughing matter, and if it can be prevented by early dietary intervention, it certainly is worth a try. I'll be including the address of HAGS at the end of this book. It could be said now in summary that:

a) Over-consumption of refined carbohydrates can lead to Reactive Hypoglycaemia in susceptible individuals, which in turn can cause all kinds of physical and mental disorders. It can contribute to hyperactive behaviour in children, attention deficit disorders and under-achievement at school, and in adults it can contribute, besides various mental and physical disorders, also to alcoholism, drug addictions and criminal behaviour.

b) Food colourings and other food additives, or more likely the synergistic effect of foods high in sugar content, which also usually contain colourings and other additives, such as various sweets, squashes and other junk food may aggravate the situation.

c) Because refined sugars are void of all nutrients, therefore in order to metabolize them, the body has to rob its own valuable vitamin and mineral reserves, which in turn leads to sub-clinical vitamin and mineral deficiencies. These in themselves can cause a myriad of mental disturbances, of which I will be talking at length in my next chapter.

d) Alcohol and crime seem to be closely connected and so is Reactive Hypoglycaemia and alcohol consumption, as many hypoglycaemics will turn to alcohol as a quick way of lifting the falling blood sugar, and in that way prevent the development of the dreaded hypoglycaemic symptoms. There is also another side to the coin, as most alcoholics seem to end up as hypoglycaemics, as alcohol is known to reduce the output of liver glycogen, which can either precipitate, or exaggerate already existing hypoglycaemia.

Now that we have finally established that Reactive Hypoglycaemia seems to be one of the main reasons for most human tragedy, it might be worthwhile taking a brief look first at how our sugar regulating mechanism decides to flip in the first place, and secondly, what we can do about it.

To put it simply: In normal healthy people insulin is released from the pancreas after a meal in response to raised blood sugar produced by the food we have just eaten. The role of the insulin is to remove all excess blood sugar or glucose which is not needed immediately by the body and store the excess in our liver as liver glycogen. Substances such as glucagon, growth hormone, glucocorticoids and adrenaline are all insulin antagonists, which means that they all raise blood sugar. The role of glucagon hormone is to stimulate the conversion of stored glycogen from the liver back to blood sugar or glucose. In a healthy individual a delicate balance is maintained at all times between insulin and its antagonists, which enables them to work together as a perfect team and keep the blood sugar on an even keel. Both in diabetes and in hypoglycaemia, for some reason or another, these gluco-regulatory hormones get all screwed up. Diabetics don't produce enough insulin, or maybe even too many insulin antagonists, and hypoglycaemics, on the other hand, either produce too much insulin, or alternatively the insulin response may be normal but insulin antagonists may be malfunctioning and not responding effectively to a low blood sugar level. And last, but not least, drugs like tranquillizers taken in long-term therapy may also lead to a chronic hypoglycaemic state, as they are known to suppress growth hormone secretion, which in turn is known to increase insulin sensitivity. Whatever the cause, it is no fun whatsoever to be a hypoglycaemic sufferer and that is pretty nearly official.

No one can really say for certain why some people become low blood sugar sufferers. In the majority of cases however, it seems to be due to some 'inborn error of metabolism', as the predisposition towards developing hypoglycaemia later in life seems to be hereditary. In my own case my dear departed mother was almost certainly a low blood sugar sufferer, and so were her parents. Also at least one of my brothers seems to suffer from the same fate.

Whatever the basic cause, Reactive Hypoglycaemia is usually 'triggered off' in susceptible individuals by over-consumption of sugary foods and an excessive use of such stimulants as tobacco, caffeine and such-like, often combined with an excessive physical or mental stress. In hindsight, it must have been due entirely to my careless eating habits combined with too much smoking which made me keel over back in 1961, and precious little to do with my father having fought on the Russian front, or my brother being three years my junior. However, to my greatest regret my old doc didn't seem to be familiar with this hypoglycaemic state, because if he had been, I wouldn't be sitting here now, reduced to poverty and writing this book. I would be right up there, filthy rich, or at least near as damn it, one of the greatest fashion designers that ever was. If you think that I must be a trifle bitter, you are right, I am.

The treatment of hypoglycaemia is solely dietary and no amount of tranquillizing, drugging, electric-shocking, name-swopping or talking to it with those old and tiresome clichés 'It is only nerves', 'Pull yourself together', or 'It is all in the mind', will make it go away. In fact drugging and tranquillizing can make it much worse in the longer run as we have already seen.

Now some explanatory words about different types of sugars and carbohydrates. First of all, all starches, dietary fibre, and sugars are known as carbohydrates, which, except fibre, can be converted in the body to blood sugar or glucose. Carbohydrates can be further divided into two separate categories: refined and complex carbohydrates. Refined carbohydrates consist of all products made of white flour, commercial sugars such as sucrose or table sugar, whether white or brown, as well as sugars known as glucose, dextrose, maltose, syrups, fructose and so on and so forth.

These refined carbohydrates are all refined from so called wholefoods or complex carbohydrates such as whole wheat, sugar cane, sugar beet etc. by stripping them of all fibre, vitamins and minerals, leaving behind nutritionless rubbish. Table sugar is in fact nothing else but a sweet pharmaceutically-pure chemical, and should be treated as such, least of all should it be eaten in bucketfulls as the present trend seems to be.

More often than not, when I talk to hypoglycaemic sufferers, the universal chorus seems to be: 'But we never eat sugar.' But little they seem to know, that instead of them being in charge of their sugar consumption, the food manufacturers now do it for them as so called 'hidden sugars'. All you have to do is to look at the labels. The higher sugar is mentioned on the list of ingredients, the higher the sugar content of that food. In fact one leaflet I picked up when I last visited my dentist claims that 'puffy sugar breakfast cereals' consist of 57% pure sugar, drinking chocolate 75%, chocolate biscuits 33%, tea biscuits 22%, tomato ketchup 22%, brown sauce 23%, strawberry jam 68% and blackcurrant drink 61%. Even our tins of soup and baked beans consist of 1% and 4% sugar respectively. As a rule of thumb one could say that the prettier the package, the more suspect the food it contains. Or in other words, the less doctored the food you choose, the less likely you will need doctoring yourself.

Both refined and complex carbohydrates can be converted in the body to blood sugar. The major difference being that with complex carbohydrates, as well as with all proteins, which also can be converted to blood sugar, this conversion happens steadily and fairly slowly. As opposed to refined carbohydrates when the pancreas is stimulated almost instantly to frenzied insulin productivity, until in susceptible individuals, it finally becomes so 'trigger happy' with its insulin production, that at the slightest provocation insulin pours out leading to a hypoglycaemic state.

Now, whereas you treat diabetic hypoglycaemia with sugar lumps, you should never do that with Reactive Hypoglycaemia, because the more sugar you stuff into yourself, the more insulin your pancreas churns out, making you more and more green around the gills. So the first rule in the treatment of Reactive Hypoglycaemia is to stop eating sugar and sugary foods altogether. You should consider breakfast as the most important meal of the day and it should be high in good quality protein.

Thorn *et al.* (158) studied the metabolic effects of several meals of varying composition with special reference to the prevention of hypoglycaemic symptoms. They found that a high carbohydrate breakfast resulted in a definite increase in blood sugar after one hour, followed by a rapid fall at the end of two hours, which was associated with hunger and weakness. Taking a high protein meal of the same calorific value, on the other hand, was followed by a definite sense of well-being and the maintenance of a normal blood sugar level throughout the six hour experimental period. In other words, blood sugar levels seem to fluctuate widely following an ingestion of a high carbohydrate meal, whereas little, or no change could be observed in blood sugar levels following the ingestion of a high protein meal. But do note that these tests were done on normal and healthy individuals, not on some poor blighter, who might be already teetering on the brink of hypoglycaemic problems. So if you wish to feel well and hearty all day long, do start your day with a good wholesome breakfast, not with a cup of strong coffee or tea accompanied with a slice of toast with a blob of jam on top. If you do the latter, you are just asking for trouble. So be warned.

A hypoglycaemic individual should also avoid all stimulants such as strong coffee, tea, cola drinks, as well as tobacco, as they all contribute to low blood sugar, but in a round-about way. All these stimulants force our adrenal glands to release adrenaline, which in turn helps to release stored glycogen from our liver, subjecting the pancreas to a frenzy of insulin production followed by a hypoglycaemic dip.

Hypoglycaemic sufferers should stick primarily to high protein foods such as meat, fish, eggs, cheese etc. providing of course that they aren't allergic to them. However, if you don't 'dig' meat, a good vegetable protein combination is mandatory. All fruits should be eaten, not drunk as juices.

Alcohol should also be avoided. But if you are determined sometimes to get sozzled, get sozzled after some food.

At least at the beginning of the treatment, the emphasis is on small multiple feedings, which means you masticate wholesome food bit by bit or being more precise, eat about six small meals daily, instead of stuffing yourself half senseless in the evening just before you are planning to go to bed. The reason for eating little and often is to allow the brain, body and central nervous system to receive a constant blood sugar supply and thereby avoid the dreaded hypoglycaemic symptoms. With that in mind it is also essential that you carry with you at all times, when leaving home, a small supply of high protein snacks such as nuts, cheese etc, because as soon as you feel a 'panic' or a hypoglycaemic attack looming on the horizon, it is easily abolished by some protein consumption. Also all allergic stresses, whether food or chemical, when identified, should be avoided. For example, if you are a smoker and suspect that you may be allergic to tobacco, for heaven's sake try to give it up, because some of the worst hypoglycaemic attacks are produced by tobacco in susceptible individuals. (125) And finally, excessive physical and mental stresses should also be curtailed, as both are known to contribute to a blood sugar fall.

You might have noticed at the very beginning of this chapter when I was giving some case samples of typical hypoglycaemic sufferers, that in both case 4 and case 7 there seemed to be a definite correlation between the frequency of hypoglycaemic attacks, and physical and/or emotional tension. For example our surgeon in the sample case 7 seemed to get his knickers into a proper hypoglycaemic knot just when he was in the middle of a serious operation and presumably under great tension. According to Conn (129) the reason tension has been thought to contribute to a blood sugar fall is that our parasympathetic nervous system, or our vagus nerve, is thought to carry secretory fibres to the islets of the pancreas which control the finer regulation of insulin secretion. Whatever the case, there is no doubt in my mind that for example agoraphobia which is sometimes 'cured' using so-called behaviour psychotherapy, comes in this hypoglycaemic category.

The success of behaviour therapy for agoraphobic sufferers is geared to the assumption that anxiety attacks should diminish as soon as the patient learns to relax when faced with his anxiety producing situation.

When I was studying behaviour psychotherapy in the Institute of Psychiatry, London, some years ago, I remember a budding head-shrinker enquiring from the lecturer what he thought was behind the claimed success of behaviour modification in the treatment of agoraphobia. I can't remember the reply precisely, but he waffled something about adrenaline secretion or a lack of it. I think I know now most of this agoraphobic mystery. First of all, as I have mentioned before, there are two types of agoraphobia: a complex and a simple one. The complex agoraphobia is caused by an addiction of tranquillizing medication and the simple agoraphobia is caused by Reactive Hypoglycaemia. Now if tension increases insulin production via parasympathetic nerve fibres, which in turn causes Reactive Hypoglycaemia, which then leads to an excessive adrenaline secretion, this is known directly to contribute to a feeling of anxiety. Adding now to that adrenaline secretion the adrenaline secretion which is directly caused by that feeling of anxiety itself, it is no longer surprising that the poor agoraphobic is now in a right old state. So by stopping the tension one also stops the adrenaline secretion one way or another. It seems to be as simple as that.

Now finally comes some good news, as according to Conn (127, 129) most troublesome hypoglycaemic symptoms can be controlled simply by dietary means even when the environmental tension persists. Or in other words, a diet high in protein and low in refined carbohydrates, all other things remaining the same, effectively stabilizes the blood sugar level and abolishes the unpredictable blood sugar dips which are responsible for the frightening symptoms. All in all, it looks now that it is entirely up to you, if you happen to be a 'simple agoraphobic', whether you prefer to be led around streets and market places by a competent behaviour therapist, or decide to leave your sugar bowl, strong teas, coffees and fags alone and at last tuck into proper and nourishing food and go out on your own as much as your heart desires. And this same pearl of wisdom goes for some alcoholics as well. Mullaney and Trippett

(159) found to their great surprise, when they studied 102 patients referred to an alcoholic treatment unit, that one third of them suffered also from disabling agoraphobia or social phobias, while a further third had 'less disabling symptoms'. Furthermore they were able to establish that the onset of these phobic symptoms preceded alcoholism more frequently than the converse. I personally am not one little bit surprised at this news, as both alcoholism and agoraphobia can be a direct result of Reactive Hypoglycaemia. Therefore if a hypoglycaemic individual is found to be suffering from both agoraphobia and alcoholism, it shouldn't be a very big deal.

Dr Stephen Gyland (132) wrote in the *Journal of American Medical Association* in 1953: 'If all doctors would read the work of Dr Seale Harris (131) on hypoglycaemia, thousands of persons would not have to go through what I did. During three years of severe illness I was examined by 14 specialists and 3 nationally known clinics before diagnosis was made by means of the 6-hour glucose tolerance test, previous diagnoses having been: brain tumour, diabetes and cerebral arteriosclerosis.'

Tuula Tuormaa writes in 1991: 'If all doctors would read the work of Dr Seale Harris (131), thousands of persons would not need to go through what I did. During over twenty years of severe illness I was examined by several doctors and specialists all over the world before a diagnosis of hypoglycaemia was made by means of a 6-hour glucose tolerance test, previous diagnoses having been: anxiety neurosis, depression, alcoholism, agoraphobia, epilepsy, psychosomatic disorder, schizophrenia, hyperventilation syndrome, cerebral arteriosclerosis, allergy, ME and last but not least, that gorgeous personality disorder, to which I am willing to plead guilty, your honour.'

Paavo Airola (121) writes: 'Since hypoglycaemia can mimic so many conditions, the correct diagnosis can be extremely difficult and time-consuming. Because incompetent or overworked doctors did not have the time or interest to make an in-depth study and a thorough testing of their patients, thousands of hypoglycaemics, whose condition would have been cured by simple dietic means, had their lives ruined, families destroyed or fortunes lost on

psychiatric couches or in mental hospitals, or were mis-
diagnosed and treated with dangerous drugs and surgery
for a long list of diseases they never had.'
Amen.

11

THE MISSING LINKS

Our mental and physical health is dependent not only on oxygen, water, natural daylight, correct temperature and a feeling of contentment, but also on a good balance of at least 45 known nutrients, which include basic proteins, carbohydrates and fats, which should supply us with all essential vitamins, minerals, amino- and fatty acids. These cannot be synthesized by the body, but should be supplied daily by the food we eat.

When I started this chapter, I nearly had a fit when I realized how much research material I had accumulated during these years dealing with Nutritional Medicine, which is similar to Clinical Ecology, which is also known as Ecological or Environmental Medicine, and which in turn may consist of Megavitamin Therapy or Orthomolecular Psychiatry. What all these names have in common is that natural nutrients such as vitamins, minerals, amino- and fatty acid supplementation can be added to basic nutritional intervention for treating both physical and mental illnesses.

Looking at the massive pile of references, my first reaction was to chicken out and to skip this chapter altogether and probably write another book at some later date. However, finally common sense prevailed and I decided to get on with it and do a quick 'hit and run job', only dealing with basics, instead of going into mind-bending revelations such as how you can become biotin deficient by drinking too many raw egg whites, which contain avidin, which has a nasty habit of immobilizing biotin. Or how phytates, or phytic acid, which forms a part of the fibre content of wheat and which is found in unleavened breads such as chapattis, forms with minerals, such as calcium, iron, zinc etc. insoluable salts, which in turn can lead to mineral deficiencies. Don't misunderstand me, all these nutritional aspects are very important, but the last thing I want is to be included in the Guinness book of records as 'that fool who wrote the longest book in the universe'. For the same reason I have also decided to shrink the reference section of this chapter to the absolute minimum. Anybody wanting to learn more about this fascinating subject of nutrition and health, should visit a book shop or a health food shop, buy books on the subject and get on with it. An excellent overall guide with ample medical references is a book called *Nutritional Medicine* written by doctors Stephen Davies and Alan Stewart (160), which covers the subject to near perfection. Besides their book, I have also used information collected from books by Dr Newbold (140), Dr Colgan (161), Patrick Holford (162), Dr Mervyn (163, 164), Adelle Davis (165) etc.

Vitamins are divided into water soluble and fat soluble vitamins. The following water soluble vitamins have been found to be essential for man: the whole B-vitamin group, which consists of thiamine (B1), riboflavin (B2), niacin or nicotinic acid (B3), pantothenic acid (B5), pyridoxine (B6), cobalamin (B12), folic acid and biotin. Inositol, choline and para-aminobenzoic acid are also mentioned in some books, but others don't regard them as true vitamins because our bodies can synthesize them. The last known water soluble vitamin is vitamin C or ascorbic acid, which, some researchers believe, shouldn't be called a vitamin at all, but a hormone, because all other animals except human beings, guinea pigs, monkeys and fruit bats seem to produce their own vitamin C from glucose in their livers. It is thought that humans were able to do the same in the past, but for some weird reason or another, they have now lost the ability, which makes vitamin C more essential than ever before.

The fat soluble vitamins include vitamins A, D, F, E and K. Vitamin D is also considered a hormone by some researchers, since it can only be produced by both animal and man by ultraviolet light reacting with cholesterol in the skin. Vitamin D can also be produced by the action of light on yeast, but far the best sources of vitamin D are foods of animal origin.

Certain vitamins can be made in our bodies, unlike

minerals which have to be supplied from the foods we eat. Minerals could be divided into four categories: macro-, trace-, research trace- and toxic minerals. Several hundred milligrams of macro-minerals are required by our bodies daily and they include calcium, phosphorus, magnesium, sodium, potassium and chloride. The trace elements include iron, zinc, copper, manganese, iodine, chromium, selenium, molybdenum, cobalt and sulphur. Although these trace elements are required by our bodies in very small amounts, they are no less important than macro-minerals, because they are needed with vitamins to act as co-enzymes, which help to catalyze all the body's vital enzymatic and hormonal reactions, as well as metabolizing ingested food into tiny sachets of energy, known as adenosine triphosphate, or ATP for short, without which we would be dead as mutton. Research trace elements include: vanadium, nickel, tin, lithium etc. which have yet to be categorically proven as essential for man, but which have been found in our bodies and which appear to have at least some part to play in our metabolism. Toxic minerals include lead, aluminium, mercury, cadmium, and an excess of copper.

Now that we have got the basics out of the way, let's take a brief look at some research studies concerning sub-clinical vitamin and mineral deficiencies. The word sub-clinical covers the vast 'grey area' existing between a slight vitamin or mineral deficiency and the final collapse, known in medical circles as beri-beri (vitamin B1 collapse), pellagra (vitamin B3 collapse), scurvy (vitamin C collapse) and rickets (calcium and/or vitamin D collapse).

I dislike speaking of specific vitamins and minerals for specific illnesses, because in reality there is never a deficiency of just one vitamin or mineral alone, just as there is never any vitamin or mineral activity by itself. It is always the multiple interaction of these essential substances which form the basis of our biochemical being. However, in-dividual deficiencies can be produced in experimental conditions, showing that certain symptoms of a certain vitamin or mineral deficiency show sooner in some tissues than in others.

Carney *et al.* (166) examined 172 successive admissions to

a psychiatric unit of a district general hospital. They found that 30% of all patients were deficient in vitamin B1. They also seemed to be the ones who were deficient in more than one vitamin, patients with affective disorders being particuarly low in B2 and B6.

Abbey (167) studied vitamin deficiencies in 12 patients suffering from agoraphobia and found out that most of them had more than one vitamin deficiency including B1, B2, B3, B6, B12 and folic acid.

These samples show how vitamin deficiencies can't really be divided, particularly the B-group of vitamins, as in nature none of the B vitamins are ever found separately from all the others, therefore if a person is found to be deficient in one of them, he is almost certainly also deficient in others.

Williams *et al.* (168) studied induced vitamin B1 deficiency in voluntary human subjects and found out that restricted B1 intake caused the following symptoms: depression, generalized weakness, dizziness, palpitations, chest pains, insomnia, anorexia, nausea, vomiting, low blood pressure, backache, muscle tenderness, a feeling of apathy, difficulty in thought and memory, sensitivity to light, headaches, abdominal distension, numbness and tenderness of the calves and feet. In all cases the capacity for work and physical activity was greatly reduced and an elevated lactic acid concentration was found, particularly after exercise. In fact, the more physically active B1 deficient subjects were, the sooner and more seriously they seemed to be affected. Less active volunteers suffered less and it took longer for them to be affected. The shortest time for the appearance of clear evidence of symptoms ranged between 12 and 48 days. They concluded their study by stating that the early stages of restricted thiamin intake closely resembles Neurasthenia, which we already know is the same as Effort syndrome, Soldier's heart, Anxiety neurosis, Hyperventilation syndrome etc.

Lonsdale and Shamberger (169) studied 20 youths suffering from thiamin deficiency, which they referred to as sub-clinical beri-beri. Symptoms, in order of frequency, included: abdominal and/or chest pains, sleep disturbances, personality changes, recurrent fever of unknown cause, alternating constipation and diarrhoea, chronic debilitating fatigue, anorexia, headache, nausea and/or vomiting, depression, dizziness and blurred vision. They write: 'Personality changes, particularly in adolescents, were very disturbing to the families since they often were aggressive and hostile in nature. The patient was described as unusually irritable, sensitive to criticism, becoming angered easily and showing poor impulse control. . . . Many of them had no breakfast at all, most had school lunch and an evening meal was provided at home. In most cases it was between meals snacking of so-called junk foods and, above all, the consumption of a variety of sweet beverages that provide empty calories. This fact constitutes a difference between our patients and those that might be expected to contract beri-beri in a deprived population. It has long been known that a high carbohydrate diet is most dangerous in the presence of thiamin deficiency. . . . ' They suggested that access to easily assimilable sweet beverages could represent a modern danger which is insufficiently emphasized and may well be responsible for personality traits and symptomatology, that are regularly overlooked and considered to be 'the personality of a growing child or adolescent'.

Sterner and Wayne (232) studied restricted vitamin B2 deficiency in six male volunteers aged between 19 to 24 years. Results indicated that a restriction of riboflavin of 39–56 days had behaviour-specific effects, which included hypochondriasis, depression, hysteria, psychopathic-deviation and hypomania. Emotional shallowness, lethargy and decreased hand-grip strength was also found.

Spies et al. (231) studied patients with various levels of vitamin B3 deficiency, a state which they named sub-clinical pellagra. They write: 'Sub-clinical pellagrins are noted for the multiplicity of their complaints, among which are many that are usually classified as Neurasthenia (which we already know is the same as Effort Syndrome, Soldier's Heart, Anxiety Neurosis, Phobic Anxiety State, Hyperventilation syndrome etc). The most common of these symptoms are: fatigue, insomnia, anorexia, vertigo, a burning sensation in various parts of the body, numbness, palpitations, nervousness, a feeling of unrest, anxiety, headache, forgetfulness, apprehension and distractibility. The conduct of the pellagrin may be normal, but he feels incapable of mental or physical effort, even though he may be ambulatory.'

Green (172) discusses sub-clinical vitamin B3 deficiency, which he calls in his paper sub-clinical pellagra. He works as a doctor near eight Indian settlements in Saskatchewan, Canada. Between November 1968 and March 1971 he diagnosed definite sub-clinical pellagra in 164 of his patients, and a further 36 patients suffering from a suspected sub-clinical pellagra. Just like schizophrenic sufferers, all sub-clinical pellagrins seemed to suffer from perceptual difficulties, at least to some degree. Vision was often affected, causing some kind of 'zoom effect', where objects seemed to move far away and then become close again, getting smaller or bigger depending on the misperception of distance. Sometimes there seemed to be a presence of fog between the object and the sufferer. In some cases buildings and trees seemed to lean over and objects seemed to change shape and become distorted. Some patients were 'hearing voices'. When walking, some patients felt the ground to be soft and 'spongy' and sometimes moving forward or sideways. The sufferer may feel that he is walking uphill or down, while he is actually on flat ground, so he may feel dizzy and have generally trouble with walking.

Being frightened is also a common symptom. He seems to be frightened of all sorts of things that previously didn't bother him. He may be also irritable and fatigued, so he tends to stay by himself becoming more and more anti-social. Anxiety and depression coexist in most cases. The difference between the illusions of sub-clinical pellagra and the hallucinations of schizophrenia seem to be only a matter of degree. The pellagrin usually knows that what he experiences just cannot be so, whereas the schizophrenic sufferer is not so sure. Furthermore, the pellagrin usually seeks medical attention, unlike the schizophrenic. Dr Green writes: 'Sub-clinical pellagra is a deficiency syndrome characterized by the presence of perceptual changes, affecting any, or all special and prorioceptive senses, which results in neurasthenia. It is caused by a deficiency of, or of an increased demand for niacin, the administration of which leads to prompt disappearance of the symptom complex. Because a disease is out of fashion there is no reason to suppose that it has disappeared. Since the addition of niacin to white flour in 1941, pellagra as a disease has gradually been dropped from the thoughts of clinicians when they consider differential diagnosis for various symptom complexes. Those of us who graduated from medical school after 1945 met with pellagra only in passing. It was mentioned in a historical fashion, as though the cause had been found, the vitamin given, and the disease cured. This is indeed a strange way to deal with a disease whose very existence depends on poverty, ignorance, and the avarice of man. It would seem to me that as long as people are poor, they buy very little red meat and other expensive high-protein items. As long as people are ignorant they eat what pleases the taste buds and satisfies the appetite. As long as there are people to whom profit means more than the health of the nation, the poor and the ignorant will be exploited by hucksters peddling puffed wheat, cornflakes and "Instant This and That", nearly all at the expense of the protein and vitamin values of food. . . . A doctor must have an open mind. If he lacks interest in the disease, he will never diagnose it. . . . It is the combination of symptoms and treatment which makes the diagnosis secure: 1) There must be complaints of a physical nature, pain, fatigue, neurasthenia and the like. 2) There must be evidence of perceptual difficulties mentioned above. 3) Diet history usually shows a low protein and a high carbohydrate intake. 4) The patient should respond to the administration of niacin or niacinamide.'

Washbourne (173) observed fifteen patients aged between 18 and 46, who were treated with vitamin B3 for their depression. Fourteen patients improved with niacin treatment and no relapses were exhibited while they were taking niacin. In eleven cases, however, it was necessary to repeat the vitamin treatment at a later date when another depression became evident. In each of these cases an improvement identical to the first was obtained on repeated niacin treatment.

Möhler *et al.* (174) found that nicotinamide, an active form of vitamin B3 seems to possess benzodiazepine-like action in rat's brain. They suggested that this finding may shed some more light on various mental disorders accompanying vitamin B3 deficiency states.

Vescovi *et al.* (175) conducted a double-blind study using either an intravenous injection of either vitamin B3 and glucose solution or a placebo on 28 people trying to withdraw from benzodiazepine addiction and found that patients receiving the vitamin B3 showed minimal withdrawal symptoms, as opposed to the placebo group, which experienced all the usual symptoms including fear, tension, anxiety, insomnia, confusion and tachycardia.

Osmond and Hoffer (176) conducted several studies using vitamin B3 in the treatment of schizophrenia. Their first comparison study started in September 1952 and consisted of 30 schizophrenic sufferers. These patients were divided at random into three separate groups, one was receiving niacin, one nicotinamide and one group was receiving a placebo. In this study the placebo group did the worst.

Another large scale follow-up study started in 1952 and finished in 1959, when Drs Osmond and Hoffer compared results between 73 schizophrenic patients treated with niacin and 98 schizophrenic patients not receiving niacin. They found during a four year follow-up that patients who didn't receive vitamin B3 spent two-fifths of a year in hospital, compared to those receiving vitamin B3 who spent only an average of one-sixth of a year. Another special double-blind follow-up study was conducted amongst 31 schizophrenic patients receiving niacin and 43 schizophrenic patients receiving placebo. All patients were followed up to six years and the results are as follows: The best results were found amongst patients who not only received niacin in hospital, but also took it for a long time after discharge. The second best were in those who did not get niacin in the hospital but had it after discharge. The third best were those who got niacin only when in hospital, while those who never received niacin at all ran a poor fourth. Drs Osmond and Hoffer write about these findings: 'This supports our contention that patients taking niacin when well or much improved, tend not to relapse. We infer from this that the vitamin protects them against schizophrenia in some way that is not yet understood . . . In our view it is a useful adjunct in the treatment of schizophrenia, both for acute cases and to reduce the chance of relapses; and we hope it will be tested on a fairly large scale, with a carefuly designed follow-up. At worst, nothing could be lost.'

Rimland *et al.* (177) studied the effect of vitamin B6 on autistic-type children. In the double-blind study each child's pyridoxine supplement was replaced during two separate experimental trial periods with either a vitamin B6 supplement or a matched placebo and it was found that behaviour deteriorated significantly during vitamin B6 withdrawal.

Carney (178) tested serum folic acid values of 423 psychiatric in-patients, consecutive admissions to a general hospital and a mental hospital unit, and 62 normal control subjects. Serum vitamin B12 estimations were also performed on 368 of the patients. It was found that patients with epilepsy, depression and organic psychoses had significantly lower mean serum folic acid concentrations than normal control subjects. The most striking association with a low serum folate were chronicity of illness, a history of medication such as barbiturates, phenothiazines or antidepressants. Also malnutrition was found to be frequently present and to a less extent, a chronic physical illness. 75.2% had received drugs during the three weeks before admission, 22.9% showed clear evidence of malnutrition, 17% were physically ill and 44.2% had been continuously ill for more than three years. This study concluded first of all, that folic acid deficiency appears to be common enough in the mentally ill to justify carrying out serum folate and vitamin B12 estimations as a routine admission procedure. Secondly, it would be wise to treat patients with subnormal serum folate values with folic acid supplements, and if indicated, vitamin B12 supplements, in the hope to secure both mental and physical improvement. And finally, that further exploratory studies should be carried out.

Gharidian *et al.* (179) explored the association between folic acid deficiency and depression. They selected 28 patients and divided them into three groups; depressed patients, psychiatrically ill, but non-depressed patients and medically ill patients. All patients were hospitalized for one week and received standard diets with no drugs or vitamin preparations. At the end of the trial period it was found that depressed patients had significantly lower serum folic acid levels than patients in the other groups. Possible reasons for low folic acid levels were thought to be either malnutrition, malabsorption syndrome, pregnancy, or a continuous use of such drugs as anti-epileptics, barbiturates, anti-cancer preparations, antibiotics and oral contraceptives.

Reynolds (180) reviewed folic acid and vitamin B12 metabolism in drug treated epileptic patients, as such drugs like phenobarbitone, diphenylhydatoin and primidone are known to have an anti-folate effect. The study concluded that drug induced disturbances of folic acid and vitamin B12 metabolism may contribute to the neuropsychiatric complications in epileptic patients. It was also suggested that a prolonged folic acid deficiency may lead to apathy, depression and ultimately, over the years, to senile dementia.

Shorvon et al. (181) compared the neuropsychiatric states of 50 patients suffering from vitamin B12 deficiency and 34 patients suffering from folic acid deficiency. Nervous system abnormalities were found in two-thirds of both groups. Peripheral neuropathy was found to be the most common condition associated with vitamin B12 deficiency. Affective disorders were associated with folic acid deficiency, which occurred in 56% of folic acid deficient patients.

Folic acid deficiency is thought to cause depression through interference with hydroxylation of such amino acids as tyrosine and tryptophan, both being responsible for the production of brain neurotransmitters like dopamine and serotonin.

Before I carry on, I would like to say a few words about anaemias. Oxygen is carried in our bodies with the help of haemoglobin which is found in our red blood cells. Iron deficiency anaemia is the most well known, which is characterized by the inability to produce sufficient haemoglobin because of lack of iron. However, anaemias can be caused by other nutritional deficiencies, because most of the components of our diet play some part in the formation of healthy blood cells, such as vitamin B2, B6, C, E etc. Vitamins B12 and folic acid are particularly involved in blood production, because deficiency of either of them leads to megaloplastic anaemia, which is characterized by the presence of immature and malformed red blood cells, which in turn will lead to a reduced oxygen carrying capacity of the blood. However, it is very important to remember that a lack of folic acid causes only anaemia, but lack of vitamin B12 causes so called pernicious anaemia, which also affects other tissues, in particular the nervous system, leading eventually to severe nerve degeneration. That being the case, it is essential that a correct diagnosis is made, as high doses of folic acid supplementation can mask pernicious anaemia allowing irreversible neurological damage to continue undetected. Also an excess of folic acid supplementation may lower vitamin B12 values. The good news is that vitamin B12 deficiency, owing to the vitamin's ability to be stored in the liver, usually takes a long time to develop, as opposed to megaloblastic anaemia caused by folic acid deficiency. Symptoms of all anaemias are similar and include a pale and sallow complexion, a feeling of weakness, shortness of breath, 'hyperventilation syndrome', general fatigue and a lack of energy. Now if we consider pernicious anaemia as a final collapse of vitamin B12 deficiency, it is believed that all sorts of mental symptoms may precede sub-clinical vitamin B12 values by several years. Let's look at the evidence.

Reynolds *et al.* (182) measured folic acid and vitamin B12 levels in 101 patients suffering from depression. Sub-normal folic acid levels were found in 24% of the patients and sub-normal vitamin B12 levels in 16% of the patients.

Shulman (183) describes ten patients admitted to a psychiatric hospital and subsequently found to have low serum vitamin B12 levels. Five patients had senile dementia, three suffered from depression, one was in a confusional state and one had hypomanic illness.

Goggans (184) describes a case of mania secondary to low vitamin B12 levels, without any of the clinical features of pernicious anaemia and which was cured completely by vitamin B12 injections.

Wiener and Hope (185) reviewed mental symptoms in

patients with low vitamin B12 levels prior to development of actual nerve degeneration. They described these symptoms as extremely variable and ranging from a mild mood disorder to overt psychotic behaviour. The milder symptoms were slight mood disturbances or mental slowness with difficulty in concentrating and remembering, ranging to the other extreme, where the sufferer may show severe agitation, paranoid and maniacal behaviour or even stuporous depression, which they considered makes it difficult to distinguish from schizophrenia.

Evans *et al.* (186) describes two patients with low vitamin B12 levels who were diagnosed as suffering from organic psychosis without pernicious anaemia. Both patients improved with vitamin B12 injections.

The basic message of these studies was that because cerebral symptoms of low vitamin B12 values may precede, sometimes by years, the actual appearance of pernicious anaemia and nerve degeneration, it would be prudent if all patients suffering from a psychiatric illness were screened for a possible vitamin B12 deficiency, always remembering that an adequate serum vitamin B12 level does not always guarantee an adequate tissue vitamin B12 level.

Now let's move to vitamin C or ascorbic acid.

Cutforth (187) discusses 11 cases of adult scurvy, consisting of 10 males and one female aged between 48 and 82, who were seen as outpatients in two London teaching hospitals. Cases fell into three different categories; seven of the patients were elderly men living alone, whose diet for various reasons seemed to consist primarily of tea, toast and bread-butter-meat-fish paste sandwiches. Three of the patients were suffering from ulcers and because of medical advice, were on a diet of fish, chicken, eggs, mashed potatoes, bread, butter and milk drinks. One patient had a diet consisting solely of wholemeal bread, margarine, cheese, honey and eggs. In all cases this insufficient diet had lasted more than six months. The chief physiological signs were small bruises on the limbs, extravasation of blood into the tissues and anaemia. The chief symptoms were pain, lethargy, anorexia and mental depression. Pain was described as 'rheumatic pain' which consisted of aching limbs, particularly the legs and in the back. Eight out of eleven patients complained of it. Lethargy was described as a feeling of tiredness or weakness or both. Six patients complained of it and it was very striking in two of them, who found it difficult to get out of bed to feed themselves. All symptoms and signs, including anaemia responded promptly to vitamin C supplementation. This study points out that not enough attention has been paid to the psychological effects of vitamin C deficiency, as more than half these patients on admission to hospital were depressed, resentful and rather unco-operative. After a few days' vitamin C supplementation, however, this state disappeared and all patients became normal and cheerful.

Kinsman and Hood (188) studied experimental vitamin C deficiency in five healthy human volunteers and found that personality changes in vitamin C deficient subjects consisted of hypochondriasis, depression, hysteria and social withdrawal, which preceded diminished psychomotor performance and physical fitness tasks.

Milner (189) conducted a controlled, blind trial of vitamin C saturation involving 40 psychiatric patients, who were found to be suffering from sub-clinical scurvy. This sub-clinical scurvy is described as a condition where the sufferer complains of excessive tiredness, depression, irritability and vague ill-health due to low vitamin C levels, which is not yet low enough to cause this 'final collapse' of vitamin C depletion i.e. scurvy. After the trial he found a statistically significant improvement in depressive, manic and paranoid symptoms complexes, together with an improvement in overall personality functioning with vitamin C supplemented patients. He concluded his study by pointing out that as both stress and anxiety, which are often found in psychologically ill patients, are known to accelerate vitamin C depletion, which in turn can further contribute to psychiatric disturbances, therefore all chronic psychiatric patients would benefit from added vitamin C administration.

All in all, anybody who is under stress of any kind, whether mental or physical, should make sure of receiving a sufficient amount of vitamin C, as even a tiny mouse manufactures in his liver 19 gr of vitamin C a day when he is harassed and a goat manages 13 gr to his body weight, unlike us, who can't even manufacture a droplet. This being the case, it wouldn't surprise me one little bit to find a sub-clinical vitamin C deficiency contributing on a large scale to our ever-expanding mental illness statistics. Now when we have looked at some of the vitamins, or being more precise, at the lack of them, let's take a brief look at minerals.

Pitts and McClure (38) conducted a double-blind study on fourteen patients suffering from anxiety neurosis and ten normal controls, using alternating infusions of lactate ions, lactate with calcium, and glucose in saline. The results indicated that infusion of lactate produced some degree of anxiety in all participants, infusion of lactate with calcium caused fewer and less severe symptoms and infusion of glucose in saline caused no symptoms. The interpretation of these results were that a marked increase in lactate production causes anxiety symptoms which can be prevented by calcium administration.

The British Medical Journal (76b) states: 'At a psychiatric section meeting of the Royal Society of Medicine on 13 February it was suggested that elderly patients generally, and also patients with neoplastic disease and psychiatric symptoms, postoperative and other confusional states, neurotic illness of late onset, and atypical depression, might be worth investigating for hypo- or hypercalcaemia. Collaboration between chemical pathologist and psychiatrist seems to indicate the pathological and pharamacological significance of calcium in human mental states.

Burnet (190) discusses in his study a possible connection between a lack of zinc and senile dementia. He points out that as most enzymes are zinc dependent metalloenzymes, especially those concerned with DNA replication, repair and transcription, all of which require an accurate transfer of information. Therefore, age-associated diminished ability to make zinc available for DNA replication, may be one of the possible causes of senility in susceptible individuals. He writes: 'A complex and highly speculative hypothesis has, however, only one legitimate function, to stimulate some of those with appropriate skills and facilities to investigate its validity. . . . For the present, the immediate requirement is to accumulate more information about the changes in zinc metabolism with age in subjects in early stages of dementia. . . . I am hopeful that a combination of such basic work with concomitant developments in neuro-pathology, along with already well-documented non-toxicity of zinc salt, will mean that a relatively early trial will be initiated.'

Bryce-Smith and Simpson (191) write about a thirteen year old girl suffering from anorexia nervosa who was found to be zinc deficient and treated with additional zinc supplementation. They write: 'There is a scientific rationale for the use of zinc in anorexia nervosa. We do not doubt that the reduced food intake initially results from social factors. However, starvation and other stresses paradoxic-ally increase urinary zinc excretion, thereby exacerbating the effect of reduced dietary intake. As zinc status declines, impairment of zinc-dependent senses of taste and smell may be expected to reduce a further desire for food. These considerations led us to the idea that zinc supplementation might be of value in anorexia nervosa. Dietary zinc deficiency may be quite common in the UK. A 1981 survey reported the zinc intake from an average diet to be about 10.5 mg daily, with risk of less for vegetarians. The US National Academy of Sciences recommends 15 mg, 20mg and 25 mg for normal adults, pregnant women and lactating mothers respectively.'

Anderson et al. (130) studied chromium supplementation in humans. Chromium is a trace element which is essential to normal carbohydrate metabolism. In refining processes however, it is completely removed from both table sugar and white flour, which is thought to be one of the main reasons for chromium deficiency, and of the present epidemic of various sugar regulatory disorders such as diabetes and hypoglycaemia. In order to study the effect of chromium supplementation in humans, Anderson and his colleagues conducted a double-blind cross-over experiment using inorganic chromium supplementation on 48 male and 28 female volunteers, ranging in age from 21 to 69 years. The results indicated that chromium supplementation seems to improve glucose tolerance, both elevated and depressed, in varying degrees. They write: 'The primary focus of nutrition with respect to disease should be on prevention and not curing responsive diseases. If chromium is involved in maintaining proper glucose metabolism, adequate dietary intake of chromium should be provided to prevent impaired glucose tolerance rather than reversing or alleviating it. . . . ' They also point out that they do not wish to imply that all glucose intolerance is the result of improper chromium nutrition, however, if chromium supplementation improves glucose utilization, it should be considered as being at least a causative factor.

Addy (192) writes about iron deficiency in the *British Medical Journal*: 'There is now substantial evidence that iron deficiency has an adverse effect on brain function. . . . Several studies have shown that iron deficiency in children with or without anaemia, is associated with abnormalities of behaviour and mental performance which improve with treatment with iron. . . . Children with iron deficiency anaemia scored less well than other children in tests of mental development, and furthermore, iron deficient children seem to be more tense and fearful and less responsive.'

Cannon (193) writes in the British Medical Journal: 'How many British children are short of iron?. . . . In 1983 the DHSS completed a national survey of the diets of 3285 boys and girls. The survey cost £650,000. Preliminary results are now available as photocopies from the DHSS Leaflets Unit (PO Box 21, Stanmore, Middlesex, HA7 1AY) price £4.50. . . . Children consuming below the UK recommended dietary allowance for iron (percentages of total sample) are as follows: 11 year old boys 81%, girls 95%. 14 year old boys 53%, girls 77%. Figures for intakes include the iron partially restored to white flour and bread in the form of iron powder ground down from old cars and other scrap metal. (K. Moock, personal communication), which is not bioavailable. . . . ' So now you know folks. Some drive them, others eat them. I don't mind telling you that this information about tucking into a powdered motor vehicle for breakfast gave me a completely new outlook on motoring offences.

Schauss (139) pointed out in his paper how iron deficiency may contribute to various personality disturbances and conduct disorders. It is thought that as iron is needed for the formation of monoamine oxidase (MAO), which is the basic inhibitor of such catecholamines as adrenaline, noradrenaline and dopamine, therefore a lack of iron may lead to an excess of catecholamine activity, which may manifest itself in heightened behavioural activity, restlessness, irritability and disruptive behaviour.

Morck *et al.* (194) studied a possible connection between iron absorption and coffee drinking, following a revelation by Disler *et al.* (195), who was able to demonstrate that iron absorption from a meal was reduced as much as 87% when a cup of tea was consumed at the same meal. Morck was able to demonstrate that no decrease in iron absorption occurred when coffee was consumed one hour before the meal, but if coffee was enjoyed after the meal, iron absorption was reduced by 39%. They felt as both coffee and tea are commonly consumed in countries where iron deficiency anaemia is prevalent, this inhibitory effect of both beverages on dietary iron absorption must have nutritional relevance. After reading all this mindblowing information I wasn't surprized any more that some British schoolkids' iron stores and demeanour are not quite up to scratch, if they prance about during their lunch break holding a scrap metal sandwich in one hand and a can of coke in the other, the latter being full of caffeine. It's surprising that they have any blood or behaviour left at all.

Now talking of caffeine, let's stay with caffeine. Greden (196) writes in his study *Anxiety or Caffeinism: A diagnostic dilemma*: 'High intake of caffeine can produce symptoms that are indistinguishable from those of anxiety neurosis, such as nervousness, irritability, tremulousness, occasional muscle twitchings, insomnia, sensory disturbances, tachypnea, palpitations, flushing, arrhythmias, diuresis and gastro-intestinal disturbances. The caffeine withdrawal syndrome and the headaches associated with it may also mimic anxiety. Patients with caffeinism will generally be identified only by routine inquiry into their caffeine intake. The psychiatrist should especially suspect caffeinism in patients who do not respond to psychopharmacological agents or who have psychophysical complaints and recurrent headaches, chronic coffee-drinking patients on inpatient psychiatric services, and "hyperkinetic" children. . . .'

So it looks now that if either you or your offspring suffer from an excessive nervousness, irritability, hyperactivity, anxiety neurosis, Effort syndrome, Soldier's heart, Hyperventilation syndrome etc., it might be pertinent also to look at your possibly excessive caffeine consumption.

Caffeine is found primarily in coffee, tea and all cola drinks, the latter containing not only a good dollop of caffeine, but also several teaspoonfuls of sugar, which must make it one of the unhealthiest thirst-quenchers around. However, coke is not all bad news, as Umpierre *et al.* (197) were able to demonstrate. They compared the effects of various formulations of coca-cola on sperm motility. They used semen from a healthy fertile donor and various formulations of coca-cola. The results showed that all samples of coca-cola markedly reduced sperm motility, a diet coke having the strongest effect, and a classic coke was found to be five times more effective than New Coke. They concluded their study saying that coca-cola as a postcoital contraceptive agent couldn't be attributed to its pH values, but more likely to some compound of coca-cola's 'secret formula'. . . . Coke as a contraceptive, the mind boggles, but I suppose it must be better than drinking the dreaded stuff.

Now let's look at fats, or being more precise, essential fatty acids or EFAs, which can't be made by the body, but must be obtained from the food we eat, and which were originally called vitamin F. EFAs are found primarily in cold-pressed vegetable oils and marine oils. The story of EFAs goes something like this: Cis-linoleic acid is converted in our bodies to gamma-linolenic acid or GLA, which is a precursor of little-known, but extremely important substances called prostaglandins, which are found in practically all our body systems. These prostaglandins are an active group of substances with a wide range of influence in our cellular biochemistry. Evening Primrose oil is used as a nutritional supplement because its active ingredient is GLA and which can accelerate our prostaglandin synthesis. Several prostaglandins have been identified so far, but I will discuss here only prostaglandin E1 or PGE1, which to date has been found to have a most profoundly positive effect on our physical and mental health.

Colquhoun and Bunday (198) who are both well-known for their work and research on childhood hyperactivity, have found that a lack of essential fatty acids may be one of the possible causes of hyperactive behaviour in children. Here is a sample of one of their case studies: Donald J. a six year old boy, from early childhood had had a disturbed sleep pattern. He was continually restless and had repeated stomach upsets. His concentration and speech were poor and he was abnormally thirsty. He was found to be sensitive to wheat products and on removing wheat from the diet he became a changed child with normal sleep, behaviour and speech. On trial introduction of wheat products he rapidly deteriorated, his pulse rate rose rapidly and his speech became almost incomprehensible. Each morning and evening he was given by mouth, three capsules of Evening Primrose oil and three tablets of combined zinc, vitamin C, pyridoxine and niacin. After two weeks on this regime he was challenged with wheat and no behavioural reaction or change in pulse rate occurred. Over the next four weeks he was gradually introduced to a normal wheat-containing diet with no evidence of previous abnormal reactions.

Dr David Horrobin has been considered one of the foremost experts in the world in connection with research into essential fatty acids and prostaglandins and has published widely on the subject. However, as this book is primarily concerned with mental health aspects, I will review here only a couple of his studies, one on schizophrenia and another on alcoholism. He writes on schizophrenia in *The Lancet* (199): 'In recent years it has been suggested that biological defect in schizophrenia may be related to excess dopamine activity, to production of an abnormal opioid or a normal opioid in excess, to prostaglandin deficiency, to a hypersensitivity to wheat proteins, to an allergic phenomenon, to a defect in zinc metabolisim, or to a pineal deficiency. The present hypothesis proposes that the various concepts are not mutually exclusive, but represent different aspects of the same problem. The final common path in schizophrenia may be a failure of formation and action of prostaglandins of the 1 series. . . . One of the great defects of the dominant dopamine hypothesis of schizophrenia is that it has proved therapeutically sterile and has simply led to the development of more and more essentially similar dopamine-blocking drugs. These drugs are much more effective against 'positive' than 'negative' aspects of schizophrenia. They have very serious side effects, including sedation, extrapyramidial disorders and tardive dyskinesias. The idea that the central problem is a PGE1 deficiency produced by opioid excess, melatonin deficiency or nutritional abnormalities, is far more promising.'

Dr Horrobin writes in his study *Prostaglandins and Essential Fatty Acids: A new Approach to the Understanding and Treatment of Alcoholism* (200): 'The most impressive results have been obtained by Iain and Evelyn Glen and their team at Craig Dunain Hospital, Inverness. They have carried out a double-blind, placebo-controlled study of Efamol (Evening Primrose oil) on patients undergoing alcohol withdrawal. The Efamol group on both patient and professional assessment consistently experienced fewer and less intense withdrawal symptoms. . . . Stephen Cunnane in Nova Scotia and David Segarnick in New York, have both found that administration of Evening Primrose oil can substantially reduce liver damage in rats, caused by alcohol administration. . . . Vid Persaud in Winnipeg showed that foetal alcohol syndrome in rats could be largely prevented if animals were given Primrose oil as well as alcohol during pregnancy. . . . Again, most impressively, in the Inverness trial Iain Glen found that liver enzyme levels returned to normal significantly faster in the Efamol group as compared to the placebo group'. . . . The study also points out that alcoholics given Evening Primrose oil showed a substantial and prolonged reduction in their cravings for alcohol. . . . Also that 4–6 Evening Primrose oil capsules taken before going to bed have a near-miraculous effect in preventing the morning after effects of alcoholic over indulgence. . . . I have personally tried this latter trick and I can assure you, it really works. . . . And now that we have fallen to this boozy level, we might as well stay on it for a while.

Alcohol is probably the most acceptable 'social poison' after tea and coffee. Alcohol provides plenty of calories in the form of carbohydrates, otherwise being almost void of any nutritional value, so it has an adverse effect on almost every vitamin and mineral in the body. Particularly affected are all water-soluble vitamins such as B1, B2, B3, B6, folic acid and vitamin C, as well as minerals such as calcium, magnesium and zinc, all of which have been found to be low in chronic alcoholics. In short, most heavy drinkers, besides suffering from a malfunctioning sugar metabolism such as hypoglycaemia, are invariably also low in most vitamins and minerals. So why do some people drink to excess? Dr Roger Williams, a famous chemist and the founder of the conception of biochemical individuality has done a great deal of research on the subject. He writes (201): 'It has been long recognized that alcoholism may give rise to serious nutritional problems in its victims, but only recently have our observations revealed that nutritional deficiencies play an important role in the aetiology of alcoholism itself.' He arrived at this conclusion while experimenting with rats. He found that individual rats on a stock diet exhibited markedly individualistic responses when they were offered a choice between water and 10 per cent alcohol. Some rats drank alcohol heavily from the start, some drank moderately and some drank none over periods of months, in spite of the fact that the positions of the bottles were changed daily, therefore forcing them to make a definite choice. However, changing diets had a revolutionary effect on the drinking pattern of these rats. When a group was placed on a marginal diet which was particularly low in B-group vitamins, all rats drank heavily within a short period of time. When they were offered a nutritious diet however, none of them consumed alcohol beyond a low level. Finally, when animals on low vitamin/mineral diet were supplied with an abundance of the missing nutrients, their alcohol consumption often dropped to zero overnight, and was maintained at this level as long as the nutrients were supplied.

Dr Williams writes: 'The obvious interpretation of these findings is as follows: Each individual animal has nutritional needs that are quantitatively distinctive. On the stock diet some rats were getting an abundance of everything, and because no deficiency existed for them, they had no marked tendency to drink alcohol. On the marginal diet all animals developed deficiencies and they all had a substantial appetite for alcohol. On the abundant diet, which contained generous amounts (several times the minimal needs) of many of the nutritional elements, none of the rats developed deficiencies and none drank appreciable amounts of alcohol.' Here we are then. If you wish to stay in the ranks of proper alcoholics, all you have got to do is to avoid nutritious food like the plague. However, if you plan to become the parent of a healthy baby, you should stop outright, otherwise your offspring might be born with a condition known as Foetal Alcohol Syndrome or FAS for short.

FAS is the term used to describe the serious mental and physical effects seen in children born to women who drink an excess of alcohol during pregnancy. There has been a considerable dispute of late about the amount of alcohol intake associated with this foetal damage, but recent evidence suggests that as little as one alcoholic drink every three days can already increase the risk of a possible miscarriage, itself a recognized indicator of toxic effects on the foetus.

The FAS child had usually the following characteristics: a small head with a flattened nasal bridge, often also combined with a neurological abnormality, developmental delay or intellectual impairment, which in a milder form may result in such behavioural problems as hyperactivity, attention deficit disorders and dyslexias. So if you are planning a family, for your kid's sake, do stay off alcohol. And this goes for your partner as well, as it has been established that children of heavy drinking males indicate a significantly higher correlation between the incidence of birth defects and the drinking behaviour of fathers (202). Whenever this subject comes up that future fathers are as responsible for the health of their offspring as future mothers, I am usually met with a smirk of disbelief. I can't understand why this is so difficult to comprehend. You don't see farmers offering their prize cows to be covered by any old bull. In fact farmers go to great lengths and trouble to select the strongest and healthiest specimen available and take it from there.

The period of sperm development in man lasts up to eleven weeks, which is then stored in the body for several days, even a week or two. A mature sperm is less sensitive to the effects of toxins such as alcohol than during formation and development. This means in plain language that if you wish to receive a healthy sperm from your mate, it would be prudent to make sure that your man hasn't been on the bottle for at least three months before the joyful event. And this goes for a future mother as well, because there is now abundant evidence that most abnormalities in foetal development are established by the eighth to tenth week of gestation, which means that the nutritional state of the future mother must be one hundred per cent during the very earliest weeks of pregnancy. Anyone who wishes to know in detail how to avoid possible birth defects should study any of the following books: *The Prevention of Handicap of Early Pregnancy Origin* (203), *Planning for a Healthy Baby* (204) or a booklet by Foresight entitled *The Next Generation: Avoiding Damage before Birth in the 1980s* (205), from which I have collected most of the following information: Foetal malformations have their origins mainly in faulty replication of cells. The replication of cells begins very soon after gestation, generally during the third and fourth week after successful intercourse. It is known that by the 26th day the foetal arm buds have appeared, followed by leg buds a couple of days later. In the third week there is already a tiny beating heart and a spinal cord. By the fourth week the tiny embryo has rudimentary eyes, ears, a mouth and a brain, followed by rudimentary kidneys, liver, digestive tract and a blood stream. It figures now, as most of the foetal malformations originate during this essential cell formation, that by the time a woman even knows she is pregnant, most of the vital cell replication has already taken place, including possible foetal malformations, which can be caused by environmental toxins combined with poor nutrition slowing down, disorganizing or depressing this cell replication process. This being the case, it is now clear that far the most important period when both future mother and father should take care of themselves particularly well is some weeks before planned pregnancy. Furthermore, the mother should not only take care of herself during the whole pregnancy, but particularly immediately some weeks after conception, while this vital foetal cell replication is in process. Now if I were in the process of starting a family, before anything else, I would contact an organization called Foresight, which is a charity promoting pre-conceptual care, and carefully follow their instructions. They will be able to help you to take all possible steps to ensure that your baby is born in perfect health by advising you and your partner how best to improve your nutritional status and if applicable, lower your body burden of heavy metals and other pollutants.

Now that we have skipped scantily through some psychological disturbances due to various nutritional deficiencies, thrown some abuse on caffeine and booze, as well as on some aspects of baby making, we might as well now take a brief look at excesses of so-called toxic minerals.

Let's concentrate first on lead, which is pure poison and which is spewed daily in abundance from our cars into our living environment. Symptoms of classical lead poisoning are manifold and include excitement, restlessness, agitation, insomnia, nightmares, impotence, hallucinations, loss of concentration and memory, depression, personality changes and intellectual disturbances, combined with an impaired psychomotor performance. However, I will not be discussing here lead poisoning as such, but some subtle and negative effects of lead pollution, which particularly affect young children's behaviour and intelligence. There is no doubt now that a human brain is one of the most complex systems in the whole universe, and it is now generally accepted that the child's brain, because of the delicate vulnerability of a newly developing central nervous system, is particularly at risk from all sorts of environmental pollutants, including lead.

Needleman *et al.* (206) conducted a carefully designed study which provides some of the strongest evidence so far, that even a relatively small amount of lead pollution in children, without any history of actual lead poisoning, can affect their learning abilities and classroom behaviour. In this study tooth lead levels were used as the indicator of long term lead exposure, rather than blood lead, which reflects only very recent exposure. Of a total school population of 3329 eligible children 2335 submitted at least one of their milk teeth for analysis. The teachers, with no knowledge of the lead level of children were asked to rate eleven different aspects of classroom behaviour for each child who had contributed a tooth. Teachers were asked to answer 'yes' or 'no' to questions which included: 'Is this child easily distracted during his/her work?', 'Do you consider this child hyperactive?', 'Is he/she over-excitable and impulsive?', 'Is he/she easily frustrated by difficulties?', 'Can he/she follow a sequence of directions?', 'In general, is this child functioning as well in the classroom as other children of his/her own age?' etc. Teachers' behavioural ratings were available for 2146 of the 2335 children. The result was that the frequency of teacher's negative ratings for every question increased with increasing dentine lead level.

For the second part of this study Needleman and his co-workers selected 58 children with lead levels higher than 20 ppm and compared them with 100 children with lead levels lower than 10 ppm. Both groups were given a battery of psychological tests. The results showed quite clearly that children with high lead levels performed significantly less well on auditory and verbal processing, attention performance and most items of the teachers' behavioural ratings.

Bryce-Smith and Waldron (207) conducted a thorough review of literature looking for a possible connection between high body lead levels and various behavioural disturbances including criminal behaviour. They summarized their work by pointing out that present evidence shows that excess lead in children can be linked directly with an impairment of fine motor and perceptual skills, including a broad range of psychiatric disturbances including hyperactivity of 'unknown cause', which can be cured simply by chelating excess lead from their system. They also found some evidence that some delinquents and some of the prison population may have higher lead levels than law-abiding citizens.

Phil and Parkes (208) measured fourteen different trace elements in hair samples from 31 learning disabled and 22 normal children and found significantly elevated lead and cadmium levels in learning disabled children compared to controls.

Capel et al. (209) found an average 25 times more cadmium in the hair of 77 British dyslexic children than in 44 control children. The dyslexic children also had significantly higher copper levels.

Now let's briefly go back to babies again. Ruth Jervis writes in the October 1985 issue of *The Journal of Alternative Medicine*: 'It was exciting to hear Professor Bryce-Smith's report on the latest findings of his research into trace elements in normal and abnormal foetal development, which is supported by Foresight. Of the nine different tissues from mother and baby, placenta has emerged as the most useful for providing relevant information. In 1981 it was found that birth weight relates directly to foetal mortality and morbidity – not just to gestational age. Tests done on obstetrically normal newborn babies related to 37 elements from nine tissue samples in each case, the most significant elements found to correlate to low birth weight were: Low zinc levels resulted in low birth weight. . . . Copper levels tended to be abnormally high in the smallest babies. . . . High lead levels coincided with low birth weight, with successively heavier babies as the lead burden decreases. . . . The cadmium graph was even more striking in its step relationship, starting very high cadmium in the smallest babies, the cadmium levels of smoking mothers being twice as high as in non-smoking mothers. . . . ' This exciting study has been now published in *The International Journal of Biosocial Research*. (210)

Now that we are on cigarettes, let's stay with cigarettes. Besides cigarette smoking being the main source of cadmium pollution and a cause of both allergic and hypoglycaemic reactions in susceptible individuals, the principal alkaloid, called nicotine, is pure poison. A mere eight drops of nicotine will kill a horse stone dead. Another poison, carbon monoxide, which is also formed during smoking has a much greater affinity to our haemoglobin than oxygen, therefore smoking results in the diminished oxygen carrying capacity of our blood, which results in a feeling of faintness and giddiness. Nicotine molecules can either stimulate or decrease acetylcholine turnover, in that way acting as a stimulant in smaller, more widely spaced doses, and as a sedative in large, more frequent amounts. (211) Cigarette smoking can stop us feeling hungry, because nicotine leads to an immediate rise in blood sugar level by stimulating adrenals, which in turn forces the release of liver glycogen, which, after a while can lead to all sorts of sugar regulatory disorders, such as hypoglycaemia. Cigarette smoking affects also our vitamin and mineral levels. For example it has been established that one cigarette neutralizes about 25 mg of vitamin C. So if you are a smoker and don't eat your greens, your body's vitamin C stores will become depleted in a jiffy, causing you to suffer from subclinical scurvy, which makes you feel tired, depressed, resentful and generally unco-operative. (187) Smoking can also deplete other nutrients such as B2, B6 and zinc. Smoking can also elevate your serum copper levels. (212) So all in all, cigarettes may make you feel good, but they are certainly not good for you.

Now that I have mentioned copper, let's stay with copper for a second. This copper business is a rummy one, as copper in minute amounts is essential for our life, but too much of it will cause all sorts of problems, besides those underweight babies we just talked about. Maybe its most harmful action is that copper is an antagonist to zinc, which means that when our body copper rises, our body zinc falls, and vice versa. Having a low zinc level is no fun whatsoever, as our body contains at least a hundred zinc dependent enzymes, which just can't function properly if we are zinc deficient. As zinc is also linked with DNA, which is our genetic information code, and to RNA which, besides being involved in protein synthesis, also complements DNA synthesis, one can appreciate the wide metabolic effects of zinc deficiency, as well as copper excess. Excess copper is also found in women using oral contraceptives, or the Pill, as it is more popularly known. Now that we are with the Pill, let's stay with it just a bit longer.

Dr Ellen Grant (213) has written a whole book about the effects of the Pill on human metabolism, which in my opinion is essential reading to every female who has chosen that form of birth control. I will say only a few words about the whole subject, as well as review briefly Dr Wynn's study, 'Vitamins and Oral Contraceptive Use', which was published in *The Lancet* (214). He writes:
'The many published reports concerning the effect of contraceptive steroids on vitamin levels reveal both the complexity of their interaction and the difficulty of inter-

pretation. Serum vitamin A levels are usually raised, but vitamin B2, B6, C, folic acid and vitamin B12 levels are lowered. . . . Only in regard to vitamin B6 and folic acid is there as yet any suggestion of an adverse clinical effect. Vitamin B6 deficiency may be associated with neuro-psychiatric symptoms, and may contribute to impaired glucose tolerance. . . . Megaloblastic anaemia due to folic acid deficiency has been described, but this interpretation has been challenged and the subject is still subjudice. . . . In view of the findings reviewed above, it has been suggested that oral contraceptive users should take additional vita-mins, and indeed a combined formulation has already been marketed in the USA.' So if you are one of the ladies presently on the Pill, for heaven's sake, don't forget your vitamins.

Dr Grant (215) has also established that a continuous use of the Pill can lead to the development of allergies, migraine headaches, to a decreased resistance of infections as well as to a decreased ability to deal with common cardiogenic substances. In short, the Pill is not just a little useful nonsense which will prevent the patter of tiny feet, but a powerful steroid hormone, which can cause besides vitamin and mineral deficiencies, many metabolic and immune system changes, which can last for years after the Pill is discontinued.

Now that we have established some of the missing links, as well as found out that this life is nothing more than a sexually transmitted disease, and a serious one at that, let's take a look at what could be done about it in order to make it more bearable.

12

EVERY TREE IS KNOWN BY ITS FRUIT

In the simplest terms a human being could be said to be a three dimensional creature: chemical, structural and emotional. The current healing profession could in turn be roughly divided into two basic categories: The Pasteurian, or germ theory of medicine, and the others. The present concept of orthodox medicine seems to be based primarily on Pasteur's germ theory of disease, which believes that the majority of human ills are caused by nasty germs, bacteria or viruses, which hover mercilessly everywhere 'out there' in trillions, just waiting to pounce on a poor, unsuspecting victim when he least expects it. The job of a good doctor is to find, drive out or kill these evil intruders by a substance called medicine, or to cut out the offending bit with the help of a surgeon's knife, or if possible, swop a bad bit for a better bit in the form of transplant operation. On the surface these methods appear to be doing wonders, as one can't but marvel at a brave kid with a brand new liver, a wonder baby straight out of a test tube, a happy man with somebody else's heart and so forth, at least until the overall yearly disease statistics are looked at.

Thomson and MacEoin (216) write in their book *The Health Crisis* in the chapter 'Serious Illness on the Increase': 'Although some "modern" diseases have been curtailed to some extent, mainly as a result of health education and health promotion measures, far too many serious illnesses are still on the increase, for example: lung cancer among women in the UK is causing more deaths than ever before and deaths from heart diseases are rising in this country, in marked contrast to world trends. Quite apart from the incidence of serious illness, there is a good deal of evidence from official statistics that our general level of health is poor, and even deteriorating. The latest WHO figures show that Britain has the worst death rate in the world from lung cancer, breast cancer and heart disease. The expectation of life in the UK at the age of 45 is among the worst in the developed world. Between 1972 and 1980, the incidence of chronic illness in this country rose from 20% to 29% in males, and from 21% to 31% in females. Bluntly stated, this means that almost one-third of the adult population at one time has a long-standing illness. High-lighting statistics like these is not to belittle the more obvious achievements of medicine in recent decades, especially in surgical techniques. But, however, as we approach these figures, we are forced to conclude that levels of health in this country amount to a national disgrace.' . . . Now what is to be done about it? What else but drugs, drugs and even more drugs. Thomson and MacEoin point out that research has shown that in the industrialized nations one in two adults take a drug every day. In this country 75% of all visits to GPs end up with a prescription of a synthetic drug and 18% of all men and 28% of all women are constantly taking prescribed medication, which amounts in this country to 15 million people. In the USA most adults are believed to swallow at least one pharmaceutical drug almost every day. . . . Fair enough if medication could really cure an illness in the real sense of the word, but more often than not it doesn't. What you and the medical profession calls 'a cure' by drugs is often merely the suppression of superficial symptoms, which is our poor body's silent way of letting us know that things aren't quite right in there. In fact any disease process could be said to be nothing more than nature's blind attempt to rid our body of unwanted rubbish, and drugs can only be used as a procedure to fill in time while waiting for our body's natural healing process to take place. All drugs can do is to either suppress, or in some cases stimulate, isolated bits of our delicate biochemistry, which isn't the same as a proper cure by a long chalk. For a sick body, which is merely asking for attention by using the only language it knows such as pain, frequent pill-popping only adds a further toxic burden to an already sickened system.

Now that we have established what drugs can't do, let's see what they can do. First of all they can make you quite ill. Let's look at the evidence collected by Thomson and MacEoin concerning medicine induced, or as they are known, iatrogenic diseases. The facts look as follows:

1) One person in ten who enters hospital as an in-patient picks up an illness they did not have before.
2) Two out of five people receiving clinical drugs have side effects and in many cases much more serious than the condition being treated.
3) The cost of dealing with the side effects of drugs in the USA has been estimated at about 3 billion dollars.
4) Obvious drug (clinical) induced deaths are not easy to estimate, but the likely figure for the UK is somewhere in the region of 15,000 per year. To give the figure some meaning, the equivalent figure for road accident deaths, again for the UK, is about 7000. In the USA, the number of people who die each year because of clinical drugs administered in hospitals have been found to be a staggering 60,000.
5) Various studies have shown that errors in medication occur in one out of six hospital wards. . . .

Furthermore people seem to think that hospitalization will reduce their pain or at best they will probably live longer in the hospital. This has been found to be not true, as research had shown that those admitted with a fatal condition to the average British clinic, 10 percent died on the day of arrival, 30 percent within a week, 75 percent within a month and 97 percent within three months. So it seems now that if one is dying, one is dying, there is not much either a hospital or a doctor can do if your number is up. In fact one US study showed that over half the people who dropped dead because of cancer or a heart attack had been declared fit in their most recent annual medical checkup, and that treatment available after detection had proved to be largely ineffective. This small but thought-provoking booklet by Thomson and MacEoin, which is well referenced by the way, finishes with these immortal words: 'The sad truth is that if doctors never saw another patient it would make no difference to anyone, other than doctors themselves perhaps. . . . For modern medicine to be a success, it would need to go somewhere towards achieving what must be its objective i.e. eliminating illness and by no stretch of the imagination is it anywhere approaching that goal. . . . A greater proportion of the population is ill today than ever before, despite there being more doctors, more powerful scientific intervention, more amazing drugs to be pumped into people and more money spent on ill-health.' I can't but agree with what has been said. There is no more question about it that orthodox medicine with all its scientificism seems to be pretty powerless in preventing our increasing ill-health statistics and may even be, with the help of powerful drug companies, one of the chief factors in promoting it, which is far from being funny.

Now that we have established the regrettable fact that even if we have been born, checked, drugged and died under hospitals and doctors, and potions, as well as being pampered by a complex assembly of nursing labour, it has hardly made a blind bit of difference. We still seem to be a very sickly lot, so it would be pertinent to ask: what on earth has gone wrong?

Harry Benjamin (84) writes about the subject: 'Although called' "a science", orthodox medicine has never been able to formulate any definite rules governing the appearance of disease in the human body and how it might be overcome. . . . When Pasteur elaborated his celebrated germ theory of disease the whole medical world enthusiastically and unhesitatingly accepted it, in the full belief that here at last was the conclusive solution to the vexed problem of disease, the solution they had long been waiting for. At last the dread cause of disease was fully established. It was germs. . . . All one had to do now was to kill the germs and the disease would disappear. But after fifty years of adherence to the germ theory, and despite literally astonishing feats in bacteriological science, disease exerts as firm a hold upon humanity as heretofore, as germs appear to thrive better than their victims. . . . The world's disease problem is still waiting to be solved at medical hands. Indeed, it appears to be growing more and more insoluble every day. Why? Because Medical Science has always looked to externals for the cause of disease, instead of to factors at work within the body of the individual concerned. Consequently, despite its skill and honesty of purpose, the medical profession continues to add error to error, and pile up enormity upon enormity, in attempting to 'cure' disease by means of administration of poisonous drugs and vaccines, and the very drastic employment of the surgeon's knife, without having the faintest idea that what it is inevitably doing is really adding to the disease bill of the nation, rather than subtracting from it. . . .' If you think that all this is nothing but old hat and you have heard all this many times before, you are right, as I cited Harry Benjamin at length in chapter seven.

Now let's stop here for a while. If it is a fact that doctors really are so misled about the basics of ill-health, why has this chaos then be allowed to continue for so long? I think one could summarize it simply: Medicine is big business and there is no vested interest in either prevention or in health. Now you might argue that at least medical researchers would surely be most concerned with what causes diseases and how to prevent them. I don't like to be the bearer of bad news, but let us never forget that the business of research is the business of researchers, and researchers get paid a tidy sum for what they are doing. It is an occupation like any other, so no wonder that the majority of researchers believe that more research is always needed. Always when I see photographs of researchers and so called 'experts' at work, clad in their white overalls, peering earnestly through a powerful microscope at some tiny blob of a molecule languishing on some glass dish or other, I can't help wondering what on earth this has to do with the ill-health of the nation? Looking at the sickness statistics, obviously not a lot.

Now let's take a brief look at the drug industry. I have collected all the following information from Charles Medawar's book *The Wrong Kind of Medicine*, which was published in 1984 by the Consumer's Association. (217)

The drug industry provides secure employment for over 70,000 people. It pays a substantial amount of taxes and by exporting its products it contributes a net £600 million a year to the UK's balance of trade. The National Health Service's drugs bill approached £2000,000,000 in 1984 alone. The scale of drug promotion is formidable and the methods used are sometimes distinctly unfair. In 1982 the drug industry in Britain spent some £150 million on drug promotion, roughly the equivalent of £4000-£5000 for each general practitioner. Just under half of the promotional budget was spent on medical representatives, one representative for eight doctors. Enough is spent on advertising to expose doctors to an average of over fifty drug advertisements each day, most of them sent in free magazines. The industry also acts as benefactor and sponsor in all kinds of medical activities; it gives support for scientific meetings and research, it funds academic and other journals, it provides information and educational materials, and supplies free medicine and equipment in hospitals and surgeries. This kind of help can be indispensible. The drug industry also lobbies vigorously, contributes substantially to party political funds and is tireless in organizing professional and public relations campaigns. The drug industry does not deny that there are imperfections, but argues that the overall benefits of its operations far outweigh any disadvantages. The benefits include therapeutic and economic advantages, including therapeutic advantages still to come. The drug industry also feels that it cannot be held responsible for putting right what is wrong, so long as governments license its products and doctors prescribe them. Now governments in turn feel that they are unable to make any real headway in promoting rational or economic drug use because this could only be done by restricting what drug companies manufacture and what doctors prescribe, which the drug industry would anyhow reject as an attack on free enterprise and the medical profession would see as a threat to clinical freedom. In the face of this combined opposition government feels pretty powerless to interfere.

As you can see now, we are not talking here about health, we are talking here about big business, which spells out simply: the more drugs we take, the higher the drug industry's profit and the bigger the government's cut. All in all, it looks to me at least, that drugs are not so much used for improving health, but improving economics.

Now how do doctors fit into this merry-go-round? In the first place, the study of medicine is the study of medicine, and doctors are not taught about health, their subject is straight forward sickness or ill-health. To be quite honest, I can't but feel sorry sometimes for the poor blighters who have selected this noble trade of caring for the sick and ailing, who are mercilessly exposed to, and brainwashed by, the bewildering incessant insistence of the drug companies, that only medicine has got the mighty power to sort out all human ills, while being at the same time a witness of the sad fact, that nothing could be further from the truth. Cancers, heart diseases, allergies, arthritis, diabetes, hypertension, respiratory disorders etc. are on the rampage, let alone all sorts of mental disorders and addictions. Hospitals, jails and mental institutions are overflowing, while our great Sickness Service seems to remain as insatiable as ever. I strongly suspect that quite a number of medical men know in their heart of hearts that they are just pouring drugs, of which they know little, into patients, about whom they know even less, which must be pretty disheartening. No wonder some surveys show doctors as being some of the unhealthiest folks around, as the futility of it all, and the pressures imposed upon them, tends to turn many of them more readily to drugs or alcohol, for which I am the last one to blame them.

The Royal College of General Practitioners' 1977 survey estimated that in an average year a general practitioner typically sees 600 patients with coughs and colds, 325 with various skin disorders, 300 patients suffering from anxiety and/or depression, one hundred patients suffering from chronic rheumatism, fifty with high blood pressure, eight with heart attacks and five each with acute appendicitis, cancers and strokes. At least twenty-five percent of all GP's consultations are thought to be unnecessary and furthermore it is estimated that at least seventy-five percent of all GP's consultations end in the prescription of a synthetic drug, many of which are admitted to be given only for their placebo effect, which, as I see it, is given to the whining patient just to keep him quiet.

Now that we have sorted out the basic politics of drugs and the plight of overworked doctors, it might be a good idea to say a few words about us, the patients.

I will never forget when I was attending a meeting in one of the London suburbs organized by agoraphobic sufferers.

About forty people were there. My part in the show was to give a short talk about the role of nutrition in the management of panic, or as I know them, hypoglycaemic attacks. I could see during my talk that folks around me didn't seem to be at all impressed by what I had to say, in fact they seemed to grow more and more irritated by the minute. When I had finished, the spokesman addressed me with these immortal words: 'Thank you, but I find it difficult to believe that nutrition, or a lack of it, has anything whatsoever to do with our panic attacks. This is a proper illness, and in order for it to be cured, medical research must come up one day with a drug or vaccination which is effective in helping us.' When she had finished, an enthusiastic clapping followed, after which the crowd scuttled back to their black coffee urn, sugar lumps and sweet biscuits, followed by a cigarette or a tablet or two of tranquillizers.

In my opinion this little tale sums up to perfection why drug companies are allowed to flourish and why the poor doctors have to write one prescription after another, whether they like it or not. It looks to me at least, that they are patients themselves who often insist on receiving a prescription, because it seems somehow to add some sort of 'credibility' to their illness, or prove a diagnosis or whatever. In other words, patients generally dislike leaving the doctor's surgery empty handed, because that would indicate the depressing possibility that they might not be ill at all, and all they are doing is shamming, which can be a pretty annoying feeling, particularly if they are not feeling well at all. A confusing state of affairs, but there it is.

I think that one reason why the role of nutrition in the treatment of various forms of ill-health seems to be so uncomprehensible to so many is simple: As we look entirely to our doctors to guide our health and doctors don't generally discuss nutrition or our diet, it seems logical to us to assume that what we eat, or don't eat, is nothing whatsoever to do with our anxiety attacks, heart problems, aches or pains. There is also another side of the coin: Nutritional treatment seems to be very unpopular, because being asked to change one's diet, interferes somehow with our personal freedom of choice. I remember when our junior health minister (then Edwina Currie) attacked the fish and chips brigade, causing damned near a national revolution, whilst the gutter press was spying on her every mouthful of fodder. When she was finally caught one morning tucking into a plateful of the greasy stuff, next morning headlines emerged with screaming print pointing out the hypocrisy of it all; how dare she lecture the nation to leave the fatty stuff alone while she is tucking into it with great relish. As I see it, all this lady was trying to do, was to point out that too much fatty food just isn't good for anybody's health, though a little bit now and then can't do any harm, which is only fair.

The simple reason why the majority of doctors don't discuss diet is that nutritional sciences are not taught in medical schools, except a few words on such serious stages of nutritional deficiencies as pellagra, beri-beri, rickets, scurvy and kwashiorkor. So naturally it is best not to talk about the subject you don't know anything about. The general argument amongst doctors seems to be that if a person eats a good, mixed diet, he shouldn't have anything to worry about. This type of argument drives me barmy. Any doctor, who is bleating about a good, mixed diet, obviously hasn't ever observed in a supermarket what 'average folk' pile into their shopping trolleys. It is really frightening to watch. The majority of trolleys are piled to the brim with various multicoloured packages with a list of ingredients which are more like chemical sets, and which are as far removed from wholesome food than planet Mars is from this earth. All right, these so called 'foods' store and keep for ever, because they are so void of any nutritional value that no self-respecting weevil, bacteria, fungi or mould would even look at the dreaded stuff. Now let's face it, if that rubbish can't support even a tiny weevil, how on earth do we expect it to support human life? And frankly speaking it doesn't support life – not properly anyhow, hence the ever-growing tide of all non-infectious and chronic diseases such as heart diseases, cancers, hypo- and hyperglycaemias, mental illnesses of all kinds etc. Only this morning, before I started to tickle my typewriter I glanced through a daily paper which reads: 'More and more young people are getting diabetes, and nobody knows why. The incidence in the young has mysteriously doubled since the 1960s. The British Diabetic Association says there are now about 18,000 diabetics under the age of twenty in the UK. The rate of diabetes in this age group is now more than twenty per 100,000 people compared with ten per 100,000 in 1968. One theory is that there are more virus infections affecting the pancreas. The report says 20,000 people of all ages die prematurely each year as a result of diabetes. Sufferers are at particular risk of heart disease, strokes and kidney failure. The Association recommends that each health district should draw up proper plans for their care, with a system of regular checks. It also calls for more research. . . .' All I can say is, for heaven's sake don't bother. I can give you all the research you want in one fell swoop and it won't cost you a farthing: The main reason why this diabetes and other sugar regulatory disorders, such as hypoglycaemia, have grown to epidemic proportions is simply excessive sugar consumption. In fact we Brits are known to polish off on average a staggering one hundred pounds of sugar per person every year, including 455,000 tonnes of confectionery worth nearly £3000,000,000. Now if we further add to this mountain of sweeties all refined flour products such as non-wholemeal breads and flaky-buffi-baffi breakfast cereals boastingly 'enriched' with a vitamin or two and maybe a few shavings of scrap iron, we are really in trouble. The reason being the following: Anyone who is familiar with the basics of biochemistry knows, that in order for carbohydrates to be metabolized in the body properly, they require not only the presence of all B vitamins but also such minerals as magnesium and chromium, both of which are milled away during the refining process and never put back. If you look at the previous chapter, Anderson and his team (130) have already suggested that lack of chromium might be one of the causes of various sugar regulatory disorders, such as hypoglycaemias and hyperglycaemias or diabetes.

I can't but feel mighty sorry sometimes for all those little innocent viruses which seem to get blamed almost for everything. We are supposed to be a reasonably educated lot, so why on earth is it so inconceivable to comprehend that illnesses can also be caused by an absence of something, not always by some positive outside factor such as a virus or bacterium. And believe me or not, because of our non-balanced refined/'enriched' diet our poor bodies are denied a hell of a lot of essential nutritional substances, such as zinc, chromium, magnesium etc which are fundamental for our biochemistry and for our physical and mental health. It is simply utter madness to remove precious vitamins and minerals from foods and then only put a few of them back, which simply invites all sorts of biochemical imbalances, which in turn are responsible for all kinds of mental and physical disorders. I bet you also would get a bit miffed if a friend borrowed a fiver from you and paid back only fifty pence. The same goes for your body as well.

Now what is that myth of 'a good mixed diet'? According to Dr Victor Herbert (218) a good mixed diet should contain the following: Each day you should eat four portions of fruits and vegetables (including uncooked), two portions of meat, fish, poultry or eggs and two to three portions of milk or milk products. And furthermore, in order to get full nutritional benefit from your 'good mixed diet', foods should be as fresh as possible, especially fruits and vegetables, because they lose their nutritional value all the way from the garden to the gullet.

Michael Colgan (161) tested the nutritional content of different raw foods. When he tested raw carrots, he found that different samples of 100 gr varied in their pro-vitamin A content from 70iu to 18,000iu. Some supermarket oranges, which obviously had been stored for a long time, didn't seem to have any vitamin C left in them whatsoever, even though they looked, smelled and tasted perfectly normal. Oranges bought directly from the grower and picked that day, contained 180 mg of vitamin C per orange. Lettuce stored at room temperature loses 50% of its vitamin C value in twenty-four hours after picking. Keeping it in the fridge results in the same loss in about three days. In fact most stable vegetables such as broccoli, peas etc. seem to lose about 50% of their vitamin C value in cold storage even before they reach our greengrocers. Cooking vegetables destroys another 25% of vitamin C, 50% of vitamin B2 and up to 70% of vitamin B1 and so on and so forth. . . . And as far as the essential mineral content of foods go, even the best organically grown vegetables contain only those minerals found in the soil in which they have grown. Unfortunatley with modern farming methods, the soil is usually so void of all essential minerals that no farmer today would consider trying to raise top-grade livestock without supplementing their feed with added vitamins and minerals. Let's face it, it all seems to get back to hard cash again, as healthy livestock, sick people and food which doesn't perish are all good for business and profit. Tough words, but unfortunately true.

The Government's Recommended Daily Allowance or RDA of vitamins and a couple of minerals is the estimated minimum amount needed by an average person in order to prevent such vitamin deficiency diseases such as pellagra, beri-beri, rickets and scurvy. Fair enough, besides strongly believing that the current RDA is far too low, the other bit which bugs me even more, is this concept of 'an average person'. Because let's face it, at least as long as I have lived, and believe me I have lived long enough, I have never yet met one single 'average person'. In fact we are all so non-average that it is nobody's business and because of it, also our personal nutritional needs are as diverse as our fingerprints. Here are some reasons why:

1) Family history or our basic biochemical individuality.
2) Past and present health history.
3) Past and present medications, whether prescribed or over-the-counter medications.
4) How much different stimulants you consume, such as coffee, tea, alcohol or tobacco etc.
5) How stressful you find your life.
6) How well you seem to absorb nutrients.
7) Past operations and/or pregnancies.
8) Your everyday living environment i.e. outdoor and/or indoor pollution including possible heavy metal toxicity.
9) And last but not least, whether you already show any sub-clinical vitamin/mineral deficiencies due either to an excessive demand, or to a possible vitamin dependency disease, whether acquired or inherited.

When all this information is mapped against your personal
food preferences, the amount of convenience foods you eat,
the amount of empty calories such as sugar you consume,
your everyday food storing and cooking methods etc. a
competent nutritionist can give you a pretty good idea
whether you might be short of any vitamins or minerals. A
good nutritionist also knows that coffee, as well as strong
tea, besides reducing dietary iron absorption, also hinders
vitamin B1 uptake and that antibiotics as well as sulpha
drugs interfere with most of the B vitamins. He could also
tell you that diuretics wash out most of the water soluble
vitamins as well as minerals like potassium, magnesium
and zinc. He would also know that smoking reduces vitamin
B2, B6, C and zinc levels. In fact it has been established that
each single cigarette neutralizes about 25 mg of vitamin C,
which I have already mentioned, but say again. If you insist
on puffing away, for heaven's sake, do take vitamin C
supplementation, otherwise you will soon be suffering from
'smoker's scurvy' with all its most unpleasant and depressing symptoms. Excessive smoking can also lead to a
condition known as amblyopia, which is an eye condition
where vision becomes, for no apparent organic reason, dim
and blurred and which can often be helped with vitamin
B12 injections.

A good nutritionist can also advise you that alcohol
depletes most of the water soluble vitamins out of the body,
as well as lowers vitamin A, vitamin D and zinc levels. He
would also know that oral contraceptives lower body's
vitamin B2, B6, folic acid, vitamin B12 and zinc levels and
increases vitamin A and copper levels, which will remain
sub-clinically either low or high at least up to three months
after discontinuing the Pill. (213) This information should
be remembered by those who have been on the Pill for years
and suddenly decide to start a family. Because if you want
to make sure that your offspring will be born as healthy as
possible, it is not wise to get pregnant immediately after
stopping the Pill, as for example low folic acid level is
directly linked with spina bifida (247) and low zinc level
with foetal growth retardation and reduced immune system
function. A good nutritionist could also tell you that you
may be magnesium deficient if you drink a lot of milk. Even

that milk is very high in calcium, it is quite low in magnesium, therefore an excessive milk consumption can create a serious calcium/magnesium imbalance, which can be harmful for cardiovascular health. He could also tell you that since all B-group vitamins work intimately together, a continuous digestion of large doses of any one of them may result into the exertion of other B-group vitamins and a consequent deficiency. I could go on and on, but I won't, as I am sure that these few examples may have convinced you that you are indeed an individual and very far away from 'an average person', with his boring average vitamin and mineral deficiencies or needs.

Are British people likely to suffer from vitamin or mineral deficiencies? Let's look at the evidence: First of all let's take a nutritional analysis which was commissioned by Booker Health Products and conducted amongst 449 British households consisting of 801 individuals, who kept an accurate record of their food and drink intake for one week. (219) The final data was analyzed at Queen Elisabeth College under Professor Ian Morton. Here are some results.

93% of all males and 98% of all females had folic acid intakes lower than the suggested acceptable RDA.
24% of males and 27% of females had a low intake of vitamin B2.
92% of all males and 95% of all females were found to have a B6 intake below US RDA.
8.6% of males and 22% of females had a vitamin B12 intake below US RDA.
The vitamin C levels were found to be noticeably low, particularly in females of the older age group.
73% of all women had calcium intakes below RDA.
60% of all females and 17% of males had iron intake below RDA.
35% of the males and 67% of the females had zinc intake below WHO recommended level.
And finally, even though there is no UK RDA for vitamin E, it was found in both females and males to be approximately half the US RDA.

Now let's look next at a survey called *The Diets of British*

Schoolchildren: Preliminary Report of a Nutritional Analysis of a Nationwide Dietary Survey of British Schoolchildren conducted by R W Wenlock and his team, which cost the taxpayer £650,000 and which will cost you £4.50 to buy, and can be obtained from the DHSS Leaflet Unit, PO Box 21, Stanmore, Middlesex HA7 1AY. (220) This survey goes on for nearly ninety pages, but the gist of it is as follows: Most school kids seem to consume a reasonably well balanced diet. There were exceptions however, as most children were found to be low in iron and most older girls were found to be low in both calcium and vitamin B2. The survey also pointed out that the DHSS has not yet made a RDA for vitamin B6, which is involved both in the metabolism of amino acids and in the conversion of tryptophan to nicotinic acid. However The National Academy of Science of the US have set a RDA for this vitamin, compared to which, all children were found to be deficient in vitamin B6. The survey added that in spite of this there seems to be no evidence of a public health problem related to B6 deficiency in Britain. I find this latter statement rather stupid, to say the least, as apart from the importance of B6 in the formation of vitamin B3 from tryptophan, and its role in the conversion of proteins to amino acids, it is absolutely vital for both our physical and mental health. Amino acids are essential for all body's repair processes as well as in the formation of the brain's neurotransmitters, which govern our mental and emotional behaviour. Anyhow, this mammoth study concluded with the following words: 'The proportion of daily energy intakes obtained by older children who ate out at cafés etc. was similar to that of children who took a midday meal at home. . . . In particular, the older boys obtained the lowest amounts of protein, calcium, iron, retinol equivalent, thiamin, riboflavin and nicotinic acid equivalent from their café meals. The older girls also obtained the lowest amount of protein, calcium, iron, retinol equivalent, thiamin, riboflavin, nicotinic acid equivalent and vitamin D from these sources . . . etc. etc.' What I think this survey is trying to tell us in a round-about way, is that most teenage kids who prance around during their lunch hour with a packet of crisps or a chocolate bar in one hand and a can of coke in the other are likely to be vitamin and/or mineral deficient compared with children who receive their lunch-time meal at school.

This £650,000 gem has obviously gone quite unheeded by the present government, because a leaflet called 'Of Little Benefit; An Update, a Critical Guide to the Social Security Act 1986' reads, under the section 'Free School Meals and Welfare Foods': 'Over half a million children will lose their current right to a free school meal. These are children whose parents currently receive Family Income Supple-ment, and children who benefit from local authority schemes for low income families. The Government say that it is better to give cash compensation through Family Credit to children whose parents earn low wages, rather than provide a free meal direct to the child. Calculating on the basis used in the White Paper on recently announced rates, the amount allowed in Family Credit for this element is £2.55 a week. This is equivalent to 66p a day for a 40 week school year.' (221) As a nutritionist and a realist I can see this present government legislation spells nothing but serious trouble. In the first place, this school meal is the main meal of the day for many inner city children, therefore abolishing it will certainly lead to nutritional disaster and to a great variety of both mental and physical ill-health. And furthermore, giving money instead of food is a pretty silly thing to do. Even I was a kid once, albeit quite a while ago, but I still remember perfectly well where my 'lunch money' went. It certainly wasn't spent on well balanced food.

I can't help reading almost daily about the ever-expanding statistics of juvenile crime and delinquency, drug addictions, classroom violence, muggings, rapes etc. while our government is bleating about tougher sentences, better police protection, armed guards on the school grounds and some such deterrents. Knowing what I know now, the only guard the kids would need is a hefty school dinner lady making doubly sure that all the kids eat every scrap of wholefood off their plates. This sensible suggestion is not based on some kind of 'food faddism' but on pure biochemical and scientific fact.

Now that we have sorted out what our diet is missing, let's take a look at what we are receiving plenty of. First of all, although our food is very short of nutrients, it seems to possess far too many calories, hence the present epidemic of obesity or overweight folk.

Let's look next at toxic metals which include lead, cadmium, aluminium, mercury and an excess of copper, all of which in various ways interfere with our bodies' essential mineral content. For example high body lead and/or cadmium levels antagonizes the body's essential mineral levels, such as zinc or calcium.

Lead comes mainly from the atmosphere polluted by traffic exhaust fumes, from old lead-based paint, from the unlined seams of food cans and from our water supply which may come through lead piping, or through copper piping where the joins of the pipes have been formed with lead-containing alloys. High body lead levels are directly linked with various disorders ranging from under achievement at school, hyperactivity and even with birth defects.

The main source of excess cadmium is cigarette smoke, yours and other people's. Also some plumbing alloys may contain cadmium. An excess of cadmium is linked with birth defects and all sorts of childhood attention deficit disorders.

Excess aluminium comes from foods cooked in aluminium pans. Especially very acid foods such as rhubarb and sour fruit which can literally take a thin layer off the aluminium pan when cooked in one. A high aluminium content can also be found in drinking water, especially in regions where aluminium sulphate is used for water clarification to get rid of a 'peaty appearance'. A high aluminium level can also be found in drinking water due to excessive sulphur pollution pumped constantly out of power stations leading to acid rain, which in turn is able to erode all sorts of heavy metals, such as aluminium from the earth's crust. Aluminium is also found in some antacid medication. A high body aluminium content is linked both with Alzheimer's disease and senile dementia.

A high mercury level is not thought to be a very frequent problem in our neck of the woods. Possibly the most extensively documented and published mercury poisoning was found in Japan, the so-called Minemata Bay disaster, where literally tons of methyl mercury was discharged into the bay with industrial waste causing hundreds of deaths and birth defects in both humans and animals. Here in the west, excess mercury has been linked with dental fillings. Jack Levenson (222) of the British Dental Society for Clinical Nutrition writes about the subject in the *Journal of Alternative and Complementary Medicine*: 'A small but unknown percentage of the population are hypersensitive to low-level chronic exposure to mercury released from amalgam fillings, and possibly to the electric current generated by these fillings. With patients who suffer from a non-attributable medical condition it would be prudent to consider mercury hypersensitivity as part of the differential diagnosis.' I can't but agree with him. A high level of mercury has also been found in some pesticides and large fish, the latter getting high on the dreaded stuff by feeding in waters containing mercury based factory effluent.

Copper in turn is absolutely essential for us in minute amounts, because it is needed in the formation of our haemoglobin. However, a high copper level has been linked with low birth weight babies, childhood hyperactivity, both with paranoid and hallucinatory schizophrenias, 'binge drinking', psychiatric depression, as well as senile dementia. (123) A high body copper level can be due to oral contraceptives, the copper contraceptive coil, excessive smoking, copper pans, kettles, bracelets and copper water pipes.

Now let's look at food additives. There are said to be between 3500-4000 different food additives available in the UK which include such things as antioxidants, bleaching and improving agents, bulking aids, colourings, emulsifiers and stabilizers, flavourings, flavour enhancers, preservatives, solvents, thickeners, artificial sweeteners, anti-caking agents and so on and so forth, used by food manufacturers in an excess of 210,000 tonnes each year. The reckoning is that by the age of five, a child might already have eaten seven pounds of all sorts of chemical food additives. One report showed that an estimate of up to 80,000 people in this country suffer from allergic reactions to common food additives. The report also points out that 41 food additives approved for use in Britain are suspected of causing all sorts of health problems. Most of these additives are already banned in other European countries. Having read this information, I wasn't surprised that some of our European neighbours have been looking a bit cockeyed when we Brits have been trying to bombard them with our precious beers and sausages. No hard feelings, only a touch of self-preservation I presume. And talking about preservation, I happened to hear during one conference that it has been found that the corpses of today decompose at a much slower rate than the corpses of our ancestors due to the high level of preservatives they contain. At last it is a blessing to know that even if these blasted chemicals may kill us long before our time is up, at least they seem to prolong the time our corpses last.

There are also other ways that additives can unintentionally find their way into our food. They are through livestock, through pesticides and finally through our drinking water. You might remember the South American scandal when it was found that young boys started to grow breasts due to an excessive hormone level given to fatten poultry. Hormones and anabolic steroids are still used in animal feed today to promote weight gain and growth, not in such hefty amounts however, that we have to worry about our young Kevin growing breasts, but enough to fatten livestock and farmers' pockets. Antibiotics may also be used in young animal feed, but not in mature animals because the drug would not only kill 'harmful bacteria', but also the 'friendly bacteria' which are essential for the ruminants' digestive process. Other additives are reserved for the mature lot, for example one is designed to modify the digestive process so that the amount of methane produced during digestion is reduced, thus saving the beast's energy reserves, which can then be used to put on precious weight instead. Penicillin is also used in the treatment of mastitis, and can sometimes be detected in milk and cause problems, particularly in people who are allergic to the drug. (223)

And last, but not least a few words about fungi called mycotoxin, of which Ramsay Tainsh (224, 225, 226) has written several thought-provoking articles. Mycotoxins are poisonous fungi which can be found in damp and mouldy cereal crops. When a harvested cereal crop is thoroughly sun-dried and kept dry, that is below a moisture content of ten percent, these mycotoxins are unable to grow and sporrulate. In 1985 alone, some twelve million tonnes of wheat was harvested in the UK, of which less than one million tonnes was fit to mill. Most of the cereal which was found to be unfit for human consumption is then usually 'doctored' and used as animal feed. The residues of this 'doctoring process' combined with mycotoxins, will then accumulate in animals fed on this unsavoury crop, and are passed on to us in our Sunday joint. These mycotoxins are said to be cumulative poisons which break down the body's natural defences leading to a myriad of health problems.

Now let's peep next at pesticides: *The Journal of Alternative and Complementary Medicine* writes in the June 1987 issue under the heading 'Retrospective':
'In 1983 well over a billion gallons of pesticide spray were dispersed over Britain and there is now increasing concern that much of it ends up in our food. Britain, with its high-intensity farming methods, uses more chemicals per acre than practically any other country and many of them are poisonous and banned in other parts of the world. We absorb pesticides along with our foods, through our skin and by inhaling them. Pesticides are fat-soluble so that they can kill the insects they are aimed at, but this also makes them able to pass via the blood into the human brain and fatty organs of the body. The Soil Association has shown that twenty percent of pesticide sprays are released in droplets so small that they drift great distances in the air. This means that people living in the countryside can be affected by spraying taking place some distance away. A Friends of the Earth report has shown that only one percent of pesticides sprayed from a tractor actually reaches the pests. In the US a research team tested the blood of 200 people for pesticide residues, partly because the medical authorities generally played the problem down. Every patient studied had some residues and the average had five different ones including DDT.'

Action Against Allergy (AAA) has also been carrying out airborne pesticide tests on people suffering from severe allergies. All these allergy sufferers tested were found to have high titres of at least four to eight different pesticides in their blood, the highest always being DDE, a derivative of DDT. Those who were found to have the highest titres were those who had been diagnosed as suffering from Post Viral Fatigue Syndrome or ME. (227)

Dr Jean Monro (228) discusses the results on the 200 patients tested for pesticide residues by Drs John Laseter and William Rea. She writes: 'DDT and DDE were found in sixty-two percent of the patient population in the United States study. It has been shown that if a blood concentration of one part is observed it would correspond to approximately 306 parts in adipose tissue, 27 parts in the liver, 3.9 parts in the white matter of the brain and 2.6 parts in the grey matter of the brain. DDT is known to damage the liver and has been implicated in the provocation of tumours. . . . The Soil Association's Pall of Poison report states: "Many pesticides are directly related to the nerve gases banned even from warfare by the Geneva Convention as a hazard to humanity. Their presence in the air we breathe as a by-product of chemical farming is a major scandal which must be ended with urgency. It could explain so many of the diseases and deformities to which our population becomes prey. Cancers, multiple sclerosis, allergies, asthma and the like."'

A report in *The Lancet* (229) and subsequent correspondence highlighted the relationship between industrial chemicals and the development of Parkinson's disease. The report claims that an irreversible Parkinsonism developed in a farmer who applied pesticides, and in a worker who manufactured pesticides.

The Journal of Alternative Medicine writes in the September 1984 issue: 'Chemical poisons, some of them carcinogenic, have been found in one-third of all fresh fruit and vegetables sampled in 1983 according to a survey by the Association of Public Analysts. Figures revealed by the *Sunday Times* show that among the chemicals found in 615 different fruit and vegetables tested in Britain last year were DDT and Aldrin, which were supposedly banned for use by farmers in the UK. Although chemical residues are commonly implicated in allergy problems, the real danger is that long-term ingestion leads to toxins being stored and accumulated in the body. DDT was banned in the USA in 1972 when it was linked with cancer. It can remain in the body for up to fifty years. It is not supposed to be used on food in Britain and is the subject of a voluntary code between producers and the Ministry of Agriculture. Yet DDT was found in 119 of 132 samples of apples, mushrooms and lettuce. . . . In 1977 ten percent of winter wheat was being sprayed more than ten times, the average number of sprays on beer hops was more than twenty-three times per season and fruit crops were sprayed more than eight times.'

As I see it, the sole reason for using all these poisons is to produce as vast a crop as possible, which, when harvested, could then be stored at enormous expense on top of already mammoth Euro-mountains and lakes of already existing farm produce, or alternatively destroyed, as my daily paper pointed out: 'Millions of pounds worth of fruit and vegetables are being destroyed on the orders of Brussels bureaucrats – to keep up prices for farmers. Almost all of it is dumped, distilled into alcohol or fed to animals. The cost in the four months to February this year was a staggering £67 million. Food destroyed during that time includes 605.518 tonnes of apples, 285.702 tonnes of peaches and 164.357 tonnes of oranges. Labour Euro MPs claim the destruction works out at 5,850 lb for every minute of the year.' I am aware that I am not an expert in these agricultural matters and therefore I should be very careful what I say, so let's just say that in my opinion what is going on out there just isn't quite cricket.

Now let's look next at our drinking water, starting first with this so called 'fluoride controversy'. The *Journal of Alternative Medicine* writes in August 1986 under their short news section: 'Two leading American doctors have claimed that fluoride in drinking water results in 35,000 deaths from cancer every year in the United States, one in ten of all cancer deaths in the country. The claim comes from Dr Dean Burk, former head of the cytochemistry division of the National Cancer Institute and a cancer researcher for more than fifty years, and Dr John Yiamouyiannis, science director of the National Health Federation, after "extensive statistical analyses" of cities across America over a ten-year period before and after fluoridation. . . . Anyone advocating fluoridation, says Dr Burk, is "advocating mass murder".'

Ray Brant replied to this alarming statement in the same

journal in November 1986: 'I read with interest your report about fluoridation and since this was a matter of some concern locally, I wrote to my MP who happens to be Norman Fowler, the health minister. Enclosed is a copy of his very detailed reply.' Norman Fowler's letter is too long for me to repeat here, but here are the very basic points: 'There is a very large amount of scientific evidence available on the safety of fluoridation. . . . You mentioned specifically work on fluoridation carried out by Dr Burk and Dr Yiamouyiannis. Their reports are well known in this country and have been extensively reviewed by leading experts in the field, who have found them invalid. . . . I hope that this will help to reassure you of the safety of fluoridation, particularly in relation to cancer. I can assure you that we continue to examine carefully the evidence of fluoridation and that we believe fluoridation to be safe.' Following Norman Fowler's letter *The Journal of Alternative Medicine* wrote directly to Dr Burk, whose reply was printed in the May 1987 issue: 'You tell me your readers want to know who is telling the truth about whether artificial fluoridation of public drinking water supplies causes increased human cancer mortality: DHSS Health Minister, Norman Fowler, who says no, or Yiamouyiannis and Burk who say yes. . . . As I see it, each reader will have to make his own choice, depending upon whether he is moved by a) skilful, long-practised bureaucratic dissimulation based mainly on political convenience, surrogate science etc. etc. or b) a decade of original scientific research articles now so numerous as to require summarizing, books, reviews and court cases of which are far beyond the scope of this letter. . . . The jewel in the Fowler bureaucratic crown would appear to be its reliance on the Knox Report of the Working Party on Fluoridiation of Water and Cancer, whose membership has stated to include some of the "eminent experts in the field". It is a little disconcerting to find that among the some fifteen party members listed, only one of them is cited in the 112 references to major scientific studies in this field. . . . In conclusion, long-term experience in large American central cities still show a strikingly prompt association and casual relationship to artificial fluoridation of public water supplies, involving large increase in human cancer deaths of the order of ten percent, now amounting to a yearly excess of thousands of cancer deaths in those parts of United States population whose drinking water has been artificially fluoridated.'

What I wanted to show you with this fluoridation ding-dong is, that even though medical science claims to rely always on so called 'scientific evidence' on all aspects of research, one 'expert' can always dig enough 'scientific evidence' to contradict another 'expert'. It is in fact quite easy, all one has to do is to set up the experiment and adjust the evidence depending on what the goal is and what one wants to prove or disprove. I must stress now that I am not talking here about any kind of distorted or 'crooked' trials, but quite straightforward and honest ones, the outcome of which can be modified using the careful art of punctuation and elimination. Therefore, at least in my opinion, out should go all those 'double-blind-placebo-controlled-crossover-trials-with-matched-controls', as well as all those ghoulish and sinister trials on our little, innocent furry friends, who have been caged, pricked, drugged, electro-cuted and disembowelled in laboratories in trillions in the name of so called 'scientific research'. In should come a holistic and individualistic approach to all human health problems, whether in the form of prevention or cure.

Now that I have managed to get this little grievance out of my system, let's go back to water. Besides the mass medication i.e. fluoride, which we are forced to swallow and which scientifically speaking does and does not cause cancer, as many as 350 different man-made chemicals have been detected in our tap water. Lead, pesticides, herbicides, aluminium and nitrates pour out from our kitchen taps. It has been estimated that in Britain over 2.5 million people drink water which exceeds the EEC maximum permitted aluminium levels. Also presently about 850,000 British people drink water with nitrate levels above EEC limits, and Government estimates say that under current condi-tions, this will continue to rise. (230) Nitrates, which are used as agricultural fertilizers are thought to be cancer producing, because once digested, they transform in our gut into substances called nitrosamines which are known to be cancer producing. I will never forget as long as I live the late Dr Geoffrey Taylor's (231) plea on our national TV network to start seriously to consider the role of nitrates in causing cancer, of which he was dying. Dr Taylor was dead the day after the interview was shown. Now whether the use of agricultural fertilizers played the major part in his cancer death, we will never known for sure, but at least I believe that there could have been a connection. If my hunch is right, how many other great men have to end their earthly careers before time just because of our blind determination to shovel even more stuff on that crazy Euromountain of food which nobody seems to want in the first place?

Not only is our drinking water polluted, our great rivers and sea water are simply a toxic torrent of filth, as untreated sewage cadmium, oils, chemicals and fertilizers pour forth. It has been estimated that more than three-and-a-half million tonnes of industrial waste is pumped into the sea every year and 90,000 tonnes of toxic waste is incinerated over it. Sludge containing 140,000 different chemicals is added to the poisonous soup at the rate of fifteen million cubic meters each year. The appalling sight of seals and dolphins dying due to some 'virus' or another is only the latest sign that our seas are on the verge of an ecological disaster, as toxic wastes are playing havoc with their immune systems. A dolphin calf which was found dead on one of our beaches was examined. It was found to have died of septic hepatitis. On examining its sad body, it was found to be loaded with chemicals including polychlorinated biphenols (PCBs), insecticides and herbicides, which are washed off from our fields into rivers and then into our seas. Not only have our seas become a death trap to our marine life, they don't seem to be any more much fun for ourselves, as frolicking holidaymakers may find that they share their bathing experience with odd blobs of human excrement, condoms and other exciting sanitary products, due to untreated sewage pouring out through too short sewage pipes.

While wallowing in our own excrement, we do also other crazy things. At present we are busily destroying the whole planet by filling our earth's atmosphere with gases such as carbon dioxide, methane, nitrous oxide etc. which trap long-wave solar radiation, causing severe climatic warming known as the greenhouse effect. When this warming becomes severe enough it causes solar ice caps to melt, which in turn raises sea levels to the extent that all low-lying land masses and nations will drown. The greenhouse effect will also create a 'dust-bowl-effect' which causes severe droughts leading to damaged crops and food shortages.

We people also burn all our rainforests, which is thought to add at least ten per cent a year to our global warming. These lush jungles are being chopped down and torched at the rate of a football field every second, destroying one hundred species of plants a day. Besides being literally our earth's lungs, these proud forests also soak up a great deal of rain gently releasing it into our earth like a tap. When these forests are cut down, rain will strip off the top soil, which will then pour directly into rivers, causing severe flooding, as happened quite recently in Bangladesh, Rio and Nepal.

There is now a continuing outcry throughout Europe because of the sulphur emissions from power stations causing acid rain, which in turn destroys the life of forests and lakes of Europe. This is particularly notable in Scandinavia and in Finland, where I come from, as most of our thousands of lakes, once rippled by fish, lie now practically empty. While this acid pollution kills lakes and fish, dissolves buildings, wipes out forests including the undergrowth with its mushrooms and berries, it would be simply stupid arrogance to claim that it doesn't affect our health the slightest.

I think that I will leave the subject of nuclear waste alone, as in my opinion it is far too explosive a subject to be discussed here. All I know is that we have umpteen barrel loads of the stuff sweating away in various parts of the country, waiting either to be thrown into the sea, or buried under somebody's cabbage patch, both suggestions being quite unacceptable. What its future will now be, is anybody's guess. Maybe one day it will just blow up and send our whole planet into the universe in tiny fragments, which in my opinion serves us right for trying to be a lot smarter than we really are. In addition, the presence of nuclear plants themselves, such as Sellafield and Duonreay, is responsible for possible radioactive contamination, and has been strongly linked with childhood leukemia.

Now let's look at so called electropollution, of which Simon Best (232) writes: 'In 1979 the first well-controlled Western study linking power line fields and childhood leukemia was reported by the University of Colorado researchers Wertheimer and Leeper. They carried out a case control study of 328 children in the Denver area. Using a wire coding and configuration assessment of the high-current electric wires near children's homes, to indicate magnetic field exposure, they found a significant correlation with childhood cancer in exposed children versus controls. In the same year in England an Aldrington GP, Dr Stephen Berry, collaborated with three American researchers led by Dr Maria Reichmanis at the Veterans Administration Medical Centre in Syracuse, New York, to link suicide in the Shropshire/Staffordshire area with residential proximity to the fields generated by overhead power lines. Further studies are in progress. In this country Perry and Pearl have just reported a higher incidence of heart disease and depression in people living near main electrical supply lines in highrise buildings and Dr David Dowson in Southampton has reported a link between depression and residence near overhead transmission lines.'

One US study involving almost 1600 pregnant women showed that there could be a connection between would-be mothers using video display units and the incidence of miscarriages and birth defects. It is thought that the low-level electromagnetic radiation linked with these units, may be able to alter or disrupt the foetus's cellular development, which was found to happen in experiments with both mice and chicks of the feathery variety.

Besides power lines and proper VDUs, also radios, TV transmissions, satellite broadcasts, CB radios, cellular telephones etc. all are said to add to this electromagnetic pollution. In fact electropollution seems to be present in a greater or lesser degree almost everywhere on our planet.

Now a few words about natural daylight, also known as full-spectrum light. My interest on the subject started when I was a mere kid. I grew up in a town called Jyväskylä, which is situated not too far from the Arctic Circle and where sometimes during the winter months proper daylight is hardly ever seen. This was the time of the year when living somehow stopped and one started to exist instead. We just mooched listlessly about philosophizing endlessly about the deep meaning of life whilst waiting for 'something to happen', not knowing exactly what. When the days finally started to lengthen, our steps lengthened and our smiles broadened accordingly. By the midsummer night, when the sun never sets, we were usually so full of vivacious mirth and jollity, frolicking around our summer huts, that all the rest of the wild life had to dive for cover, in order not to be trampled underfoot during this show of endless merriment. At first I thought that we Finns were just a bit weird. It was not until I studied works by Hollwich (233), Ott (234, 235) and Tibbs (236) that everything started to fall into its proper place.

I think that everybody knows by now the importance of natural daylight in helping our skins to manufacture vitamin D. However, there is more. Full-spectrum daylight seems to have a direct effect on our mental and physical functions through its effect on our 'third eye', known as the pineal gland or neuro-endocrine transducer gland, which is a shorthand way of saying that it translates nerve signals into different hormonal messages. The chief messenger hormone is melatonin, which has a direct regulatory influence on our master gland known as the pituitary gland, which in turn controls most of our hormonal functions, such as sex hormones, thyroid and adrenals, as well as effecting the synthesis and release of some of our brain's neurotransmitters, such as serotonin, adrenaline and noradrenaline. Some American researches have also been able to link electropollution with disruption of melatonin synthesis, which may explain some of the adverse effects of electromagnetic fields on both human and animal health. Now if lack of both full-spectrum light as well as electropollution can cause disruption in melatonin synthesis, thus decreasing both our hormonal as well as some neurotransmitter production, constant lack of full-spectrum light combined with the use of all sorts of electric gadgets, such as are found in most public buildings, may be one of the causes of so called 'sick building syndrome', where workers complain about feelings of depression, headaches, tiredness and other major or minor ills.

Even though sun is good for us, too much of the good thing can be bad. As everybody knows by now, we have been apparently busily puncturing our precious ozone layer using CFCs or chlorofluorocarbons, thus inviting the sun's harmful ultraviolet radiation to enter the earth causing skin cancers and such like. Are we all mentally ill?

I think that words with which HRH The Duke of Edinburgh finished the 1989 Richard Dimbleby lecture says it all: 'In the end it is up to us as procreators, predators, manipulators, exploiters and consumers to realize that we have to live off the limited land of our planet. We have to learn to accept that any further growth in the human population, any further increases in the exploitation of the Earth's limited natural and mineral resources, and any further degradation of the physical and biological systems of our planet, are bound to cause very serious problems for the generations that we have every reason to believe will come after us. Nearly 140 years ago a very perceptive leader of a group of Indian tribes in the western United States wrote these words:

> This we know,
> the earth does not belong to man,
> man belongs to the earth.
> Whatever befalls the earth,
> befalls the sons of earth.
> Man did not weave the web of life;
> he is merely a strand in it.
> Whatever he does to the web,
> he does to himself.

13

MENS SANA IN CORPORE SANO

Whenever anyone asks what I am doing and I tell them that I am involved in a medical research project, primarily concerned with mental health issues, the very first thing people usually ask is whether I am a doctor. When I tell them that I am not a medical man, I am usually dismissed as some sort of a crank. I can never understand this strange either/or attitude, because let's face it, once stripped of its jargon and Latin phrases, medical science is not very difficult to understand. As Dr Catherine MacFarlane puts it: 'It doesn't take universal intelligence and brilliance to be a doctor. It does take common sense and hard work.'

All I possess, is a hell of a lot of common sense and I have worked in this project very hard already for some years now, which, I admit, doesn't make me a doctor, but it shouldn't make me a crank either. On the other hand one has to be a bit of an oddball to start to study a subject one doesn't know very much about in the first place and furthermore, to stick one's nose into a subject only designed for 'experts'.

Whenever I talk about the importance of nutrition in both the prevention and treatment of physical and mental ill-health, the majority of people seem to consider the whole subject most boring gibberish, because only doctors know, and medicine cures, and that is the end of it. They also seem to support this argument constantly using the same factors; primarily that it is only due to the brilliance of modern medical science that our life expectancy has nearly doubled since the beginning of this century, not forgetting such marvels as coronary bypass surgery, kidney dialysis, pacemakers, extra-uterine fertilization, kidney, liver, lung and heart transplants. I personally find this attitude rather strange, as it is indeed one thing to be mighty impressed by all these technological achievements, but quite another to ask why so many people need new hearts, livers, by-passes, pacemakers etc. a question which I have never yet been asked.

Dr Colgan (161) writes about life expectancy: 'Doctors are proud that the average life expectancy of a baby born in the UK today is seventy-three years, where in 1900 it was only fifty years. So we now enjoy an additional twenty-three years. What is seldom revealed however, is that almost all this increase took place before 1950. By then the average life expectancy had already risen by eighteen years to sixty-eight years. This huge improvement occurred without the benefit of mass immunization, antibiotics or the super technology of modern medicine. Most of the increase of life expectancy came from reducing infant mortality, not from reducing disease in adults. Every baby who dies at birth drastically reduces life expectancy. For example, if we take one hundred people who live to the age of eighty, then their average life is eighty years. If we take one hundred babies who die at birth (age zero), then their average life expectancy is zero years. In 1900 many babies died in infancy, so the average life expectancy looked very low. Once past childhood however, people lived nearly as long as they do now. . . . ' So much about current life expectancy statistics. Now looking at present illness statistics, it looks to me anyhow, that since most infectious diseases such as diphtheria, tuberculosis, scarlet fever, whooping cough etc. came under control, primarily due to improved hygiene, a colossal army of non-infectious diseases such as cancers, heart diseases, arthritis, respiratory illnesses, allergies, ulcers, mental illnesses and sugar regulatory disorders such as hypoglycaemia and diabetes have taken their place.

Dr Alan Kellas (237) writes in his article that among men, bronchitis, ischaemic heart disease, mental illness (depression), arthritis, nervous diseases and musculoskeletal problems all figure highly. Among women, on the other hand, mental illnesses (depression), respiratory illnesses, arthritis, pregnancy complications, nervous diseases, bronchitis and ischaemic heart disease are the most significant reasons for asking for a doctor's help. Ten of the most common causes of death here in Britain are, in order: ischaemic heart disease, cerebrovascular disease, pneumonia, other heart diseases, cancers of the trachea, lung, intestine, rectum and breast, bronchtis, emphysema and asthma. Between 4-5000 people commit suicide in Britain every year, with men being on average twice as likely as women to kill themselves. And finally, figures produced by the 1980 Hospital In-Patient enquiry emphasized the large number of beds occupied by those with a mental disability, both mental illness and mental handicap, which was found to be more than a staggering forty-two percent of the total, compared with nineteen percent for surgery cases and less than eighteen percent for the geriatric and chronically sick. Just to add to these statistics, according to the Hyperactive Children's Support Group (101b) in one year alone 60,000 children were diagnosed as mentally handicapped or mentally ill, 13,000 were admitted to psychiatric units and institutions, and a further 66,700 were 'in care'. And finally the Department of Health and Social Security's 1981 figures show peri-natal deaths of 8427 and congenital abnormalities 12,951. I don't know about you, but at least in my opinion, all these sickness statistics prove that somebody must have goofed somewhere.

I am painfully aware that I have strayed a hell of a way off course with my writing, as this book is supposed to be primarily on mental health issues. However, it can't be helped, as I am a firm believer that mental and physical ill-health can't really be separated, as both of them have the same basic cause: internal and external pollution combined with a lack of proper nutrition. In short, a faulty diet is responsible one way or another for majority of patients lying horizontal on psychiatric couches or on hospital beds when they should be sitting vertical at lunch counters. Unfortunatley food, or a lack of it, seems to be the last thing the orthodox medical profession suspects and more often than not, the poor undernourished blighter is branded as 'neurotic' or some such psychiatric label, just because the poor soul fails conventional laboratory tests or treatment. I find this quite sad.

Now more words about that 'labelling business', as I would like to review such a 'label' as schizophrenia from four different angles: medical, nutritional, vested interests and self.

Snyder (238) writes about schizophrenia in *The Lancet* publication 'Neurotransmitters and CNS disease': 'Several neurotransmitter systems have been evaluated for possible roles in schizophrenia. The most consistent findings involve the influence of drugs that regulate the dopamine system. However, no unequivocal abnormalities in dopamine systems have been demonstrated in schizophrenic patients.... Though schizophrenic symptoms can be worsened or improved by increasing or decreasing dopamine activity, this by no means establishes that an abnormality in dopamine systems is at the root of the disease.'

Pfeiffer (239) writes about schizophrenia in a book called *Mental Illness and Schizophrenia: The Nutrition Connection*. The main biotypes of the schizophrenias are five in number. These are:

1) Histapenia – low blood histamine with excess copper; fifty percent of schizophrenias.
2) Histadelia – high blood histamine with low copper; twenty percent of schizophrenias.
3) Pyroluria – a familial double deficiency of zinc and vitamin B6; thirty percent of schizophrenias.
4) Cerebral Allergy, including wheat-gluten allergy; ten percent of schizophrenias.
5) Nutritional Hypoglycaemia; twenty percent of schizophrenias.

These percentages do not add up to exactly one hundred percent because many patients have more than one disorder. In our Princeton Brian Bio Centre clinic we have treated over 5000 patients labelled schizophrenic. Of these, ninety-five percent can be categorized into the five types described above. When the exact biotype guides the appropriate treatment, ninety percent of these patients will attain social rehabilitation.'

From so called 'vested interests' angle I would like to review David Pilgrim's (240) well researched article 'The Myth of Schizophrenia'. The article suggests four possible reasons why such a label as schizophrenia is still taken seriously by psychiatrists, by many patients and by their relatives. The first and most obvious party being that of medicine. This label of schizophrenia was first constructed within German psychiatry when medicine was consolidating its claim to have authority over so called 'madness', even though then, as now, not a shred of evidence was supplied to substantiate the view that madness is a medical phenomenon, or that the main focus of medical scrutiny (the body) is the domain where its cause can be identified. ... The second vested interest lies of course with drug companies, as the biological response to madness in the form of all sorts of 'anti-schizophrenic medication' is a vast business.

In the US alone one prescription of one of the major tranquillizers is made for every ten people in the general population per year. Being such a lucrative business, it is not surprising that drug companies are also keen to sponsor elementary textbooks on the topic of 'schizophrenia' and to fund all sorts of drug treatment research with 'schizophrenics' as subjects. This shores up the fairly generally held view that mental distress in any form is nothing but a medical matter and that diagnoses such as 'schizoprehnia' are then correspondingly made by the medical profession on 'rational and scientific grounds'.

Clinical psychology has of course also a vested interest to keep 'schizophrenia' alive so to speak, as during the seventies, when the profession was struggling to become autonomous of psychiatry, it opted increasingly to work with so called 'lesser disturbed populations', when the leaders of the profession made it clear that a division of labour could be made between psychiatrists who are supposed to be in charge of psychoses and such like, and clinical psychologists, who are in charge of lesser ills such as 'neuroses' etc.

The fourth, and the final group of people often interested in retaining the concept of 'schizophrenia' as a disease amenable to medical explanation and treatment, are the relatives of 'mad people'. One vital issue here is that 'madness' is usually considered a form of deviance, which is both offensive and disruptive to the 'non-mad'. Indeed, any close study of the identification of 'madness' shows that it is in the 'lay area' that a judgement is made first. Experts are then called upon to rubber stamp this lay labelling and hopefully control the offending or distressing behaviour.

This is quite an understandable reaction, because when people behave in ways which cannot immediately be understood (the core hallmark of madness), fear and disruption is caused in everyday life. However, we should not be hypocritical about how we typically respond to this disruption. For example, when 'mad people' are sectioned under the Mental Health Act and given drugs to control their disturbing behaviour, relatives, social workers and psychiatrists should be honest about the venture they are involved in. This is a version of social control and no amount of paternalistic talk about 'treatment', especially 'compulsory treatment', can alter this fact. The recent lobbying on the part of the Royal College of Psychiatrists and the National Schizophrenia Fellowship to extend 'compulsory treatment' to the community, thankfully not supported by the 1987 MIND AGM, reveals this type of hypocrisy at its worst. At a time when the real issues about the quality of life of psychiatric patients relate to material opportunities, such as jobs, decent housing, supportive professional and lay relationships etc. and because the segregation of 'madness' is crumbling with the Victorian hospitals, an honest re-appraisal of the nature of 'schizophrenia' is required.'

However, according to David Pilgrim, while the four vested interests he highlighted above are in prominence, they will very likely impede the progress of this exercise. Unfortunately I have to agree with him. However, I must say that at least I wouldn't take kindly to the thought, if one day when I was shuffling along the dreary corridor of a mental hospital, my drooling mouth hanging open, face grimacing, tongue clicking and my whole body fidgeting and shaking uncontrollably due to the side effects of my medication, some smart Alec informed me, that the only reason I am in such a frightful state is because auntie Agnes thought I was a bit weird and drug companies want to see healthy profits on their balance sheets, as well as mental health professionals needing jobs.

Let's face it, it was a bit touch and go in Sweden all those years ago that I wasn't sucked into this appalling system, and once in, presumably forced to swallow masses of major tranqillizers with their most devastating side effects. The only reason for being admitted in the first place would have been that I was suffering at the time from the horrendous withdrawal symptoms of minor tranquillizing medication. We have been pretty quick to criticize the Russians for their past willingness to send their politically unsavoury folks to mental institutions, while we Westerners don't seem to have any qualms whatsoever about filling our institutions in the name of financial gain. Such is life.

These past years I have made a point of listening equally to both 'schizophrenics' and their relatives and I can fully sympathize with those relatives or carers, where the 'schizophrenic' member of the family is either violent or abusive. I can also sympathize with the so called 'schizophrenics' themselves, particularly with those who have been labelled 'schizophrenics' against their own will. It s a very delicate issue indeed. However, as we have seen here, the 'anti-schizophrenic' medication is definitely not a solution. However, Dr Pfeiffer's biochemical approach seems to be ninety percent successful, so why not try it in this country? Pharmaceutical industries should start manu-facturing more vitamins, minerals, amino- and essential fatty acids, which psychiatrists should learn to administer. Psychotherapists, psychologists as well as counsellors should carry on giving their talking therapies, the combina-tion of which would make patients better and relatives happier and most importantly, nobody would be out of pocket at the end of the day. So there is food for thought.

Now that we are with mental health issues, let's stay with them a bit longer and look briefly at a condition known as senile dementia, a condition where some old, and some not so old folk slowly 'lose their marbles'.

Shaw *et al.* (241) investigated the dietary intakes of twenty-nine patients suffering from senile dementia (mean age seventy-eight years) and thirty-five healthy volunteers (mean age seventy-four years). The results showed that one third of the control group was receiving less than the recommended daily allowance for ascorbic acid, thiamine, riboflavine and pyridoxine, whereas the proportion of patients with senile dementia with low intakes of these vitamins was found to be even higher. Most patients in both groups received less than the recommended allowance for vitamin D and folic acid.

Another study by Rivlin (242) also points out that most elderly people do not eat adequately. A recent analysis of several surveys concluded that a substantial segment of the elderly population as a whole, perhaps as high as 50%, is consuming less than two-thirds of the currently recommended dietary allowances for several important nutrients. These key nutrients include calcium, iron, thiamine, riboflavin, niacin, vitamin A and vitamin C. Also caloric intake has been noted to be below the recommended level in many of these persons.

Professor Millard (243) writes: 'Doctors do themselves and their patients an injustice if they believe that a failing memory is a sign of old age. In examining the elderly may we not find what we expect to find? Because we see old age as a problem, do we report only negative findings? If a patient has a loss of memory, the first question should be: "Is anything I am prescribing causing it?" The doctor should suspect all drugs: Digoxin, barbiturates, short and long acting benzodiazepines, tricyclic antidepressants, antihistamines, diuretics, indomethacin and recently naproxen and ibuprofen. Septrin, cimetidine, the anti-Parkinsonian drugs levodopa, promocriptine and benzhexol and tranquillizers may all cause confusion. The list is endless. Indeed, it is surprising that the medicated aged pass any mental tests at all. . . .' Thank you Professor Millard.

Garrison (244) writes in the 1984–85 *Yearbook of Nutritional Medicine* under the heading 'Drug-Nutrient Interactions: 'All drugs must be detoxified or undergo biotransformation in order to be excreted. The biochemical reactions involved in this process are mainly enzymatic, and, as such require certain vitamins and minerals as co-factors. Individuals at risk for vitamin and mineral adequacy, especially the elderly on poly drug therapy, may have impaired ability to metabolize certain drugs. . . . In the first step of drug detoxification or biotransformation, the following nutrients play key roles: ascorbic acid, calcium, copper, glycine, iron, magnesium, nicotinic acid, pantothenic acid, protein, riboflavin and zinc. If any of these nutrients are deficient, incomplete drug metabolism is possible, leading to prolonged drug action or side effects from incomplete drug metabolites. In the second phase of drug biotransformation, the following vitamins, along with carbohydrates, amino acids and fats play a key role: vitamin B12, nicotinic acid, folic acid, lipoic acid and pantothenic acid. It is important for the practitioner to note how essential vitamins and minerals are in drug metabolism. Drug-induced nutritional deficiencies may actually impair the metabolism of the drug and alter the expected therapeutic outcome.'

My interest has always been problem solving. In high school I loved maths, geometry in particular, because of its great problem solving potential. Having that type of mind, I found this whole biochemical research journey oodles of fun. That aside, it doesn't need much brain power to figure out what the final outcome of these last four studies are. Elderly folks, who don't consume an adequate diet and are on multi medication are in grave danger of suffering from senility. First of all, because vitamin and mineral deficiencies alone can lead to all sorts of mental health problems, but when combined with multi medication, they really are in trouble. For two reasons: first of all because drugs themselves, during their detoxifying process, further deplete their already low vitamin and mineral reserves, and secondly because of accumulation of side effects of incomplete drug metabolites. If your granny is also keen on cooking her rhubarb in an aluminium pan, mixes her daily tipple with tap water, as well as cures her heartburn, hangover or whatever with daily antacid medication, all known sources of aluminium, it is hardly surprising if she ends up half dead from the neck up, which is far from funny.

Now let's go back to a more unripe generation, being precise, to Welsh schoolchildren.

Benton and Roberts (245) conducted an interesting double-blind study lasting for eight months, on ninety Wrexham schoolchildren aged twelve and thirteen, to test a hypothesis as to whether possible dietary vitamin and/or mineral deficiencies might be preventing their optimum psychological function. The study used the American RDA as their yardstick because the British RDA covers only a limited range of vitamins and minerals. All children kept dietary diaries for three days, from which the researchers were able to establish that in most cases the average intake of vitamins was close to the US RDA, the lowest intakes being of vitamin D and folic acid. With minerals however, the situation was found to be less satisfactory, the average intakes being around half of the RDA with correspondingly more subjects having low values. These ninety children were then divided into three groups, matched by their form teacher for sex, school performance and home background. They were then randomly assigned, three at a time, to one of the three following groups: no tablets, vitamin/mineral supplementation and a placebo group. The placebo and vitamin/mineral supplementation were then administered to children double-blind i.e. no parent, teacher or child knew whether he was receiving an active or a placebo tablet. Both the verbal and non-verbal intelligence was tested of all children taking part before and after the experiment. When the final results were analyzed, the vitamin/mineral supplemented group showed a striking increase in non-verbal intelligence score, without a change in verbal intelligence. The authors concluded their study by pointing out that as their findings indicate that dietary deficiencies seem to hamper non-verbal intelligence in these sample children, the study should be replicated, and if provocative conclusions are confirmed, the underlying mechanism should be established.

Because I haven't as yet had time, as I have been so busy with my studies and research, to acquire plenty of letters after my name, I should be very careful what I say, so I will say nothing but what has already been insinuated. It looks as if today's 'adequate diet' is not quite adequate enough to support the optimal performance of non-verbal intelligence of schoolkids from Wrexham, nor does it seem to be adequate for most of us, as the DHSS study of 3285 schoolchildren showed definite deficiencies of iron, calcium and vitamin B2. Most adolescents have been found to be commonly short of zinc, iron, vitamin C and vitamin A. (246) When we add to this list the elderly folk who seem to be more often than not short of calcium, iron, most B-group vitamins as well as vitamins C and A, there is no question any more that we really are a malnourished lot, and that seems to be pretty nearly official.

Not only are Wrexham children suffering from a definite lack of optimal non-verbal intelligence because of an inadequate diet, but Welsh mothers sometimes give birth to malformed babies because of the same plight.

Laurence *et al.* (247) conducted a randomized controlled double-blind trial on women in South Wales who already had had one child born with neural-tube defect or spina bifida. The trial was undertaken to find out whether 4 mg of folic acid daily, before conception and during pregnancy could prevent the recurrence of neural tube defects. The final result showed that none of the forty-four women who received folic acid before and during pregnancy, had babies born with spina bifida, whereas there were found to be six recurrences among sixty-seven mothers who received a placebo tablet. The study pointed out that women receiving a poor diet and who are at risk of a recurrence of foetal neural-tube defects, can reduce this risk either by improving their diet or taking folic acid supplementation. The study concluded that folic acid supplementation might be a cheap, safe and effective method of primary prevention of neural tube defects, but that this study should be confirmed in a large, multi-central trial.

In my opinion these types of trials are quite unethical. I don't know whether these mothers taking part were fully aware about the nature of the experiment. If they knew perfectly well what they were in for, well and good and that is then their business. However, if I were in the process of starting a family, no amount of flanelling would make me play Russian roulette with the health of my future baby. Sadly, medical research has never been famous for its ethics, and as long as there is a fool or an innocent animal born every minute, they seem to get away with it, which I find quite depressing.

I think that I have mentioned before how much I dislike talking about specific vitamin or mineral deficiencies, as there is never just one vitamin or mineral activity on its own. It is always the multiple interactions of all these essential substances as found in all raw, unprocessed foods, which are the basis for both our mental and physical biochemical function. It looks to me as if the most frequent mistake the majority of doctors, as well as non-doctors make, when they first become interested in nutrition, is to emphasize a single nutrient supplement, expecting it to prevent or cure some particular symptom. This attitude seems to stem from identifying vitamins and minerals with drugs, which they are definitely not. Nor are they pep-pills or backbones for Mensa brains, and most importantly, they are not substitutes for food, nor can they be assimilated without digesting food. That in mind, let's make it quite clear from the start that no amount of folic acid without eating anything else, will prevent your child from being born with spina bifida, just the opposite, both of you would soon be dead as a doornail. Furthermore Professor Bryce-Smith and his team suggest that a low folic acid level may be directly caused by zinc deficiency, even when dietary folate intakes are normal. They write: 'The importance of correct balance between zinc and folate may need to be borne in mind when supplementation with either nutrient in pregnancy is under consideration'. (210)

The reason I decided to discuss vitamins and minerals as a separate entity in my book, is to show the sceptic medical man, that the use of additional vitamins are not only helpful in the treatment of scurvy, pellagra, beri-beri and such like. This use has never come in for much criticism by the medical profession. But heaven help the poor blighter who dares to mention vitamins and minerals being helpful outside this narrow context.

Before we get down to the basics, let's take a brief look at the number one reaper in this country, which is heart disease. This is when most doctors usually utter the word 'diet', to be more precise 'a low cholesterol diet'. This word cholesterol seems to strike terror on the lips of many men, but I wonder if many men are aware that cholesterol is essential for our health. In fact cholesterol is made by practically every tissue in our body, adults synthesizing daily two to four times the amount of cholesterol absorbed from food, adjusting the production to meet demand i.e., the more cholesterol you eat, the less cholesterol your body produces. Some of the reasons why our bodies are so busy manufacturing cholesterol is that it is an essential substance needed for cell membrane structure, the formation of bile, production of steroid hormones as well as the manufacturing of vitamin D with the help of sunshine. However, having said that, too much dietary cholesterol is not good for you, particularly if you are hereditarily prone to cholesterol related heart diseases, nor is too little cholesterol good for you as the following study points out.

Dr Emmanuel Cheraskin (248) writes about the subject: 'A group of Japanese investigators (249) question the practice of maintaining the total serum cholesterol level as low as possible in order to prevent coronary heart disease and cerebral stroke. From a ten-year study they reported a significant negative correlation between total serum cholesterol level (from 150 to 200 mg/dl) and both cerebral haemorrhage and cerebral infarction. According to these authors, the mortality rate for stroke increases in groups with a total serum cholesterol level lower than 160 mg/dl. Our results suggest that the desirable level of total serum cholesterol in men may be somewhere between 180 and 200 mg/dl, where incidence rates of both coronary heart disease and stroke are low.' So all in all, a mad obsession about dietary cholesterol can be a waste of time, except of course with those individuals whose cholesterol level has been found to be disturbingly high. However, if I were one of those unfortunates, before I would consider changing my beloved pat of butter for a dollop of margarine with all its hydrogenated fats and additives in order to control my cholesterol level, I would look first at other alternatives, such as coffees and sugars.

Forde *et al.* (250) assessed the effects of coffee consumption and coffee brewing methods on the serum cholesterol concentration of thirty-three men with hypercholesterolaemia. These men were randomly assigned to the following procedures; continue with the usual coffee intake, stop drinking coffee altogether, stop drinking coffee for five weeks, thereafter drinking either boiled or filter coffee. The results showed that cholesterol concentrations fell significantly in all subects abstaining for the first five weeks, compared with subjects not giving up, and continued to fall in those abstaining for ten weeks. Cholesterol concentrations rose again in subjects returning to boiled coffee. They concluded their study that abstention from heavy coffee drinking is an efficient way of reducing serum cholesterol concentrations in men with hypercholesterolaemia, the extent of brewing methods affecting the relation requiring further study.

John Yudkin, Emeritus Professor of Nutrition at London University, an author of many medical articles and an excellent book *Pure, White and Deadly* (251, 252) has done a great deal of research on the connection of refined sugar and heart disease. His experiments have shown a direct correlation between dietary sugar consumption and a rise in both serum cholesterol and triglycerine level in both animals and humans. He writes (252): 'In our first experiments with nineteen young men, the sugar-rich diet produced an increase in blood triglycerine in all of them after two weeks. In addition, six of them showed other changes; they put on about five pounds in weight, the level of insulin in the bood rose, (remember hypoglycaemia), and there was an increase in the stickiness of the platelets. All of these changes disappeared entirely, or almost entirely, two weeks after the men went back to their usual diet. . . . Three aspects of these results we found especially interesting. The first was the fact that about a quarter or a third of our subjects showed this special sensitivity to sugar, while the remainder did not. This suggested to us the idea that only a proportion of men are susceptible to coronary thrombosis through eating sugar. Secondly, the rise in the level of insulin recalled to us that there had been two or three British research workers who had suggested that a raised level of insulin could be a key factor in the production of atherosclerosis. Thirdly, we were intrigued that men who were susceptible to sugar, as shown by the rise of insulin, also put on a lot of weight while on sugar, and lost it within two weeks of going back to their normal diet. This reminded us of the association between overweight and the liability of coronary thrombosis. Indeed, it has been argued that, if eating sugar does increase the risk of heart attacks, this is only an indirect effect, since dietary sugar predisposes people to become overweight, and it is being overweight that predisposes to the disease. We tested this suggestion by getting some young men to overfeed by increasing either the sugar in their diet or the starch. With the sugar, there was an increase in the concentration of both triglycerine and cholesterol in the blood; with starch giving the same number of additional calories, there was no change in the concentration of either of the fatty substances. . . .' The very next day when I finished reading this great gem of wisdom, I saw, when I opened my daily paper, the headlines hollering at me: 'Sweet times are here. Sweet-toothed Britain is on top of the world. We eat more sweets than anyone else, and next year sales are expected to top £3,300 million. Above ninety-four percent of the population buy chocolates, sweets and mints at least once a month. And it's adults who eat the most.' Need I say more?

Even though I had decided not to talk any more about the effect of any single nutrient on any diseases, I would like to mention briefly the effect of vitamin C, vitamin E and magnesium deprivation in connection with our tickers. I have collected the following information from Barbara Griggs's book *The Food Factor*. (253)

Dr Emil Ginter of Bratislava in Czechoslovakia and his team studied vitamin C deprivation on the arteries. Ginter used guinea-pigs who, like men, cannot synthesize their own vitamin C. Pre-study photographs of their aortas, using an electron-scan microscope showed beautifully regular rows of endothelial cells lining healthy aortas. After just a fortnight on diets deprived of vitamin C, the aortas now looked like bare lunar landscapes, with eroded cells, and debris beginning to accumulate. Two months later, they suggested scrapyards, choked with a jetsam of cell debris, fibrin and cholesterol. Ginter and his team went on to show that in the absence of vitamin C, the liver continues to produce cholesterol, but can no longer convert it into bile acids for excretion, and it begins to pile up in the arteries.

Canadian doctors, the brothers William and Evan Shute successfully treated thousands of their heart patients using vitamin E supplementation. Vitamin E appears to work for hearts in several ways; it helps to stop blood platelets sticking together to form clots and helps to dissolve them if they form. It also increases the blood supply of oxygen, as well as helping to keep cholesterol down.

The heart muscle needs calcium to contract and magnesium to relax; and a series of complex chemical interactions keeps this calcium/magnesium balance carefully tuned. A magnesium deficiency can wreck this balance as the cells then take up too much calcium, or alternatively are unable to pump it out, causing a vasospasm, sometimes with fatal results. Cow's milk is an excellent source of calcium, but unfortunately a poor source of magnesium, therefore, an excessive milk consumption without additional magnesium supplementation could also lead to calcium/magnesium imbalance and therefore contribute to cardiovascular disorders.

Doctors Crouch and Freed investigated milk products in the connection of heart diseases yet from a different angle. They conducted a survey in order to find out whether cow's milk protein and egg protein could be specifically artherogenic. They selected forty-four patients aged between forty-five and seventy-five who were already suffering from coronary heart disease and/or hypertension, who agreed to embark on a diet free of all cow's milk and other bovine products and all foods including egg. After one month of the diet thirty-three reported that they felt either well or noticeably improved. After six months on the diet, thirty-eight reported improvement in their symptoms, seventeen of them feeling virtually asymptomatic. They concluded their study by pointing out that the beneficial effects of this milk-free, egg-free diet could have not been only due to the changes in dietary fat, but also the avoidance of bovine and egg antigens. This interesting study was published in July 1984 in *The Practitioner*.

As early as the seventeenth century milk drinking had been linked with 'melancholy' and now recently with schizophrenia (106), psychological disturbances in young children (99), childhood hyperactivity (97) and even juvenile delinquency.

Alexander Schauss (138) compared cow's milk consumption between thirty juvenile offenders and control subjects and found a statistical difference between these two groups milk being consumed in considerably higher quantities by juvenile delinquents. Another research reported in the March 1981 *Journal of Behavioural Ecology* by the Law Enforcement Administration US Department of Justice, corroborated Schauss's discovery concerning cow's milk consumption in relation to juvenile offenders. In a programme conducted by the San Luis Obispo (California) Country Probation Department, juvenile offenders' pre-natal, post-natal and early childhood development was evaluated. Nearly ninety percent of the offenders were found to have a symptom history associated with milk intolerance and allergy. Further physical examination and biochemical testing revealed eighty-eight percent having evidence of milk allergy. After these findings Alexander Schauss stresses that he is not suggesting that children should not drink milk, as cow's milk is considered a nutritious source of both calcium and protein. However, those children who react either physically or mentally adversely to milk, because they are allergic to it or they have an inability to break down opioid peptides found in it, should avoid all milk and milk-based products. I must stress here that anyone who either decides to give up milk or doesn't drink milk for whatever reason, should make sure that their calcium intake is adequate. All wholegrains, vegetables and pulses contain a fair amount of calcium. Or if one still would like a supplement, dolomite tablets, if they come from a pure source, are good because they contain both calcium and magnesium in right proportions.

All I can say is, poor old cow. She is trying to do her best, and it isn't her fault if her milk is not universally suitable to everyone, except her own offspring who are, because of our greed, denied their hereditary rights. Serves us right.

Now back to our hearts. I hate to think how many more years and how many more billions of pounds will still be spent financing heart experts to peer earnestly in their cosy laboratories through their impressive gadgets, while millions of folk outside are croaking their last breaths. One has only got to look at these few research studies I have selected on the subject, to cotton on, that heart diseases don't have just one cause, but several. Furthermore, that most causes seem to be primarily nutritional. Take us Finns for example. Before prevention and nutritional education became the flavour of the day, our heart disease statistics were the wonder of the world. And knowing what I know now, I am not surprised one little bit. The combination of boiled coffee continuously simmering on the stove, our

liking of sweets and, because of our climate, the comparative lack of fresh fruits and vegetables, leading to vitamin C
deficiencies. When you add to this over-processed foods
nearly void of vitamin E, our great liking of cow's milk and
fried foods, I am surprised that destiny spared me at all to
tell you this little tale. However, before we lynch our poor
old cows and bury our coffee pots, let's take first a brief look
at a couple more aspects of this hearty saga.

Newman *et al.* (254) point out that arteriosclerosis can in
fact begin very early in life, as fatty streaks have been found
in aortas of some three year olds, as well as in the coronary
arteries during the second decade. More advanced coronary
arteriosclerosis was also found in the majority of young
adults, in whom autopsies were performed during the
Korean and Vietnam wars.

Kuller *et al.* (255) studied sudden natural deaths, i.e.
deaths which happened unexpectedly within twenty-four
hours, among Baltimore residents in US between 15 June
1964 and 14 June 1965. Of the total 3648 deaths, 1178, or
32.3% were sudden and unexpected, of which arteriosclerotic heart disease (ASHD) accounted for 58.1%. They write:
'With respect to the possibility of the reduction of ASHD
mortality in the forty to sixty-four age group, several
important facts reported in this study should be
re-emphasized:

1) Sixty percent of deaths attributed to ASHD were sudden.
2) Only 18.9% of the individuals who died from ASHD in
   Baltimore City survived longer than twenty-four hours
   in a hospital, and one third of these had been previously
   admitted with another diagnosis.
3) Of those who died suddenly from ASHD 50% had a history of heart disease, 11.4% of diabetes, 27.8% of hypertension and finally.
4) Approximately 24% had seen a physician within a week
   prior to death.'

This study mentioned also a further 8.2% who died without
any warning whatsoever within a couple of hours. None of
these had had any history of either heart disease, diabetes,
hypertension or stroke, nor had they seen a doctor or been
hospitalized within one year prior to their deaths. They

were also able to work until the moment the death occurred. The study concluded that these particular deaths may represent the sudden and unexpected cardiac deaths in apparently healthy individuals.

What these two last studies seem to be telling us is that dying of heart disease can start at a very young age. Also that no doctor or hospital can do much for us once our ticker has decided to give up, not even visiting a doctor a week before the fatal incident. Furthermore, that sometimes even 'apparently healthy individuals' can die from a heart attack without any prior warning whatsoever. This being the case, one can only conclude that prevention of dying from a heart disease must start very early in life. This means that all people from juveniles to adults, who don't want to die before their time due to a dicky heart, should all tuck into good and wholesome food including plenty of fruits and vegetables and avoid excessive use of refined sugars as well as other stimulants such as coffee, strong teas, tobacco and alcohol. Fish foods such as mackerel, herring and sardines as well as all cold pressed vegetable oils are particularly good because they are a rich source of fat soluble vitamins as well as of essential polyunsaturated fatty acids, both being vital for our optimal health. Eicosapentaenoic acid (EPA), found particularly in oily fish and fish liver oils have been found to prevent blood platelets clumping together as well as to promote the production of high-density lipoproteins, which in turn are able to remove excessive cholesterol deposits from artery walls and promote their return to the liver to be excreted as bile. Sadly however, fish and chips, our beloved British diet is not good for us, because oil which is used in frying the stuff, besides being commercially purified and bleached, has also been hydrogenated, which alters the composition of the oil from its health promoting cis-form to its non-health promoting trans-form. All cis-oils, which consist of all natural cold pressed vegetable and marine oils are excellent for our health, because their high vitamin and essential fatty acid content, including their ability to be transferred to prostaglandins. All processed oils which contain trans-fatty acids and which are found in most margarines and commercial cooking oils are not good for us because these trans-fatty acids interfere with the process of prostaglandins' production. Prostaglandins, as you might remember, are an active group of essential substances which have a vital influence on our healthy cellular metabolism, including our hearts. Dr David Horrobin (256) writes about this subject: 'It is unfortunate that many doctors are unaware of the existence of trans-fatty acids. Recommending a switch from butter to margarine for example, may actually increase the ratio of potentially harmful fats. If margarines are recommended it is important to insist that they contain polyunsaturated fatty acids in which the cis-bonds remain intact.' So for your heart's sake, check your margarines.

Finally, exercise is essential for a healthy heart. All muscles weaken and wither if they are not sufficiently used and our heart muscles are no exception.

14

PASS THE BUG PLEASE

Now that we have tackled both mental health issues and physical health issues 'separately' so to speak, let's look again at a condition known as Post Viral Fatigue Syndrome, Royal Free Disease, Epstein-Barr Virus Syndrome, Chronic Fatigue Syndrome, Myalgic Encephalomyelitis etc. but known as ME for short. Its hallmark is an excessive feeling of tiredness not helped by rest, combined with a plethora of both mental and physical symptoms. The reason for this puzzling illness is thought to be a persistent virus infection. Before I go any further with this subject, I would like to mention that I have been personally diagnosed positively as an ME sufferer, as a laboratory test detected the presence of enteroviral group protein (VP1) in my blood.

When I first became acquainted with this ME subject, the very first thing which struck me, was the uncanny similarity between ME and Reactive Hypoglycaemia. All one has to do is to compare the description of ME leaflet 'Guidelines for Sufferers' which you find in chapter 5 and compare it with Dr Dunne's description of Reactive Hypoglycaemia, which you find in chapter 10 and you can see what I mean. Another condition ME seems to resemble is a severe allergy or the 'brain fag' as described by Dr Randolph and which you find in chapter 8. Now when you compare the similarity between mental and physical symptoms arising from ME, which I was discussing in chapter 5 to the mental and physical symptoms arising from Anxiety Neurosis, Agoraphobia, Effort Syndrome, Hyperventilation Syndrome, Neurocirculatory Asthenia etc which I was discussing in chapter 2, you will find the similarity striking. Also when you compare physical and mental symptoms of 'non-organic diseases' as described in chapter 5 to physical and mental symptoms of ME you will find again that they are nearly identical. And finally, when you compare the physical and mental symptoms of both ME and the addiction and/or withdrawal of tranquillizing medication, which I was discussing at length in chapter 6, you will find the similarity pretty close.

Now what are we supposed to learn from this? Not a lot, except, as I see it, ME could be alleviated simply by eliminating the tendency to both Reactive Hypoglycaemia and Allergies, and where applicable, by withdrawing gradually from tranquillizing medication. I would find this particular approach useful in those situations where the hunt for a virus has been unsuccessful. And let's face it, this nutritional approach could be just as useful to folks like me, who have got 'a proper virus' to fall back on. In fact ME is already treated nutritionally in some circles by working on the hypothesis that ME may be caused by a yeast infection, known as candida albicans, of which I shall now mumble a few selected words.

Candida is a yeast which is present in all of us. It is a pure parasite and it resides primarily with our so called 'friendly bacteria' in our digestive system, largely in the intestine. Our digestive tract is inhabited by upwards of five pounds of various micro-organisms which we call 'friendly bacteria' because amongst other useful things, they are able to manufacture a fair amount of various vitamins. When our doctor prescribes us antibiotics in order to destroy harmful bacteria, the 'friendly bacteria' will also then either be destroyed or at least severely damaged in the process, which, besides lowering the person's vitamin status, also gives the parasitic candida yeast much more space to proliferate.

The effects of candida infection are primarily found in the mouth, on the skin and around the reproductive organs, when it is known as thrush. When candida spreads, it puts out all sorts of toxins, even acetaldehyde, which, besides being toxic in itself, also has been thought to have an ability to act as a hapten or a protein carrier leading to allergic reactions. These same toxins are also thought to affect our immune system, leading to a diminished immune system function. It has been also suggested by Dr Truss (257) that when candida spreads, it can change from its simple form into what is called its mycelial form. When this happens, it develops long root systems which are able to penetrate into the tissues it is growing on. When this takes place in the bowel, this penetration may also allow any incompletely digested food proteins an easy access into the blood stream, which can lead to further allergic reactions.

A possible ongoing presence of candida infection is notoriously difficult to establish, primarily because candida yeast can be found in all of us. The diagnosis is usually based on a patient's past history of long term use of broad spectrum antibiotics, steroid drugs such as cortisone and the Pill, a number of pregnancies, possible present fungal infections etc. When all this information is then combined with a dietary history, if particularly found to be high in sugary foods, yeasty foods such as cheeses, pickles, brewers yeast and fermented substances such as alcoholic beverages and so on and so forth, candida infection can be suspected. The final diagnosis however, can only be confirmed by the patient's own response to the anti-candida treatment, which includes an anti-fungal drug called Nystatin which has the ability to kill the yeast by direct contact, combined with sugar-free diet. A sugar-free diet is used literally to starve the yeast of its favourite food, as yeasts practically live on sugar. Many ME sufferers have been said to be helped considerably with this approach. Whether it was the candida albicans which bothered them in the first place, or whether they started to feel perkier because this same sugar-free diet is used in the treatment of Reactive Hypoglycaemia, is now just anybody's guess. . . . Anyone who wishes to learn more about candida albicans and how this yeast could affect one's health should read any of the books by the following authors: Chaitow (258), Truss (257) and Crook (9).

I will be approaching next one of the most controversial subjects of modern medicine; the dreaded virus theory. Heaven will hopefully help me if I get it seriously wrong. I must stress here again, that all ideas, whether right or wrong, have been put by me on these pages by following my own final conclusions, so naturally I am also solely responsible for all errors which may appear. The basic knowledge of this virus business I have collected, besides from several research studies on the subject, also from an excellent and thought provoking book written by Leon Chaitow and which is called *Vaccination and Immunization: Dangers, Delusions and Alternatives*. (259) I like to recommend this book as essential reading to anyone planning to be vaccinated, whether an infant or a grown-up.

Now back to ME and its viruses. As I have mentioned before, it has been suggested that ME symptoms in some people are caused by an underlying viral infection, particularly by an infection caused by a group of so called enteroviruses, which can be usually isolated from the intestinal tract and which consist of about seventy different strains. Also Epstein-Barr virus has been linked with ME.

Yousef (260) and his team studied faecal samples of seventy-six ME patients and compared them with matched controls. Positive cultures of enteroviruses were obtained from seventeen (twenty-two percent) of patients and two (seven percent) of controls. When the same investigation was repeated one year later, five of the seventeen patients still were found to have positive cultures of the same serotype as previously, furthermore thirteen out of seventeen still had detectable enterovirus-specific IgM antibodies, a further nine having detectable VP1 antigen in their serum. In the second experiment Dr Yousef and his team tested for a possible presence of VP1 antigen in a group of eighty-seven ME sufferers, out of which forty-four (fifty-one percent) gave positive results. It was also found that the number of patients positive to VP1 antigen was greater when IgM complexes were detectable than when they were not. The study concluded that a chronic infection with enterovirus seems to occur in many ME patients, and furthermore, there has been found to be correlation between clinical improvement and the disappearance of both VP1 and IgM complexes.

All well and good. However, the more I mulled over this Yousef's study, the more restless I became. I suppose what got me particularly pensive was the fact that the presence of these blasted enteroviruses can be obviously detected also in perfectly normal and healthy people. This worrying news in mind I decided to burrow myself back into my pile of literature. After a spell of intense concentration I finally came to the following conclusion: Enteroviruses, which can be isolated from the intestinal tract are non-tumour inducing viruses, which includes subgroups like coxsackie, polio and echo viruses. All these viruses are involved in a variety of diseases, ranging from common colds to pneumonia, meningitis and paralytic poliomyelitis. They are often present in sub-clinical infections, are distributed worldwide, and are present in most people. I don't mind telling you that this little news shook me a bit. Now that I had established that most of us seem to be virus-ridden, how come that some unfortunates develop ME or some such thing, and others don't turn a hair?

In order to find a satisfactory answer to this controversial puzzle, I dived back into my literature and after an intensive research emerged with the following gem: Virus particles themselves are models of biological minimalism, consisting of a simple core of genetic material, either DNA or RNA molecule which is nesting in a protective envelope of protein. Now as I see it, these virus particles can be found sitting quietly, minding their own business, inside the cells of most of us, without any specific alterations of that cell's function or structure. When this virus DNA is languishing happily, without causing any trouble whatsoever, with a human cell DNA, this virus is known as a provirus. These proviruses could nestle in a person quietly for eternity, only getting troulesome under adverse conditions, when these proviruses wake up from their peaceful sleep. When this happens, they become angry and activated and start to proliferate, producing more and more viral DNA, even trying to take over the host cell's DNA. This pathogenic, or angry and activated state of the viral protein can be generated either within the body itself, or it could be transmitted from an external source. This pathogenic state can be created by excessive use of drugs, both prescribed and non-prescribed, vaccinations, general anaesthetics, surgery, other infections, toxic chemical overload, including cigarettes, pesticide residues, food additives as well as other excessive physical or mental stresses.

When these hazards are then combined with poor nutrition and defective immune system function, the activated virus will have a ball, whether it is an irksome enterovirus or the dreaded AIDS virus. I am sure that most of us are aware that being an AIDS virus carrier doesn't necessarily mean that the person is going to develop full blown AIDS. Leon Chaitow and Simon Martin write in their excellent book *A World Without AIDS* (261)

'AIDS is no more caused solely by the virus currently claimed to be its trigger, than the smell of a dustbin is caused by the flies that feed on it. – Yes, "the" virus (HIV) and others are present in most people with AIDS. But HIV is also present in many people who have not developed, and will not develop AIDS. What's more, "the" virus is not present in everybody who does develop AIDS . . . The HIV virus, if it causes AIDS, only does so if the health of the individual affected is already compromised. Our general state of health and the efficiency of our immune systems should be the real focus, not "the" virus. The truth is that it is easier to be afraid of the virus than to do something positive about our wretched general health. It is also a lot more likely to win a Nobel Prize for aspects of research related to "the" virus, than for telling people to eat correctly and to confine themselves to monogamous relationships. There are no research rewards and mind-boggling fortunes to be made, by drug companies, from the promotion of good health through positive living and an adequate diet, but there are from the research for drugs which modify the symptoms of AIDS or which alter the behaviour of HIV. This appalling tragedy will result in a polarization of efforts in which alternative healing will point to the true enemy, and the ways in which this can be dealt with while, Nero-like, the medical establishment and its official cohorts in government fiddle along the old tune of "kill the bug" while millions continue to destroy themselves through ignorance.'

This is now enough of AIDS, as this chapter is not supposed to be about AIDS or HIV viruses, but ME and enteroviruses. The sole reason why I cited Chaitow and Martin at length is that I also believe that enteroviruses or Epstein-Barr virus, which can be found also in perfectly healthy individuals, if they cause ME, *only do so if the health of the individual infected is already compromised*. Therefore our general health and the efficiency of our immune system should be the real focus, NOT the enterovirus or Epstein-Barr virus.

Our health and immune system can become disarrayed through the following factors:

1) Diet high in refined carbohydrates. In fact Sanchez and his team found that refined sugars directly hinder the ability of the immune system to deal with bacteria and viruses. (262)
2) Diet low in protein, complex carbohydrates, vitamins, trace minerals and essential fatty acids.
3) Denatured food, food additives and contaminants.
4) Air, water and electromagnetic pollution. Also pesticides and toxic metals.
5) Extended use of drugs, both prescribed and non-prescribed.
6) Allergies, where immune system is chronically stimulated by a high antigenic load.
7) Lack of sufficient exercise and relaxation.
8) Physical and psychological stresses.
9) Number of previous illnesses, yeast infections such as candida albicans, bacterial and virus infections, pregnancies, surgeries, anaesthetics, vaccinations and immunizations.

Now that we are with vaccination and immunization, we might as well stay with them a bit longer, particularly as our present government has proposed in their latest White Paper to achieve 'specific' target levels of vaccination and immunization.' I can only guess that whoever dreamt up that kind of 'health promotion campaign' isn't familiar with Leon Chaitow's book: *Vaccination and Immunization: Dangers, Delusions and Alternatives*, from which I have collected most of the following information. However, before I start I would like to point out that both decline and prevalence as well as the severity of most major infections we are today vaccinated against seemed to have occurred after improvement in sanitation and hygiene and much before any national vaccination and immunization programme. (161, 263)

Chantler *et al* (264) isolated rubella virus from 7 of 19

children with chronic arthritis in contrast with 16 controls. They found that in no case was there a history of recent rubella infection, although most children had received rubella vaccination in the past.

Ogra and Herd (265) were able to isolate the rubella virus from the affected joints of children vaccinated with rubella vaccine strain for several months after the vaccination procedure. They concluded their study saying that rubella virus could be one of possible aetiologic agent in chronic rheumatoid disease in children.

Tingle *et al.* (266) studied the effects of rubella virus vaccine in 13 adults with 'failed' rubella immunization and found striking evidence of auto-immune disease, connective tissue disorders and chronic forms of arthritis, in all of which an immuno-regulatory mechanism is thought to play a primary pathogenic role. They concluded their study by pointing out that failed rubella immunization in adult populations may have more clinical significance than has been previously recognized.

Miller *et al.* (267) describes 9 cases of multiple sclerosis which were apparently provoked by vaccination or innoculation. They also discussed in their paper various German authors who have described the apparent provocation of multiple sclerosis by protective innoculation or vaccination against smallpox, typhoid, tetanus, poliomyelitis and tuberculosis.

Zintchenko (268) in turn had reported 12 patients in whom multiple sclerosis became evident after a course of anti-rabies vaccinations.

Chaitow (269) writes about Sudden Infant Death Syndrome (SIDS) 'Many workers have noted that the sudden, inexplicable, death of an apparently healthy baby often takes place within hours or days of vaccination of one kind or another (but with some cases showing more of a link than others). Time and again this has called forth warnings and protests without any real impact on the consciousness of the medical fraternity, or the public at large. . . . Dr Robert Mendelsohn has stated categorically: 'My suspicion, which is shared by others in my profession, is that the nearly 10,000 SIDS deaths that occur in the United States each year are related to one or more of the vaccines that are routinely given to children. The pertussis (whooping cough) vaccine is the most likely villain, but it could also be one of the others.' It was noted by Dr William Torch, of the University of Nevada School of Medicine, that the DPT (diphtheria, pertussis, tetanus vaccine) may be responsible for SIDS deaths. He noted in one survey that two thirds of 103 children, who died of SIDS, had been immunized with DPT vaccine within three weeks of each death. Many died within one day of the procedure.'

Chaitow (259) writes about allergies: 'Many allergists speculate as to the link between the vast array of allergic symptoms, seen in children today and the use of toxic foreign proteins in vaccination procedures. There is evidence that it is indeed so. For example, in adults receiving flu immunization, there have been observations of a worsening of allergic symptoms. This was noted in one survey to occur in six out of seven people immunized. A variety of other symptoms were also seen to be worse after immunization, including aggravation of high blood pressure, diabetes, gout and Parkinson's disease. The allergic factor though seemed to receive the greatest exacerbation.'

Chaitow and Martin (261) also point out that some cases of AIDS could have been directly caused by contaminated polio vaccine containing SV40 (Simian Virus number 40) which is commonly found in the kidney cells of African Green Monkeys. These contaminated kidney cells were used in the past in preparing batches of polio vaccine. It was Dr Eva Snead's research work (269) which eventually led to the discovery that HIV and SV40 virus are in fact very similar. This disturbing fact was verified by Dr Andrew Scott. (270) He writes: 'The current most favoured hypothesis is that all human AIDS viruses are related to a type of virus called "Simian Immunodeficiency Virus (SIV), which is known to cause an AIDS-like disease in monkeys. SIV is genetically similar, though clearly distinct from, all types of human AIDS virus. This similarity suggests that the first seed of the current AIDS pandemic was sown when a monkey virus somehow gained access to humans in central Africa.'

Another speculation about the adverse effect of vaccination programmes could be that they may be seeding our own cells with an excess of proviruses which could cause our cells to alter their genetic code to the extent that our immune system doesn't recognize these cells any more as our own, but foreign, causing all kinds of auto-immune diseases, multiple sclerosis, cancers etc. or even so called 'provocation diseases' as explained by Sir Graham Wilson: (271) 'Provocation disease takes place when there is already present in the body of the individual being vaccinated, a latent or incubating infection, which might either become manifest, or with which the defence mechanism of the body would deal adequately without patent infection being displayed. Should vaccination against, say diphtheria, be received at such a time, the incubation period of the other disease, say polio, is shortened, or a latent infection which might not have ever been seen as an active disease, is activated, and the symptoms of infection by this micro-organism may become evident in an acute form. The two diseases in which this form of provocation has been most noted are typhoid fever and poliomyelitis, the latter becoming evident immediately after vaccination against diphtheria or pertussis. Paralysis which results from such infections is often noted in the limb which was used for the innoculation. Should there be a latent virus present, in a suitable susceptible individual, say, someone with nutrient deficits or generally lowered vitality and well being, then a variety of possible changes could occur.'

Whether these revelations about the possible side effects of vaccination and immunization procedures are eventually found to be correct or not correct, remains to be seen. Until then however, at least this author will completely ignore the government's 'specified target levels of vaccination and immunization in order to promote better health', and stick firmly on my own health promoting measures, which are: To keep my immune system functioning the best I can, which can be achieved by many different approaches. Leon Chaitow mentions in his book (259) homeopathy, botanic medicine, osteopathy, acupuncture as well as optimum nutrition. And last, but not least a positive mental attitude. And even if in future some scientifically-based-double-blind-placebo-controlled-do-dahs will try to change my mind, I think I'll still refuse, knowing now from what kind of nauseating materials vaccines are made out of. For example diphtheria toxin and antitoxin is derived from putrifying horse blood, pertussis vaccine from mucus taken from throats of infected children, typhoid vaccine from decomposed faecal material taken from typhoid victims and Salk polio serum from infected monkey kidneys and so on and so forth. This concentrated filth may make drug companies' balance sheets look rosey but I am already feeling a bit green around the gills just writing this sentence.

I must stress here that I am certainly not insinuating that either drug companies, doctors or government would deliberately endanger lives or would knowingly cause ill-health in the world by either altering or falsifying research. This certainly is not so. However, I have personally been long enough in this research business to realize that one can prove almost anything and get any kind of evidence one wants, determined principally by how the investigation has been loaded. Furthermore, quite a lot of so called 'scientific evidence' can be open to different forms of interpretation. Now taking doctors and drug companies for example, they obviously deal only with the scientific evidence which is most suitable for their purpose, just as I am concentrating on that scientific evidence which is most helpful for my line of research. So who is then telling the truth? I can't say anything else except that I certainly would always look cock-eyed at any statements which are contaminated either by commercial or political considerations. Besides pure commerce, there is also another reason why some folks, particularly many doctors of orthodox persuasion, often continue to support old-fashioned methods and ideas long after they have been subjected to criticism. It seems to stem from their compassionate need to show a united front to all outside influences, and where this 'rocking the boat of unity' or 'stepping out of line' is usually met by their other peers and colleagues by utmost disapproval, and sometimes even by complete rejection.

Now a few words about how a positive mental attitude can boost our immunity and overcome illness. This fairly recently acknowledged science of medicine has acquired the name of psycho-neuro-immunology or psycho-immunology.

Dr Paul Martin (272) writes: 'The notion that psychological stress makes us more likely to fall ill is at last beginning to be taken seriously. Even the most sceptical of scientists are having to admit that there is something in this idea, long enshrined in folklore. A new and rapidly developing field of research known as psycho-immunology, is uncovering ways in which the brain and immune system interact to influence our susceptibility to disease. . . . In Britain, the subject still tends to be regarded with suspicion, perhaps because it is often tarred with the same brush as psychosomatic medicine. Yet psycho-immunology differs fundamentally from psychosomatic medicine, which stems from the notion that certain diseases are caused solely by psychological, as opposed to "organic" factors. Psycho-immunology is based on the subtler idea that the brain influences the immune system, and therefore, our resistance to disease. . . . Psychological stress can elicit changes in the levels of many different hormones, neurotransmitters and neuromodulators, including growth hormone, insulin, vasopressin, testosterone, prolactin, adrenaline, noradrenaline, endorphins and enkephalins. Many of these substances also affect the immune system. Furthermore, there is mounting evidence that the cells of the immune system carry receptors on their surface that recognize various hormones and neurotransmitters. When the right substance binds to a receptor, it initiates a chain of events that alters the activity of the lymphocyte. In principle, then, psychological factors could influence the immune system via any or all of these chemical messengers.'

The Lancet (273) writes about depression, stress and immunity: 'There are neuronal pathways between the brain and the immune system. Lymphocyte production of and receptors for hormones suggest there is also an important two-way relation between the brain and the immune system, with hormones as the messengers. Thus immune changes may be mediated either by altered concentrations of corticosteroids, prostaglandins and opioid peptides, or by enhanced sympathetic activity, acting alone or in unison.'

Bartrop et al. (112) were able to demonstrate in their study a defective T-cell function in 26 recently bereaved individuals.

As seen above, no fancy language can hide the fundamental fact that a positive mental attitude is essential for both our mental and physical health. This in mind, any 'talking therapies' used as a treatment should always be positive and constructive, and should not, as often seems to happen, particularly in the mental health field, leave the poor patient quite impotent and unable to contribute anything positive to help his own plight. More often than not the poor blighter is first stripped of his own personality and neatly labelled as an anxiety neurotic, agoraphobic, manic depressive, personality disorder or some such gibberish, after which one 'expert' or another pompously informs the already bewildered individual that he is like he is because his mother didn't love him or because he was playing with himself when young. To cap it all, he is then shackled into a chemical straight-jacket and told not-to-ask-questions-and-keep-on-taking-the-tablets. A bewildering state of affairs, to say the least.

Another condition, so called 'non-organic disease' doesn't seem to receive much better response. The patient is usually told that 'it-is-all-in-the-mind'. This approach, yet again, doesn't leave the distressed patient any room to maneouvre whatsoever, as what on earth can one do with an illness which is 'all in the mind'? Not a lot. Then there is that 'psychosomatic brigade', which may be fair enough, but not yet good enough. The simple reason being that because this psychosomatic concept yet again stems from a notion that a disease is caused solely by psychological factors, which, yet again, leaves the poor soul to blame his tiny mind for the cause of his bewildering aches and pains, which must be quite frustrating. And finally, there are us ME sufferers, some with a 'proper virus' and some without, who at least have been given a permission by some medical men to rest under an umbrella of having a disease of 'an organic origin', however, vague.

Dr Ramsay, the foremost expert on ME emphasizes that patients with ME can be much helped by the knowledge that their persistent and vague complaints could have organic basis. What do we learn from this? No more, except that Dr Ramsay seems to have the art of psycho-neuro-immunology all buttoned up, as every patient likes to be believed and taken seriously by their doctor, whether they complain of 'non-organic' feeling of faintness or pain. The patient doesn't like to be told by their doctor when they are feeling like a dizzy corpse all warmed up, that there is nothing whatsoever wrong, except 'it-is-all-in-the-mind' or he is only suffering from a bout of anxiety neurosis, agoraphobia, personality disorder, so 'just-pull-yourself-together-and-keep-on-taking-the-tablets'. One tends to become frightfully dispirited after such a shoddy treatment and according to the science of psycho-neuro-immunology, the more dispirited one becomes, the less effective becomes one's immunity. One day the immune system might feel so dispirited and knackered that it just can't any more be bothered to keep non-activated enteroviruses, Epstein-Barr viruses or HIV viruses at bay and they become activated and before one knows what is what, the formerly dispirited agoraphobic with a personality disorder might just end up as an ME sufferer with a virus, or even die of AIDS.

Now what I think could be done about this distressing state of affairs is quite simple: I would like to suggest first of all, that all doctors should gradually start to acknowledge the existence of both non-antibody mediated allergies and Reactive Hypoglycaemia, both conditions being easily treated by the patient himself, following his doctor's sound nutritional advice. This would make the patient feel that he is able to participate in his own treatment, which is all positive. Secondly I would like to suggest that doctors could try to start to behave a bit less arrogantly and with less hostility towards anything mildly unorthodox and unconventional. Because whether one likes it or not, there is an alternative and drugless healing world out there, which no amount of abuse will destroy and which interestingly enough seems to become more and more popular as time goes by. It may be just that the success of this 'quack-brigade' stems from this new science of psycho-neuro-immunology, because, amongst other things, patients are usually given time, taken seriously and listened to, all of which can be very healing and comforting. Whatever the case, orthodox medics should stop harassing us alternative medics, because very sad but very true, there will be plenty of work for both approaches, until people come to their senses and stop treating their bodies as if they were some sort of banger vehicles, which can be driven as recklessly, fast or hard as one pleases, and when trouble looms, expect a medical man, whether an alternative or an orthodox, either to repair it, patch it up, or at worst, to sign a death certificate.

Our future king The Prince of Wales puts the whole sentiment in his speech to the British Medical Association's 150th Anniversary Dinner in 1983 by using the following words: 'I have often thought that one of the less attractive traits of various professional bodies and institutions is the deeply ingrained suspicion and outright hostility which can exist towards anything unorthodox or unconventional. I suppose that human nature is such that we are frequently prevented from seeing that what is taken for today's unorthodoxy is going to be tomorrow's convention. . . . Paracelsus believed that the good doctor's therapeutic success largely depends on his ability to inspire the patient with confidence and to mobilize his will to health. He constantly repeated the old adage "Nature heals, the doctor nurses", and it is well remembered that these sort of healers still treat the majority of patients throughout the world. I would suggest that the whole imposing edifice of modern medicine, for all its breathtaking successes is, like the celebrated Tower of Pisa, slightly off-balance. It is frightening how dependent upon drugs we are all becoming and how easy it is for doctors to prescribe them as the universal panacea for our ills. Wonderful as many of them are, it should still be more widely stressed by doctors that the health of human beings is so often determined by their behaviour, their food and the nature of their environment.' Thank you Prince Charles, one just couldn't wish for a more intelligent king.

Now briefly back to our enteroviruses, Epstein-Barr viruses, HIV viruses etc.

Leon Chaitow writes (259): 'That infection can result from externally arriving bacteria or virus is not contested, but that it can also arise spontaneously, in a suitably compromised body, is strongly suggested by the range of viral "infections" which exist, and the fact that these viruses, and many bacteria, can be found in obviously healthy individuals. Even the externally delivered infective agent, of whatever degree of virulency, will not produce infection as a matter of course, but only if the host is unable to contain its activities, and provides it with a suitable environment for replication.'

Harry Benjamin (84) puts the same sentiment into these following words: 'One would imagine, from the way the medical profession speak, that one tiny little germ or bacillus (countless thousands of which could scarcely cover the head of a pin) has only to enter the body of a healthy individual, for that individual to be stricken with some fell disease or another. Perhaps typoid. Perhaps cancer. And modern man goes around terrified out of his life because of the existence of these tiny creatures which he endows with such malevolent properties, and which he believes are always threatening him, and which only the most powerful microscope can reveal to his shuddering gaze. . . . What nonsense it all is. Our bodies are always full of germs and bacteria; they play a most important part in the working of the body, especially in the destructive processes. For constructive and destructive processes are always going on within the body, night and day, asleep or awake, whether we know it or not.'

So what should one do if a virus of any description has been found messing about in our bodies? The most sensible thing to do is to start to strengthen our immunity that it can in turn start to deal with the rebelling virus effectively. In my opinion poor nutrition is the commonest single factor for an inadequate immune system function. Therefore the first thing is to start to feed both ourselves and our immune system daily with good wholesome food, which must include a sufficient source of protein, whether animal or vegetable, combined with fresh vegetables, fruit, essential oils and clean water. Avoid also poisoning your immune system with drugs and stimulants, whether prescribed or non-prescribed, such as tranquillizers, repeated doses of antibiotics, alcohol, caffeine, tobacco etc. Particularly avoid refined sugars; because they have been found to hinder directly our immune system function in dealing with viruses and bacteria, as shown in an experiment conducted by Sanchez and his team (262). Keep your immune system healthy by exercising within your personal limits in the open air, as well as learning the art of relaxation. Avoid environmental pollution as much as you are able to, particularly polluted food and water. Avoid if you can such stressful procedures as vaccinations, immunizations, surgeries, anaesthetics etc. Since wholesome food grown in naturally mineralized soil is not easy to obtain, I would suggest that everyone should take for 'insurance purposes' a balanced vitamin and mineral supplementation daily, vitamin C and zinc being of particular importance. (274) And last, but not least, do try to keep a positive attitude, because feeling negative and dispirited can simply play havoc with your precious immunity.

15

ABF

I am now fully convinced that most chronic diseases, whether mental or physical are due to a lack of knowledge about the vital importance of a proper diet. I am convinced likewise that no chronic condition, whether mental or physical, has only one cause, but is usually the result of the following stressful events: nutritional deficiencies, polluted food, water and environment, toxic drugs and lack of sufficient exercise, rest and relaxation. I am also a firm believer that as brain cells are also cells and a part of the living organism, the malnutrition of these cells due to careless nutritional habits and the other factors mentioned above, also affect the working of the mind, leading to disordered behaviour, memory, perception, thinking and feeling. I would stick my neck out as far as to say that the majority of psychological problems may be only chemical problems, and once we are able to normalize the brain's biochemistry, all so called 'mentally ill' people would benefit. I would also say that whenever we are confronted with any mental or physical disorder of an 'unknown cause', we must always consider diet as a factor, because years of unnecessary suffering on the part of the patient is a terrible price to pay for a doctor's failure even to consider that simple possibility. Let's face it, you can't diagnose it unless you first consider it.

This nutritional approach is also safe, after all one of the rules of the Hippocratic Oath is: 'First do no harm'. And let's not forget either, that with the exception of stress, nutrition is the only factor which can be safely controlled in most diseases, therefore it certainly should be the number one target in all treatments. The basic rule should be; whenever in doubt, always try nutrition first. Furthermore, this approach should be adopted universally amongst the medical profession, because whenever doctors differ, the patients are the only ones who suffer.

Besides being safe, this nutritional approach is relatively inexpensive, as literally billions of pounds are being spent presently by pharmaceutical companies, who, in spite of enormous profits, still want more of the same, and by doing so, keep on using quite unethical animal experiments in trying to develop even more drugs for already saturated drug markets. I wouldn't mind so much if these drugs were safe, or even able to cure diseases, but as far as I can gather, after antibiotics came on the market during the last war years, most drugs invented since are only able to control the underlying symptoms to some degree, often at the cost of unpleasant and sometimes even dangerous side effects. Further billions of pounds are spent on umpteen double-blind- placebo - controlled- crossover - trials - with - matched-controls, which may then one day be published in some scientific journal, which is then left unread to gather dust in some vast medical archive or other. In fact I have never really understood this fervent desire and obsession with conducting these so called 'scientific proofs' or double-blind-matched-do-dahs, which are almost invariably conducted using groups of people. Fair enough, one might just about be able to match a child by sex, and even by school performance, which, let's face it, is already pretty doubtful, but when they start spouting that they have matched them by home background as well, I can't help but cringe. It would make perfect sense to me however, if these medical trials were conducted using the person tested as his or her own control, i.e. before and after the 'treatment procedure'. But let's be realistic, this would be far too cheap and simple, which just isn't proper science. And finally, still talking about the vast expense of modern medicine, at least as I see it, however much extra cash is injected into our beloved National Sickness Service, it seems to remain as insatiable as ever. The basic reason being that more people are sick today than ever before. In fact I read somewhere that with its £22 billion budget, the NHS is already twice as rich as Egypt, and more than four times as rich as Bangladesh. All in all, not only are we getting sicker, but our sickness is costing us a fortune, quite apart from the suffering in human and animal terms to which it is quite impossible to put a figure on. Besides the evergrowing plague of the usual chronic diseases, such as heart diseases, cancers, diabetes, respiratory diseases etc. also such ailments as mental illnesses, alcoholism, drug addictions and crime are at an all time high and seem to be increasing almost daily. More mentally defective children are born than ever before and looking at the growing number of elderly people sitting or lying out their last monotonous or agonizing days in our thousands of old people's homes, one wouldn't even view this alleged increase in the human life span with such unmitigated pride. Presently our hospitals, mental institutions, drug addiction centres and jails are overflowing, more are planned to be built, and even more seem to be needed. Quite a shocking state of affairs, you have got to admit.

As I am now a firm believer that the great majority of human ills are directly caused by inadequate nutrition, you just might like to know why I think we are eating so badly in the first place. I think that the primary reason is due to various vested interests, combined with our own approach to food. This latter suggestion was offered to me by my friend Jane, whilst we were strolling around the Surrey countryside and while I was racking my brains as to why particularly some British youths have been singled out as real troublemakers by our European cousins. Jane reminded me of the great differentiation betwen continental and British eating habits. The more I thought about it, the more convinced I became that she was talking sense. All one has to do, is to compare our lukewarm interest to food with that of our European neighbours, who seem to spend hours shopping for fresh ingredients, hours preparing the feast, and even more hours consuming it, usually complimented with lots of laughter, merriment and gallons of wine.

We Brits, on the other hand, generally don't seem to associate food with fun and festivity, therefore we tend either to drink or eat, both activities seldom going together, except during Xmas or such like. We usually go to our local pub to meet friends, to drink and have fun, and when we think that we have had enough of all three, we scurry back to our homes and to our boringly overcooked meats, vegetables boiled to a pulp, followed by a sweet and stodgy pud. The only fresh foods we may consume are either an occasional fruit or a salad, which usually consists of a limp and tired looking lettuce leaf languishing forlornly on a plate, accompanied by a dollop of salad cream.

In some cases food comes so far down on the list of life preferences, that one only thinks about it when practically half faint with hunger, which then means stuffing oneself at a moment's notice with some nosh, whether it means staggering to some take-away or jazzing up a tin of beans on the stove, or if lucky tossing some convenience food into a microwave. I must stress now that I am not talking here about Mrs Helen Humanoid and her family from Herts, but another human specimen known nowadays as Lager Louts who apparently scare the pants off ordinary peace-loving citizens by their rowdy and disgusting behaviour.

So what, I hear you say, has this meal picking got to do with loutish behaviour? In my opinion, a hell of a lot. Primarily because drinking alcohol while tucking into wholesome food is considered amongst these Lager Louts, if not sissy, at least a complete waste of good drinking time, I wouldn't be surprised one little bit if the majority of these troublemakers are suffering from serious vitamin and mineral deficiencies, coupled with a Reactive Hypoglycaemia, both known to be a cause of a myriad behavioural disorders, as described in my book in chapters 10 and 11. Now let's look at some concrete evidence: First of all Barbara Reed, a probation officer and author of an excellent book *Food, Teens and Behaviour* (137), after reviewing the diets of thousands of probationers found the following dietary pattern amongst the offenders:

1) No breakfast.
2) High consumption of sugar and other refined carbohydrates.
3) High consumption of processed foods.
4) Low consumption of lean proteins.
5) Low consumption of fresh fruits and vegetables, and finally
6) High milk consumption.

Dr Vicky Rippere (275) examined the diets of eight typical psychiatric patients, finding all diets sharing some of the following points:

1) Breakfast was either based on refined cereal products including sugar, or consisting solely of cups of stimulant drinks, or was non-existent.
2) These people eat very little, if any, fresh fruits and vegetables.
3) Apart from alcohol, the only beverages were coffee, tea, coke and other sweetened artificial drinks.
4) Refined sugar was the major dietary stable.
5) Diets contained very little fibre, if any.
6) For several, alcohol provided most of the day's calories.
7) The main meal of the day was usually taken in the evening, when it is of least use in providing energy for the day's activities.
8) Processed foods containing many chemical additives played a disproportionate role for many.
9) The diets were restricted to a small number of convenience foods consumed repetitively.
10) The diets were deficient in major sources of essential nutrients, such as vitamins, minerals, essential fatty acids and high grade protein.
11) The diets which contained solid food tended to contain much saturated fat.

You have to admit that there are more similarities than differences between these diets which eventually lead a person into the arms of the law or a psychiatrist.

I think that the ancient proverb *mens sana in corpore sano* or 'a sound mind in a sound body' is just as relevant today as when it was first invented. So even though we have now come up in the world by learning to fly, built massive atomic reactors and ever so complicated computers, and even clambered briefly on top of the moon, our own brain seems to be still as backward as it was thousands of years ago because we seem to only be able to think straight with the aid of undercooked cabbage and a load of old lentils. So if we want to avoid seeing young Kevin in the nick, or ourselves waiting to be drugged up to our eyeballs by some shrink, it looks as if we had better take heed and sort out our diet a bit sharpish. We should also take heed and look carefully at what we eat, or don't eat, if we happen to suffer from some other chronic condition such as a dicky heart, breathing problems, digestive disorders, arthritic pains, sugar regulatory disorders and so on and so forth.

So why don't doctors advise us about diet? As I said before, the study of medicine is a study of medicine, not a study of old lentils, and as far as I can gather, this multidisciplinary science of nutrition is far too vast a subject to be included in an already crowded medical curriculum, which in my opinion is quite wrong.

The Lancet (276) discusses nutrition in medical education in the United States, mentioning the 1975 survey which indicated that both doctors as well as medical students gleaned most of their knowledge of nutrition from the popular press, which was not surprising, since most medical schools gave nutrition education a low priority, as only about fifteen out of 143 medical schools in US and Canada list courses in nutrition as a graduation requirement. The suggestion to include nutritional education into medical discipline was met by one influential physician with the following statement: 'There are all kinds of worthwhile interests like nutrition that well-intentioned people want to include in medical education. However, it is difficult to find space and time to satisfy these people. It is simply impossible to fit everything in.'

This in the United States, but what about the United Kingdom? A booklet called *Nutrition in Medical Education – Report of the British Nutrition Foundation's Task Force on Clinical Nutrition* (277) points out that nutrition, once a minor speciality, can now be seen as a major force both in the prevention and management of many present day diseases and in the promotion of health. In many public health problems today the role of nutrition has become the subject of much long-term academic research.

Doctors need to be aware of this and training should therefore include some experience in assessing these important research areas. It is also essential that the training of doctors today should reflect the current climate where the prevention of disease and the promotion of health are recognized as being of increasing importance.

The lifestyles which we lead, including the type and amount of food which we eat, are now generally accepted to play an important role in the disease seen in today's society. Nevertheless, until now in the doctor's training, much of the emphasis on diet has been placed on the treatment of disease and on convalescence rather than on prevention.

The general practitioner, who is generally regarded by the public as the irrefutable authority on matters relating to health, is likely to be faced with increasing requests for information on eating in relation to health, in the light of increasing consumer curiosity about nutrition and the proliferation of various health fads involving nutrition. It is recommended therefore that general practitioner training should emphasize more strongly the importance of nutrition. It is also recommended that there should be closer associations, both in research and teaching, between academic centres of research in nutrition, which are not directly associated with medicine, and the medical schools.

In conclusion, it is suggested that there is a need for the Royal Colleges, either singly but preferably jointly, to appoint a working party to review the present scope for education in nutrition to students and junior doctors, and a need to strengthen academic departments to enable more research and teaching in nutrition to be organized. I can't but agree wholeheartedly with all that has been said, but what bugs me, is that ever since that report was written in 1983, the vital role of nutrition in the prevention of disease and the promotion of better health seems to have been utterly ignored by the majority of doctors and the government alike. One has to only glance through a shortened version of the government's latest white paper on the subject named *Promoting Better Health* (278) to see what I mean. All the paper points out is that as general practitioners are in the best position to promote good health and prevent ill-health, therefore it proposes to pay a special fee to encourage doctors to provide health checks on patients registered for the first time with an NHS doctor. It also considers incentives to achieve specified target levels of vaccination and immunization, as well as to clarify doctor's role in the provision of health promotion services and the prevention of ill-health. This is all very amicable, but if doctors are not acquainted with nutritional sciences, how on earth can we expect them to be able to promote better health, let alone to prevent illness?

In my opinion we are faced with this sorry state of affairs only for one single reason: profit. Let's face it, there is neither glamour, glory, nor profit in preventive medicine. First of all the pharmaceutical industry seems to have a mighty say in modern medical education, and as long as they are in charge, preventive medicine will have no place whatsoever in medical curriculum. Except of course vaccination and immunization procedures because they bring in loads of money. Secondly; as far as our nutritional habits are concerned, the mighty food industry seems to be entirely in charge and as long as they are able to persuade us through their massive advertising, that all the worldly goodness can be found in a packet of potato crisps, not in a sack of ordinary spuds, both costing damned near the same, they are laughing all the way to the bank. The mighty food industry also promotes and finances most nutrition research both here in England and in the United States, the published results naturally being hardly ever unfavourable to the financing host. All in all the complexity and the power of the food industry is simply enormous.

One only has to read Geoffrey Cannon's book *The Politics of Food* (279) to be able to appreciate why the food industry is able to play continually Russian roulette with the health of our nation and nobody can do a damned thing to prevent it. I suggest that anyone interested in this wicked subject should read the book above, or alternatively *The Food Scandal* (280), the co-author being Caroline Walker. Both these books consist of the following message: Private wealth seems to come before public health, as only food that is good for you goes bad quickly, which means that it is bad for business. Therefore artificial additives are used to prolong shelf life and to increase profits. Unfortunately however, this long shelf life leads to a shortened human life. Additionally as a general rule, the worse a food is for your health, the more money seems to be spent on advertising it. And finally, the present food policy seems to be primarily controlled by civil servants working in harmony with the food giants. So now we know. Will all guilty parties kindly stand up now please. Thank you.

The Lancet (281) writes under the heading 'Britain Needs a Food and Health Policy: The Government must face its Duty': 'Never since the Dig for Victory campaign in the 1939–45 war has Britain experienced such public awareness as it now displays of the importance of food to health. Despite this attention among its citizens its Government has of late produced little in the form of a national policy for healthier eating. The ministers responsible often seem reluctant to face their duty, which undoubtedly includes the promotion of wiser eating habits. As the Faculty of Community Medicine has lately reminded the country, Britain's mortality and morbidity statistics for such diseases as coronary insufficiency, diet related cancers, and obesity make dismal comparisons with those of other industrialized countries. The National Food Survey (an outstanding example of how to compile national data on consumption) continues to identify the British diet as one of the least likely, among intakes of comparable countries, to promote health and longevity. . . . The signs of Government reluctance to promote health through better diet run against the Department of Health's own evidence.

In the spring of this year the Department published an analysis of schoolchildren's diets. The study was commissioned after the Government removed in 1980 the legal requirement to provide school meals of prescribed nutritional standards. The data were published after public criticism of delay in their emergence. The findings show that ten to fifteen year olds in Britain consumed large amounts of cakes, biscuits, crisps and chips. Over 70% of boys and 80% of girls ate more than 35% of their energy as fat, and many children were below the recommended levels of most vitamins and minerals. Despite the scientific uncertainties which abound, the Government could, on the evidence available, adopt a less ambiguous stance. The vested interests which gain from the Government's recent reticence are a shrinking section of the food industry, but they are still influential. A first step would be to identify healthy eating as the responsibility of a single Minister. At present it is orphaned, passed to and fro between MAFF and DHSS, neither of them admitting or seeking responsibility. The Minister for Health seems the most appropriate owner of this charge. He could establish an interdepartmental committee to promote liaison. A national food and health policy should be developed identifying the Government's co-ordinating responsibility between all areas of national policy which affect food consumption. Most urgently, the Government should produce and promote national dietary guidelines, scientifically acceptable to the professions concerned and expressed in as precise terms as possible, which can then be interpreted, for the benefit of the public, in official pronouncements in newspapers and magazines, on radio and television, and in other ways. A regular view of such guidelines would then be instituted, and the responsible Minister would prepare and publish an annual report on the state of the national diet and the operation of his food and health policy.

So what about it Prime Minister? And while you are at it, nutrition education should be incorporated into all medical schools, as well as seeing that good dietary principles are observed in all schools, hospitals and local authority establishments, instead of the greasy stuff lolling around slimy vegetables boiled to a pulp, followed by a stodge pud, which they call food, and which seems to be pretty characteristic of most institutional catering establishments. Furthermore, instead of withdrawing school meals, the Government should make sure that all school kids have access to the healthiest fodder possible, because like it or not, those kids are our future, and if their brains and behaviour gets all screwed up because of malnutrition, it looks as if we have only ourselves to blame. Present evidence also indicates that whether our Kevin ends up in front of a judge, or as one, depends a lot on his ability to differentiate between health promoting foods and junk foods, therefore a basic nutritional education should be incorporated at an early age into all school curricula.

And last but not least, can the Government enlighten me, why is it that chemical-free, wholesome organically grown food, which tastes good and is good, is more difficult to obtain than nuggets of gold? I find this a pretty crazy state of affairs, to say the least, as I want organically grown food, you want organically grown food and Mrs Bloggs wants organically grown food. But nobody is getting any, because farmers are forced to flood their produce with all sorts of toxic agri-chemicals, which get more and more potent as the years go by, because bugs get resistant to the old ones. They must do this because they apparently need to produce as much food as possible, which nobody really wants and which then ends up stored at great expense on top of already colossal Euromountains of already existing produce. I think the people responsible for this madness should have their heads tested for two reasons. First of all, because all life on our planet is sustained only by a mere dozen inches of soil cover, we should lovingly cherish it, not negligently poison it entirely with these dreaded toxins. Furthermore, Europe covered with a wine lake and surrounded by cereal, butter and meat mountains will look a bit odd. In my opinion, what governments should do, instead of subsidizing farmers to produce food which nobody seems to want, they should subsidize farmers to wean their land off these frightful chemicals so that farmers could then start to produce wholesome organic food which everyone wants. In order to achieve that, the Government should at long last revise its national food policy, which would only encourage whole, fresh and organically grown food and discourage the rubbish we are presently forced to masticate. If I understand right, our Government is all for profit and self-sufficiency, and what is more profitable and self-sufficient than a farmer growing good and wholesome crops, which is good for him and for the rest of the world.

Sir Robert McCarrison (232) one of the greatest physicians of this century and a pioneer of nutritional medicine and 'father' of the McCarrison Society lectured in 1936: 'If I have convinced you of the fundamental importance of food in relation to public health, it will become obvious that one of the most urgent problems of our time is how to ensure that each member of the community shall receive a diet that will satisfy his or her physiological needs. It is clear that to achieve this much-to-be-desired end, many barriers, poverty, unemployment, apathy, ignorance, prejudice and habit, must be surmounted and many interests, agricultural, industrial and economic, readjusted. It is for us so to instruct ourselves that we may use our newer knowledge to end that customs and prejudices may be broken and more adequate diets secured for those under our care. A subject that is an integral part of preventive medicine must in future be given a place in the medical curriculum commensurate with its importance. . . . The continued use of properly constituted food, from the earliest period of development throughout life, is the surest means we have acquiring and maintaining that necessary condition of the body: good health.'

Naturopath Harry Benjamin (84) wrote in 1936: 'All forms of disease are due to the same cause, namely, the accumulation in the system of waste materials and bodily refuse, which has been steadily piling up in the body of the individual concerned throughout years of wrong habits of living, the chief of these being wrong feeding, improper care of the body, and habits tending to set up enervation and nervous exhaustion, such as worry, overwork, excesses and abuses of all kinds . . . '

Both these great men seem to emphasize that a lack of properly constiuted food is the single main cause for both mental and physical ill-health. Time must have simply leapt by, as now, fifty years later, most modern ills are not supposed to be caused by the lack of properly constituted food, but by the shortage of doctors, research, nurses, hospital beds, tranquillizers, transplant organs, kidney machines etc. That, I suppose, is what is called progress.

Because this book is meant to be primarily about mental health issues, I feel obliged at least to finish it with mental health issues: As it happened, last night I was watching a programme on TV where all sorts of folk and sundry were arguing about what to do with all those thousands of mentally ill patients now when most large mental institutions have been either closed, transformed into proper prisons, demolished, or just locked up, leaving the poor blighters outside to fend for themselves the best they can. The usual motley crew took part; the distressed carers, the medical mafia, police, prison and other government officials, and finally the so called 'users', or people, who at some time in their lives have been accused of suffering from schizophrenia and such like. The actual tirade went on for yonks, but the very gist of things sounded to me as follows: Some carers wanted firmer and clearer diagnostic labelling, some carers wanted more knowledge about these illnesses, but all wanted more individual support and funds for better community care facilities, some with treatment orders, and some without.

The medical mafia naturally wanted more money for further research. The police in turn felt that they already have quite enough on their plate without needing to take care of vagrant schizophrenics as well. Whereas prison officers were peeved because prison places needed for proper criminals are presently filled with the mentally ill. And as always, while this mêlée was going on, the hoarse voices of present government officials could be heard bleating at frequent intervals how everything must be just hunky-dory, because everyone has already been given so much money 'in real terms' that it is just unbelievable, which nobody naturally believed. The accused mentally ill in turn didn't wish to be labelled nor locked up, but helped and cared for just like any other individuals experiencing distress.

While this mad palaver was going on, I thought fondly of Dr Pfeiffer and his Princeton Brain Bio Centre in New Jersey, where, until his death on 18 November 1988, he saw over 1000 patients a year, rehabilitating 85% of those institutionallized for various mental illnesses using simple nutritional intervention and counselling. During his forty years of research he and his research team identified several biochemical causes for various mental illnesses which include: Histadelia (genetic overproduction of histamine), Copper and other heavy metal toxicities, Pyrolyria (combined zinc and vitamin B6 deficiency), Brain Allergies (usually milk, wheat or corn), Histapenia (low blood histamine with an excess of copper), Reactive Hypoglycaemia, Folic acid/B12 deficiency, Drug intoxications, Hypothyroidism, Chronic Candida infection etc. To date over 200 articles of their research results have been published throughout the world in leading journals. Dr Pfeiffer is also the author of many books which include *Mental and Elemental Nutrients* (123) and *Mental Illness and Schizophrenia* (239). Whenever this great man came to lecture here in England, this middle-aged groupie followed him like a shadow. There was I found sitting always on the front row, hanging on his every spoken word as though my life would depend on them. In my opinion he was the greatest and most humane scientist of this century. When I heard about his death, my entire world just seemed to fall apart. All I can do now is to pray that his work will not be forgotten and that before long everyone who has had the misfortune to be labelled as suffering from a mental illness of any description, will have the possibility of being treated by Dr Pfeiffer's simple but effective methods of Biochemical Psychiatry.

Dr Pfeiffer writes: (123) '"Wastebasket diagnoses" abound in medicine and psychology. The excuse often given by the medical and psychological fraternities is that a label on the patient saves the patient's (or his parents') money in that they don't go shopping around among doctors for a cure that doesn't exist. However, the search for more effective treatment should never be relaxed by patient, parent or doctor. Biological science is at best only a progress report, so that the "wastebasket" of today maybe the goldmine of tomorrow. . . . Clinical diagnoses such as minimal brain damage, learning disability, neurological deficit, mental retardation, schizophrenia, neurosis, psychosis, maladjustment reaction, autism, emotional disorder, alcoholism, drug addiction, schizoid, juvenile delinquency and senility can all be wastebaskets. . . . Psychiatric diagnoses are only diagnoses of elimination. In the well-studied mental patient, the internist and radiologist and neurologist apply all the tests they know as of the present time. If all are negative they may suggest psychiatric help. . . . One must always ask the individual who makes a 'psychogenic' diagnosis (diagnosis of elimination) this question: What, in your handling of a thousand such cases, would make you state positively that one case was not of psychogenic origin? This positive yardstick is applied constantly by the inquiring scientist and should be used more often in medicine. At present there probably isn't a Freudian psychiatrist (or psychologist) who could give a valid and scientifically acceptable answer to this simple question.'

I can't but agree with Dr Pfeiffer. However, on the other hand I have always found it mighty strange that whenever we feel out of sorts, we are expected to cart our mind and body around to be presented to 'a medical expert' for assessment, 'labelling' and medication. Surely our own health, whether mental or physical, is so personally precious, that whenever it shows any signs of failing, instead of relying on strangers, we should be in possession of enough basic knowledge to take care of ourselves. The first step of course being an adequate knowledge of Nutritional Medicine.

BIBLIOGRAPHY

Besides Dr Pfeiffer's work, I have found the following books excellent value:

Belinda Barnes and Suzanne Gail Bradley: *Planning for a Healthy Baby: Essential Reading for all Future Parents.* (Ebury Press, 1990)

Leon Chaitow: *Vaccination and Immunization: Dangers, Delusions and Alternatives. (What Every Parent Should Know.)* (C W Daniel Co, 1987)

Belinda Barnes and Irene Colquhoun: *The Hyperactive Child: What the Family can do.* (Thorsons, 1984)

Barbara Reed: *Food, Teens and Behaviour.* (Natural Press, USA, 1983)

Alexander Schauss: *Diet, Crime and Delinquency – New Breakthrough to Crime Control.* (Parker House, USA, 1981)

Dr Stephen Davies and Dr Alan Stewart: *Nutritional Medicine – The Drug-free Guide to Better Health.* (Pan Books, 1987)

Dr Theron Randolph and Ralph Moss: *Allergies, Your Hidden Enemy. How the New Field of Clinical Ecology can Unravel the Environmental Causes of Mental and Physical Illness.* (Thorsons, 1981)

Dr Richard Mackarness: *Not All in the Mind – How Unsuspected Food Allergy Can Affect Your Body and Mind.* (Pan Books 1990)

Dr. Jonathan Brostoff and Linda Gamlin: *The Complete Guide to Food Allergy and Intolerance.* (Bloomsbury, 1989)

Dr Keith Mumby: *The Food Allergy Plan – A Working Doctor's Self-help Guide to New Medical Discoveries.* (Unwin, 1985)

Dr Vicky Rippere: *The Allergy Problem: Why People Suffer and What Should be Done.* (Thorsons, 1983)

Paavo Airola: *Hypoglycaemia: A Better Approach.* (Health Plus Publishers, Phoenix, AZ, USA, 1977)

Martin Budd: *Low Blood Sugar (Hypoglycaemia) – The 20th Century Epidemic?* (Thorsons, 1981)

Shirley Trickett: *Coming off Tranquillizers – A withdrawal Plan Which Really Works.* (Thorsons, 1986)

Dr Michael Lesser: *Nutrition and Vitamin Therapy: The dietary Treatment of Mental and Emotional Ill-health.* (Thorsons, 1985)

Jacqueline Steincamp: *Overload: Beating ME.* (Fontana/ Collins, 1989)

Leon Chaitow and Simon Martin: *A World Without AIDS – The Controversial Holistic Health Plan.* (Thorsons, 1988)

Dr Melwyn Werbach: *Nutrition Influences on Illness – A Sourcebook of Clinical Research.* (Thorsons, 1989)

Edward Goldsmith, Nicholas Hildyard, Peter Bunyard and Patrick McCully: *5000 Days to Save the Planet.* (Hamlyn, 1990)

USEFUL ADDRESSES

Many of the following organizations are charities relying entirely on membership fees and donations to carry on with their useful work. Therefore if you write to any of them for information, please remember to enclose an SAE with your enquiry to keep down administration costs. More members always welcome.

AAA (Action Against Allergy)
Greyhound House,
23/24 George Street,
Richmond, Surrey TW9 1JY

To promote the study of the causative role of food and chemicals in chronic illness.

Advisory Committee on Pollution of the Sea,
3 Endsleigh Street,
London WC1H ODD

'Ark'
498-500 Harrow Road,
London W9 3QA

Popular mass movement working to protect life and the natural environment.

Biolab Medical Unit,
The Stone House,
9 Weymouth Street,
London W1N 3FF

A biochemical test laboratory. Requests for testing must be referred by a doctor.

The Biosocial Therapy Association
115 Hampstead Way,
Hampstead Garden Suburb,
London NW11 7JN

To promote the study of the causative role of food and chemicals on crime
and delinquency.

The British Association for Counselling,
37a Sheep Street,
Rugby
Warwickshire CV21 3BX

The British Association of Psychotherapists,
121 Hendon Lane,
London N3 3PR

British Trust for Conservation Volunteers,
36 St Mary's Street,
Wallington,
Oxon OX10 OEU

Campaigns to involve the public in practical conservation activity, particularly urban clean ups and countryside conservation.

The Body Shop

These shops are found world-wide and they specialize in natural beauty,
skin and hair products.

CLEAR
3 Endsleigh Street
London WC1H ODD

Campaigns for lead-free air.

Council for the Protection of Rural England
4 Hobart Place,
London SW1W OHY

Campaigns to protect the countryside.

The Environmental Medicine Foundation
Symonsbury House,
Bridport,
Dorset DT6 6HB

Research into and treatment of illness caused by environmental factors.

Foresight – The Association for the Promotion of Pre-conceptual Care,
The Old Vicarage,
Church Lane,
Witley,
Godalming,
Surrey GU8 5PN

The association has been formed to see that all possible steps are taken to ensure that every baby enters the world free from congenital deformity and mental damage and in perfect health.

Friends of the Earth,
26-28 Underwood Street,
London N1 7JU

Campaigns to protect the environment and to promote sustainable alternatives with the help of local and national groups.

The Green Party,
10 Station Parade,
Balham High Road,
London SW12 9AZ

Greenpeace
30-31 Islington Green,
London N1 8XE

Campaigns against pollution through lobbying and non-violent protests.

HAGS – The Hyperactive Children's Support Group,
71 Whyke Lane,
Chichester,
West Sussex PO19 2LD

The aims of the Group are to help and support hyperactive children and their parents, to conduct research and promote investigation into the incidence of hyperactivity, its causes and treatments, and to disseminate information concerning this condition.

Here's Health,
Victory House,
Leicester Place,
London WC2H 7BP

A monthly magazine available in bookshops and health-food shops which is committed to alternative or holistic medicine, which treats people rather than disease. It recognizes that given the chance the body will heal itself.

The Institute for Complementary Medicine
21 Portland Place,
London W1N 3AF

Runs public information points on alternative and complementary medicine practitioners.

The Institute for Optimum Nutrition
5 Jerdan Place,
London SW6 1BE

The institute trains nutritionists. It runs short courses and seminars for anybody interested in nutrition. It also offers nutritional treatment advice.

Journal of Alternative and Complementary Medicine
Mariner House,
53A High Street,
Bagshot,
Surrey GU19 5AH

This monthly magazine is for practitioners of all forms of healing who subscribe to the belief that a person cannot be divided into parts and must be treated as a whole.

Larkhall Laboratories,
225 Putney Bridge Road,
London SW15 2PY.

Sells dietary products and has a Nutrition Centre for cytoxic testing for food allergies.

Living Earth,
10 Upper Grosvenor Street
London W1X 9PA

Promotes conservation of the rainforests through education and discussion in schools and with the public.

The London Food Commission
88 Old Street,
London EC1V 9AR

Promotes better food.

Marine Conservation Society,
9 Gloucester Road,
Ross-on-Wye,
Herefordshire HR9 5BU

Protection of the marine environment through research and lobbying.

The McCarrison Society for Nutrition and Health
24 Paddington Street,
London W1M 4DR

The Society which is named after Sir Robert McCarrison (1887-1960) aims to bring together professional workers who share their views on the fundamental importance of Nutrition and Health.

ME Action Campaign,
PO Box 1126,
London W3 ORY

The policy of the ME Action Campaign is to research and investigate useful treatments and therapies, whether orthodox or alternative, which are beneficial to ME sufferers.

MIND – The National Association for Mental Health,
22 Harley Street,
London W1N 2ED

MIND is concerned with extending the services available to the mentally ill and providing support and advice. It also has a network of local groups.

Myalgic Encephalomyelitis Association (ME Association)
PO Box 8,
Stanford-le-Hope,
Essex SS17 8EX

The prime aim of the ME Association is to raise funds for further research and to offer ME sufferers support and local meetings.

The National Anti-Fluoridation Campaign,
36 Station Road,
Thames Ditton,
Surrey KT17 ONS

The National Society for Clean Air,
136 North Street,
Brighton BN1 1RG

Campaigns for clean air and noise reduction.

The Natural Medicines Society,
Edith Lewis House,
Back Lane,
Ilkeston,
Derbyshire DE7 8EJ

The Society was formulated to protect the future of licensed natural medicines and to inform and educate the Government and general public of the value and worth of natural medicines.

Parenets For Safe Food,
Britannia House,
1-11 Glenthorne Road,
Hammersmith,
London W6

Non-profit making organization promoting improvement, safety and quality of our food.

The Research Council of Complementary Medicine,
Fifth Floor
60 Great Ormond Street,
London WC1 3HR

Promotes alternative and complementary medical research.

The Royal Society for Nature Conservation,
The Green,
Nettleham,
Lincoln LN2 2NR

Manages nature reserves and promotes conservation awareness in local communities.

The Royal Society for the Prevention of Cruelty to Animals,
The Causeway,
Horsham,
West Sussex RH12 1HG

The Royal Society for the Protection of Birds,
The Lodge,
Sandy,
Bedfordshire SG19 2DL

'Sanity'
Robina,
The Chase,
Ashley,
Dorset BH24 2AN

A voluntary organization to raise funds to further research into the nutritional and biochemical factors in mental illness.

The Schizophrenia Association of Great Britain,
Bryn Hyfryd,
The Crescent,
Bangor LL57 2AG
Gwynedd,
Wales.

The Association supports research into the genetics of schizophrenia and biological psychiatry with the help of the Biochemistry Department of the University College of North Wales.

Society for Environmental Therapy,
521 Foxall Road,
Ipswich,
Suffolk IPS 8LW

A scientific society dedicated to discovering the environmental causes of disease and to low technology medicine. Membership is open for both lay people and doctors.

The Soil Association,
86 Colston Street,
Bristol BS1 5BB.

The Soil Association promotes organic farming and the reduction of pesticide usage.

Sustainability,
31 Cambridge Road,
Barnes,
London SW13 OPE

An environmental communications company.

Tidy Britain Group,
The Pier,
Wigan WN3 4EX.

Government agency and registered charity acting to control litter.

Transport 2000,
Walkden House,
10 Melton Street,
London NW1 2EJ.

Lobbies central and national government for a transport policy which protects natural resources and provides decent public transport facilities.

TRANX – National Tranquillizer Advice Centre
25a Masons Avenue,
Wealdstone,
Harrow,
Middlesex HA3 5AH

TRANX supports and advises people on how best to withdraw from tranquillizing medication.

Wholefood,
24 Paddington Street,
London W1M 4DR

This shop specializes in whole foods and organically grown meat. It also has a well-stocked book shop on subjects of nutrition and alternative and complementary medicine.

The World Wide Fund for Nature,
Panda House,
Weyside Park,
Godalming,
Surrey GU7 1XR

Conservation of natural resources in the UK and abroad.

York Medical and Nutritional Laboratory,
Tudor House, Suite 2,
Lysander Close,
North York Trading Estate,
Clifton,
York YO3 8XB.

A biochemical test laboratory including cytoxic testing for allergies.

Zoocheck,
Cherry Tree Cottage,
Dorking,
Surrey RH5 6HA.

Animal charity pledged to investigate and monitor the suffering of animals in zoos.

REFERENCES

1. Payne J. *All in the Mind* MIND publications, 1976
2. Gould D. *The Medical Mafia* Sphere Books Ltd. 1985
3. Kendell R.E. The stability of psychiatric diagnoses. *Brit. J. Psychiatry*, 124: 352–356, 1974
4. Kaelbling R. and Volpe P.A. Constancy of psychiatric diagnoses in re-admissions. *Comp. Psychiatry*, 4: 29–38, 1963
5. Odegaad O. An official diagnostic classification in actual hospital practice. *Acta Psychiatrica Scandinavica*, 42: 329–337, 1966
6. Barbigian H.M. Gardner E.A. Miles H.C. and Romano J. Diagnostic consistency and change in a follow-up study of 1215 patients. *Am. J. Psychiatry*, 121: 895–901, 1965
7. Cooper J.E. Diagnostic change in a longitudinal study of psychiatric patients. *Brit. J. Psychiatry*, 113: 129–142, 1967
8. Cheraskin E. **The Name of the Game is the Name.** *A Physician's Handbook on Orthomolecular Medicine.* Eds: R.J. Williams and D.K. Kalita, Keats Publishing Inc. 1977
9. Crook W.G. *The Yeast Connection.* Professional Books, Jackson, Tennessee 38302, 1983
10. Mackarness R. *Chemical Victims.* Pan Books, 1980
11. Marks I. and Lader M. Anxiety States (Anxiety Neurosis):A review. *The J. of Nerv. and Ment. Dis.* Vol 156, No 1: 3–18, 1973
12. Cohen M.E. and White P.D. Life situations, emotions and neuro-circulatory asthenia. (Anxiety Neurosis, Neurasthenia, Effort Syndrome.) *A Res. Nerv. and Ment. Dis. Proc.* 29: 832–896, 1950
13. Hardonk H.J. and Beumer H.M. Hyperventilation Syndrome. *Handbook of Clinical Neurology*, Eds: P.J. Vinken and G.W. Buen Vol 38, 309–360, 1979
14. Harper M. and Roth M. Temporal lobe epilepsy and the phobic anxiety depersonalization syndrome. Part I: Comparative Study. *Comprehensive Psychiatry*, Vol 3, No 3: 129–151, 1962
15. Magarian G.J. Hyperventilation syndromes: Infrequently recognized common expressions of anxiety and stress. *Medicine*, Vol 61 No 4: 219–236, 1982
16. Da Costa J.M. On irritable heart: a clinical study of a form of functional cardiac disorder and its consequences. *Am. J. Med. Sci.* 61: 17–52, 1871
17. Wood P. *DaCosta's syndrome (or effort syndrome).* Brit. Med. J. 24 May, 767–773, 1941
18. Wheeler E.O. et al. Neurocirculatory Asthenia (Anxiety Neurosis, Effort Syndrome, Neurasthenia). *J.A.M.A.* 142: 878–888, 1950
19. Herman S.P. Stickler G.B. and Lucas A.R. *Hyperventilation syndrome in children and adolescents: Long-term follow-up.* Paediatrics, Vol 67, No 2: 183–187, 1981

20. Westphal C. Die Agoraphobie: Eine neuropatische Erscheinung. *Archiv fur Psychiatrie und Nervenkrankenheiten*, 3: 138–161, 1871
21. Benedikt V. 'Uber Platzschwindel.' *Allgemeine Wiener Medizinische Zeitung*, 15: 488, 1870
22. Fenichel O. *Psychoanalytic Theory of Neurosis*. Norton, New York, 1945
23. Goldstein A.J. and Chambless D.L. A re-analysis of Agoraphobia. *Beh. Ther.* 9: 47–59, 1978
24. Burns L.E. and Thorpe G.L. Fears and Clinical Phobias: Epidemiological aspects and the National Survey of agoraphobics. *J. Int. Res.* 5, Supplement (1), 132-139, 1977
25. Hove G. *Schizophrenia: A fresh Approach* David and Charles, 1986
26. Rosenhan D.L. On being sane in insane places. *Science*, Vol 179: 250–258, 19 January 1973
27. Marshal H.E.S. Incidence of physical disorders among psychiatric in-patients. *Brit. Med. J.* 468–470, 27 August 1949
28. Herridge C.F. Physical disorders in psychiatric illness. *The Lancet*, 949–951, 29 October 1960
29. Maguire G.P. and Granville-Grossman K.L. Physical illness in psychiatric patients. *Brit. J. Psychiatry*, 115: 1365–1369, 1968
30. Comroe B. Follow-up study of 100 patients diagnosed as 'neurosis' *J. Nerv. Ment. Dis.* 83: 679–684, 1936
31. Hall R.C.W., Gardner E.R., Stickney S.K., LeCann A.F. and Popkin M.K. Physical illness manifesting as psychiatric disease. *Arch Gen. Psychiatry*, Vol 37: 989-995, September 1980
32. Bonn J.A., Redhead C.P.A. and Timmons B.H. Enhanced adaptive behavioural response in agoraphobic patients pretreated with breathing retraining. *The Lancet*, 665–669, 22 September 1984
33. Garssen B, Venendaal W. and Bloemink R. Agoraphobia and the Hyperventilation Syndrome. *Beh. Res. Ther.* Vol 21, No 6: 643–649, 1983
34. Hibbert G.A. Hyperventilation as a cause of panic attacks. *Brit. Med. J.* Vol 288: 263–264, 28 January 1984
35. Lazarus H.R. and Kostan J.J. Psychogenic hyperventilation and death anxiety. *Psychosomatics*, Vol 10: 14–23, January/February 1969
36. Lum L.C. The syndrome of habitual chronic hyperventilation. *Modern Trends in Psychosomatic Medicine*, Vol III, Ed: O. Hill, Butterworth, 1976
37. Lum L.C. Hyperventilation and anxiety state. *J. of The Royal Soc. of Med.* Vol 74, January 1981
38. Pitts F.N. and McClure J.N. Lactate metabolism in anxiety neurosis. *New Engl. J. Med.* Vol 277, No 25: 1329-1336, 1967
39. Wendel O.W. and Beebe W.E. Glycolytic activity in schizophrenia. *Orthomolecular Psychiatry*, Eds: D. Hawkins and L. Pauling, W.H. Freeman & Co., San Francisco, 1973
40. Lum L.C. Respiratory alkalosis and hypocarbia: The role of carbon dioxide in the body economy. *The Chest, Heart and Stoke Journal*, Vol 3, No 4, Winter, 1978/79
41. Roberts K.E., Poppell J.W., Randall H.T., and Vanamee P. Respiratory Alkalosis. *Ann. N.Y. Acad. Sci.* 66: 955–965, 1957

42. Lum L.C. *Personal communication.*
43. Bell G.H., Emslie-Smith D. and Paterson C.R. *Textbook of Physiology* Churchill Livingstone, 1980
44. Huckabee W.E. Relationships of pyruvate and lactate during anaerobic metabolism. II: Exercise and formation of 02-dept. *J. Clin. Inv.* 37: 255-263, 1957
45. Eichenholz A. Mulhausen R.O. Anderson W.E. and MacDonald R.M. Primary hypocapnia: A cause of metabolic acidosis. *J. Applied Physiology*, 17: 283–288, 1962
46. Huckabee, W.E. Relationships of pyruvate and lactate during anaerobic metabolism. I: Effects of infusion of pyruvate or glucose and of hyperventilation. *J. Clin. Inv.* 37: 244–254, 1957
47. Frommer J.P. Lactic Acidosis. *Medical Clinics of North America*, Vol 67, No 4: 815-829, 1983
48. Bueding E. and Goldfarb W. Blood changes following glucose, lactate and pyruvate injection in man. *J. Biol. Chem.* 147: 33-40, 1943
49. DiSalvo R.J., Bloom W.L., Brust A.A., Ferguson R.W. and Ferris E.B. A comparison of the metabolic and circulatory effects of epinephrine, nor-epinephrine and insulin hypoglycaemia with observations on the influence of autonomic blocking agents. *J. Clin. Inv.* 35: 568-577, 1956
50. Randolph T.G. and Moss R.W. *Allergies, Your Hidden Enemy* Thorsons, 1981
51. Philpott W.H. and Kalita D.K. *Brain Allergies: The Psychonutrient Connection.* Keats Publishing Inc. New Canaan, Connecticut 06840, 1980
52. Beebe W.E. and Wendel O.W. Preliminary observations of altered carbohydrate metabolism in psychiatric patients. *Orthomolecular Psychiatry*, Eds: D. Hawkins and L. Pauling, W.H. Freeman & Co, San Francisco, 1973
53. Cappo B. and Holmes D. The utility of prolonged respiratory exhalation for reducing physiological and psychological arousal in non-threatening and threatening situations. *J. Psychosomatic Res.* Vol 28, No 4: 265–267, 1984
54. Lloyd G. Medicine without signs. *Brit. Med. J.* Vol 287: 539–542, 20 August 1983
55. Gottlieb, B. Non-organic disease in medical outpatients. *Update, 1.* 917–922, 1969
56. Ramsay A.M. *Postviral Fatigue Syndrome – The Saga of Royal Free Disease.* Gower Medical Publishing, 1986
57. Behan P.O. Behan W.M.H. and Bell E.J. The postviral fatigue syndrome – an analysis of the findings in 50 cases. *J. of Infection*, 10: 211–222, 1985
58. Arnold D.L. Bore P.J. Radda G.K. Styles P. and Taylor D.J. Excessive intracellular acidosis of skeletal muscle on exercise in a patient with postviral exhaustion/fatigue syndrome. *The Lancet*, 1367–1369, 23 June 1984
59. Ramsay A.M. ME – a baffling syndrome to diagnose. *Pulse*, 48, 15 January 1983
60. Mackarness R. *Not all in the Mind.* Pan Books, 1990

61. Forman R. *How to control your Allergies.* Larchmont Books, N.Y. 1979
62. Wolpe P. and Jellet J. *Allergy Survey Report* Action Against Allergy Publications, December 1986
63. Smith F. The Immune System: The governing factor in Health *Society for Environmental Ther. Newsl.* Vol 6, No 4, December 1986
64. *Action Against Allergy Newsletter,* No 30, July 1987
65. Wyke A. Pharmaceuticals: Harder going. *The Economist,* 3–7 February 1987
66. Catalan J. and Gath D.H. Benzodiazepines in general practice: Time for decision. *Brit. Med. J.* Vol 290: 1374–1376. 11 May 1985
67. Ashton H. Benzodiazepine withdrawal: an unfinished story. *Brit. Med. J.* Vol 288: 1135–1140, 14 April 1984
68. Ashton H. Adverse effects of prolonged benzodiazepine use. *Adverse Drug Reaction Bulletin,* No 118, June 1986
69. Coleman V. *Life without Tranquillizers.* Judy Piatkus Publication Ltd. 1985
70. Jerome J. *Cry of the Innocent.* (A) *Personal communication.* (B)
71. Lader M.H. Ron M. and Petursson H. Computed axial brain tomography in long-term benzodiazepine users. *Psychological Medicine,* 14: 203–306, 1984
72. Lader M.H. Dependence on benzodiazepines. *J. Clin. Psychiatry,* 44: 4, 121–127, April 1983
73. Petursson H. Bhattacharya S.K. Glover V. Sandler M. and Lader M.H. Urinary monoamine oxidase inhibitor and benzodiazepine withdrawal. *Brit. J. Psychiatry,* 140: 7–10, 1982
74. Trickett S. *Coming off Tranquillizers.* Thorsons, 1986
75. Murphy S.M. Owen R.T. and Tyrer P.J. Withdrawal symptoms after six weeks' treatment with diazepam. *The Lancet,* ii, 1389, 1984
76. *British Medical Journal.* Tranquillizers causing aggression. 18 January 1975 (A) Calcium in Psychiatry. 6 April 1968 (B)
77. Lacey R. and Woodward S. *That's Life Survey on Tranquillizers.* BBC in association with MIND, 1985
78. Cryer P.E. Glucose Homeostatis and Hypoglycaemia. *Textbook of Endocrinology,* Chapter 25, Ed: R.H. Williams, W.B. Saunders & Co, 1985
79. Braestrup C. and Nielsen M. Anxiety. Neurotransmitters and CNS Disease. *The Lancet Review* 1982
80. Bender A.E. Institutional malnutrition. *Brit. Med. J.* Vol 288, 14 January 1984
81. Butterworth C.E. Malnutrition in the hospital. *J.A.M.A.* Vol 230, No 6, 879, 11 November 1974
82. Weinsier R.L., Hunker E.M., Krumdieck C.L. and Butterworth C.E. Hospital malnutrition: A prospective evaluation of general medical patients during the course of hospitalization. *The Am. J. Clin. Nutr.* 32: 418–426, February 1979
83. Smith D.G. *Understanding ME* Robinson Publishing, 1989
84. Benjamin H. *Everybody's Guide to Nature Cure.* Health for All Publishers Co, 1936
85. Orr J.B. The development of the science of Nutrition in relation to Disease. *The Brit. Med. J.* 883–886, 23 May 1931
86. Williams R.J. *Biochemical Individuality.* Texas University Press, 1976

87. Pirquet C.V. Allergy. *Munch. Med. Wochenschr.* 30: 1457, 1906
88. Food Intolerance and Food Adversion. – A joint report of the Royal College of Physicians and the British Nutrition Foundation. *J. of The Royal College of Physicians*, Vol 18, No 2, April 1984
89. Rippere V. *The Allergy Problem: Why People suffer and What could be done.* Thorsons, 1983
90. Crook W.G. *Are you Allergic?* Professional Books, Jackson, Tennessee 38302, 1975
91. Mumby K. *The Food Allergy Plan.* Unwin Paperbacks, 1985
92. Smith L.H. *Improving Your Child's Behaviour Chemistry* Pocket Books, N.Y. 1977.
93. Mandell M. *Lifetime Arthritis Relief System.* Arrow Books, 1983
94. Nathan-Hill A. *Against Unsuspected Enemy.* Action Against Allergy Publications
95. Weiss G. Hechtman L. Perlman T. Hopkins J. and Wener A. Hyperactives as young adults: A controlled prospective ten-year follow-up of 75 children. *Arch. Gen. Psychiatry*, Vol 36: 675–681, June 1979
96. Weiss J.M. and Kaufman H.S. A subtle organic component in some cases of mental illness: A preliminary report of cases. *Arch. Gen. Psychiatry*, Vol 25: 74–78, July 1971
97. Egger J. Carter C.M. Graham P.J. Gumley D. and Soothill J.F. Controlled trial of oligoantigenic treatment in the hyperkinetic syndrome. *The Lancet*, 540–545, 9 March 1985
98. Egger J. Carter C.M. Wilson J. Turner M.W. and Soothill J.F. Is migraine food allergy? *The Lancet*, 865–869, 15 October 1983
99. Buisseret P.D. Common manifestations of cow's milk allergy in children. *The Lancet*, 304–305, 11 February 1978
100. Crook W.G. Food additives and hyperactivity. *The Lancet*, 1128, 15 May 1982
101. Hyperactive Children's Support Group (HAGS) *Personal communication.* (A) *The HAGS Journal*, No 31, Spring 1988 (B)
102. Grant E.C.G. Food allergies and migraine. *The Lancet*, 966–968, 5 May 1979
103. Jones V.A. McLaughlan P., Shorthouse M., Workman E. and Hunter J. Food intolerance: A major factor in the pathogenesis of irritable bowel syndrome. *The Lancet*, 1115–1117, 20 November 1982
104. Darlington L.G., Ramsey N.W. and Mansfield J.R. Placebo-controlled blind study of dietary manipulation therapy in rheumatoid arthritis. *The Lancet*, 236–238, 1 February 1986
105. Finn R. and Cohen H.N. 'Food Allergy': Fact or fiction? *The Lancet*, 426–428, 25 February 1978
106. Dohan F.C. and Grasberger J.C. Relapsed schizophrenics: Earlier discharge from the hospital after cereal-free and milk-free diet. *Am. J. Psychiatry*, 130: 685–688, June 1973
107. Philpott W.H. Maladaptive reactions to frequently used foods and commonly met chemicals as precipitating factors in many chronic physical and chronic emotional illness. *A Physician's Handbook on Orthomolecular Medicine.* Eds: R.J. Williams and D.K. Kalita, Keats Publishing Inc., 1977

108. Hall K. Allergy and the nervous system: A review. *Annals of Allergy*, Vol 36: 49–64, January 1976
109. Ziodruou C. Streaty R.A. and Klee W.A. Opiod peptides derived from food proteins: The Exorphins. *J. of Biol. Chem.* Vol 245, No 7: 2446–2449, 10 April 1979
110. Hemmings W.A. The entry into brain of large molecules derived from dietary protein. *Proc. R. Soc. Lond.* B.200, 175–192, 1978
111. Tuormaa T.E. A brief review of the immune system and its function to: Post Viral Fatigue Syndrome (ME), non-antibody mediated Allergy, Autoimmunity and Immune Deficiency. *Nutrition and Health*, Vol 6, No 1: 53–61, 1988
112. Bartrop R.W. Luckhurst E. Lazarus L. Kiloh L.G. and Penny R. Depressed lymphocyte function after bereavement. *The Lancet*, 834–836, 16 April 1977
113. Rinkel H.J. Role of food allergy in internal medicine. *Annals of Allergy*, 2: 115–124, 1944
114. Rowe A.H. Food allergy: Its manifestations, diagnosis and treatment. *J.A.M.A.* Vol 91, No 21: 1623–1631, 24 November 1928.
115. Coca A.F. *The Pulse Test.* Arco Publishing Inc, 1982
116. Smith F. A basic guide to allergy. *Society for Environmental Ther. Newsl.* Vol 7, No 4, December 1987
117. Selye H. General adaptation syndrome and the disease of adaptation. *J. Allergy*, 17: 231–247, 289–323, 352–398, 1946
118. Selye H. *Stress* Acta, Montreal, 1950
119. Dunne A.P. *Hypoglycaemia – the hidden factor in Allergy.* Action Against Allergy Publications.
120. Cheraskin E. and Ringsdorf W.M. *Psychodietics.* Bantam Books, 1974
121. Airola P. *Hypoglycaemia: A better Approach.* Health Plus Publishers, Phoenix, Arizona, 1977
122. Budd M.L. *Low Blood Sugar (Hypoglycaemia) The 20th Century Epidemic?* Thorsons, 1981
123. Pfeiffer C.C. *Mental and Elemental Nutrients.* Keats Publishing Inc, New Canaan, Connecticut 06840, 1975
124. Salzer H.M. Relative hypoglycaemia as a cause of neuro-psychiatric illness. *J. of the Nat. Med. Assoc.* Vol 58, No 1: 12–17, January 1966
125. Berry M.G. Tobacco Hypoglycaemia. *Ann. Int. Med.* 50: 1149–1157, 1959
126. Breidahl H.D. Priestley J.T. and Rynaerson E.H. Clinical aspects of Hyperinsulinism. *J.A.M.A.* 198–204, 21 January 1956
127. Conn J.W. and Selzer H.S. Spontaneous Hypoglycaemia. *Am. J. of Med.* 460–478, September 1955
128. Rynaerson E.H. and Moersch F.P. Neurological manifestations of Hyperinsulinism and other Hypoglycaemic states. *J.A.M.A.* Vol 103, No 16: 1196–1199, 20 October 1934
129. Conn J.W. The diagnosis and management of spontaneous Hypoglycaemia. *J.A.M.A.* 130–139, 10 May 1947
130. Anderson R.A. Polansky M.M. Bryden N.A. et al Chromium supplementation of human subjects: Effects on glucose, insulin and lipid variables. *Metabolism*, Vol 32, No 9: 894–899, September 1983

131. Harris S. Hyperinsulinism and Dysinsulinism. *J.A.M.A.* 83: 729–733, 1924
132. Gyland S. Possibly neurogenic Hypoglycaemia. *J.A.M.A.* 1184, 18 July 1953
133. Phillips K. Clinical studies on the Hypoglycaemic Syndrome. *Am. Pract. Digest. Treat.* 971–977, June 1959
134. Chalew S.A. McLaughlin J.V. Mersey J.H. Adams A.J. et al. The use of plasma epinephrine response in the diagnosis of idiopathic postprandial syndrome. *J.A.M.A.* Vol 251, No 5: 612–615, 3 February 1984
135. Jones M.S. Hypoglycaemia in neuroses. *Brit. Med. J.* 945–946, 16 November 1935
136. Fredericks C. and Goodman H. *Low Blood Sugar and You.* Charter Books, N.Y. 1983
137. Reed B. *Food, Teens and Behaviour.* Natural Press, PO Box 2107, Manitowoc, USA, 1983
138. Schauss A. *Diet, Crime and Delinquency.* Parker House, Berkeley, California 94714, USA, 1981
139. Schauss A. Nutrition and Behaviour: Complex interdisciplinary research. *Nutrition and Health,* Vol 3, No 1/2, 1984
140. Newbold H.L. *Meganutrients for your Nerves.* Berkley Books, N.Y. 1975
141. Landmann H.R. and Sutherland L. Incidence and significance of hypoglycaemia in unselected admissions to a psychosomatic service. *Am. J. Dig. Dis.* 105–108, April 1950
142. Hall K. Orthomolecular Therapy: A Review of Literature. *A Physician's Handbook on Orthomolecular Medicine,* Eds: R.J. Williams and D.K. Kalita, Keats Publshing, 1977
143. Meiers R.L. Relative hypoglycaemia in schizophrenia. *Orthomolecular Psychiatry,* Eds: D. Hawkins and L. Pauling, W.H. Freeman and Co., San Francisco, 1973
144. Langseth L. and Dowd J. Glucose tolerance and Hyperkinesis. *Food and Cosmetics Toxiology,* 16: 129–133, 1978
145. Wilder J. Psychological problems of Hypoglycaemia. *Am. J. Digest. Dis.* Vol 10, No 11: 428–435, November 1943
146. Rojas N. Hipoglucaemia en delinguentes. *Arch. de Medicina Legal,* 11: 29, 1941
147. Hill D. and Sargant W. A case of matricide. *The Lancet,* 526–527, 24 April 1943
148. Bovill D. A case of Functional Hypoglycaemia – A medico-legal problem. *Brit. J. Psychiatry,* 123: 353–358, 1973
149. D'Asaro B. Dietary habits in jail inmates: Report of Morris County Jail rehabilitation program. Sheriff's office, Morristown, New Jersey, November, 1973 *J. of Orthomolecular Psychiatry,* 4(3): 212–222, 1975
150. Schoenthaler S.J. The effect of sugar on the treatment and control of antisocial behaviour: A double-blind study of an incarcerated juvenile population. *Int. J. Biosocial Res.* 3(1): 1–9, 1982
151. Schoenthaler S.J. Diet and crime: An empirical examination of the value of nutrition in the control and treatment of incarcerated juvenile offenders. *Int. J. Biosocial Res.* 4(1): 25–39, 1983

152. Schoenthaler S.J. The Alabama diet-behaviour program: An empirical evaluation at Coosa Valley Regional Detection Centre. *Int. J. Biosocial Res.* 5(2): 79–87, 1983

153. Schoenthaler S.J. The Los Angeles Probation Department diet-behaviour program: An empirical analysis of six institutional settings. *Int. J. Biosocial Res.* 5(2): 88–98, 1983

154. Schoenthaler S.J. The North California diet-behaviour program: An empirical examination of 3000 juveniles. *Int. J. Biosocial Res.* 5(2): 99–106, 1983

155. Schoenthaler S.J. The effects of citrus on the treatment and control of antisocial behaviour: A double-blind study of an incarcerated juvenile population. *Int. J. Biosocial Res.* 5(2): 107–117, 1983

156. Virkkunen M. Insulin secretion during glucose tolerance test in antisocial personality. *Brit. J. Psychiatry*, 142: 598–604, 1983

157. Bryce-Smith D. Environmental chemical influences on behaviour personality and mentation. *Int. J. Biosocial Res.* Vol 8(2): 115–150, 1986

158. Thorn G.W., Quinby J.T. and Clinton M. A comparison of the metabolic effects of isocaloric meals of varying composition with special reference to the prevention of post-prandial hypoglycaemic symptoms. *Ann. of Int. Med.* Vol 18, No 6: 913–919, June 1943

159. Mullaney J.A. and Trippett C.J. Alcohol dependence and phobias Clinical description and relevance. *Brit. J. Psychiatry*, 135: 565–573, 1979

160. Davies S. and Stewart A. *Nutritional Medicine* Pan Books, 1987.

161. Colgan M. *Your Personal Vitamin Profile* Blond & Briggs, 1984

162. Holford P. *Vitamin Vitality.* Collins, 1985

163. Mervyn L. *The Dictionary of Vitamins.* Thorsons, 1984

164. Mervyn L. *The Dictionary of Minerals.* Thorsons, 1985

165. Davis A. *Let's get Well.* Unwin Paperbacks, 1974

166. Carney M.W.P. Ravindran A. Rinsler M.G. and Williams D.G. Thiamine, Riboflavin and Pyrodoxine deficiency in psychiatric in-patients. *Brit. J. Psychiatry*, 141: 271–272, 1982

167. Abbey L.C. Agoraphobia. *J. of Orthomolecular Psychiatry II* 243–259, 1982

168. Williams R.D., Mason H.L., Wilder R.M. and Smith B.F. Observations in induced Thiamin (B2) deficiency in man. *Arch. of Internal Med.* Vol 66, No 4: 785–799, October 1940

169. Lonsdale D. and Shamberger R.J. Red cell transketolase as an indicator of nutritional deficiency. *The Am. J. of Clin. Nutrition*, 33: 205–211, February 1980

170. Sterner R.T. and Price W.R. Restricted Riboflavin: Within subject behavioural in humans. *The Am. J. of Clin. Nutrition*, 26: 150–160, February 1973

171. Spies T.D., Aring C.D., Gelperin J. and Bean W.B. The mental symptoms of pellagra: Their relief with nicotinic acid *Am. J. of Med. Sci.* Vol 196, No 4: 461–475, 1938

172. Green R.G. Subclinical Pellagra. *Orthomolecular Psychiatry*, Eds: D. Hawkins and L. Pauling, W.H. Freeman and Co, San Francisco, 1973

173. Washbourne A.C. Nicotinic acid in the treatment of certain depressive states: A preliminary report. *Ann. Int. Med.* 32: 261–269, 1950

174. Mohler H. Polc P. Cumin R. Pieri L. and Kettler R. Nicotinamide is a

brain constituent with benzodiazepine-like actions. *Nature*, Vol 278, April 1979

175. Vescovi P. et al. Nicotinic acid effectiveness in treatment of benzo-diazepine withdrawal. *Current Ther. Res.* 41: 1017, 1987

176. Osmond H. and Hoffer A. Massive niacin treatment in schizophrenia. *The Lancet*, 316–320, 10 February 1962

177. Rimland B. Callaway E. and Dreyfus P. The effect of high doses of vitamin B6 on autistic children: A double-blind crossover study. *Am. J. Psychiatry*, Vol 135 No 4: 472–475, 1978

178. Carney M.W.P. Serum folate values in 423 psychiatric patients. *Brit. Med. J.* 512–518, 2 December 1967

179. Ghadirian A.M. Ananth J. and Engelsmann F. Folic acid deficiency and depression. *Psychosomatics*, Vol 21, No 11: 926–929, November 1980

180. Reynolds E.H. Anticonvulsant drugs, folic acid metabolism, fit frequency and psychiatric illness. *Psychiatria, Neurologia, Neurochirurgia*, 74: 167–174, 1971

181. Shorvon S.D. Carney M.W.P. Chanarin I. and Reynolds E.H. The neuropsychiatry of megaloblastic anaemia. *Brit. Med. J.* Vol 281: 1036–1038, 18 October 1980

182. Reynolds E.H. Preece J.M. Bailey J. and Coppen A. Folate deficiency in depressive illness. *Brit. J. of Psychiatry*, 117: 287–292, 1970

183. Shulman R. Vitamin B12 deficiency and psychiatric illness. *Brit. J. of Psychiatry*, 113: 252–256, 1967

184. Goggans F.C. A case of mania secondary to vitamin B12 deficiency. *Am. J. Psychiatry*, Vol 141 No 2: 300–301 February 1984

185. Wiener J.S. and Hope J.M. Cerebral manifestations of vitamin B12 deficiency. *J.A.M.A.* Vol 170, No 9: 1038–1041, 27 June 1959

186. Evans D.L. Endelsohn G.A. and Golden R.N. Organic psychosis without anaemia or spinal cord symptoms on patients with vitamin B12 deficiency. *Am. J. Psychiatry*, 140: 218–220, February 1983

187. Cutforth R.H. Adult scurvy. *The Lancet*, 454–456, 1 March 1958

188. Kingsman R.A. and Hood J. Some behavioral effects of ascorbic acid deficiency. *The Am. J. Clin. Nutrition*, 24: 455–464, April 1971

189. Milner G. Ascorbic acid in chronic psychiatric patients: A controlled trial. *Brit. J. of Psychiatry*, 109: 294–299, 1963

190. Burnet F.M. A possible role of zinc in the pathology of dementia. *The Lancet*, 186–188, 24 January 1981

191. Bryce-Smith D. and Simpson R.I.D. Case of anorexia nervosa responding to zinc sulphate. *The Lancet*, 350, 11 August 1984

192. Addy D.P. Happiness is Iron. *Brit. Med. J.* Vol 292: 969–970, 12 April 1986

193. Cannon G. Happiness is Iron. *Brit. Med. J.* Vol 292: 1599, 14 June 1986

194. Morck T.A. Lynch S.R. and Cook J.D. Inhibition of food iron absorption by coffee. *The Am. J. of Clin. Nutrition*, 37: 416–420, March 1983

195. Disler P.B. Lynch S.R. Charlton R.W. Torrance J.D. and Bothwell T.H. The effect of tea on iron absorption. *Gut*, 16: 193–200, 1975

196. Greden J.F. Anxiety and Caffeinism: A diagnostic dilemma. *Am. J. Psychiatry*, 131: 1089–1092, October 1974

197. Umpierre S.A. Hill J.A. and Anderson D.J. Effect of 'coke' on sperm motility. *The New Engl. J. of Med.* Vol 313, No 21: 1351, 1986

198. Colquhoun I. and Bunday S. A lack of essential fatty acids as a possible cause of hyperactivity in children. *Medical Hypothesis*, 7: 673–679, 1981

199. Horrobin D.F. Schizophrenia: reconciliation of the dopamine, prostaglandin and opioid concepts and the role of the pineal. *The Lancet*, 529–531, 10 March 1979

200. Horrobin D.F. Prostaglandins and essential fatty acids: A new approach understanding and treatment of alcoholism. *Psychiatry in Practice*, 19–21, August 1984

201. Williams R.J. Alcoholism as a nutritional problem. *Am. J. of Clin. Nutrition*, 1: 32–36, 1952

202. Badr F.M. and Badr R.S. Induction of dominant lethal mutation in male mice by ethyl alcohol. *Nature*, Vol 253: 134–137, 10 January 1975

203. Wynn M. and Wynn A. *The prevention of handicap of early pregnancy origin.* The Foundation for Education and Research in Childbearing, 1983

204. Barnes B. and Bradley S.G. *Planning for a Healthy Baby.* Ebury Press, 1990

205. *The Next Generation: Avoiding damage before birth in the 1980s.* Foresight Publications, 1983

206. Needleman H.L. Gunnoe C. Leviton A. Reed R. et al. Deficits in psychological and classroom performance of children with elevated dentine lead levels. *New Engl. J. of Med.* 300: 689–695, 29 March 1979

207. Bryce-Smith D. and Waldron H.A. Lead, behaviour and criminality. *The Ecologist*, Vol 4 No 10: 367–377, 1974

208. Phil R.O. and Parkes M. Hair element content in learning disabled children. *Science*, Vol 198: 204–206, October 1977

209. Capel I.D. Pinnock M.H. Dorrell H.M. Williams D.C. and Grant E.C.G. Comparison of concentrations of some trace, bulk and toxic metals in the hair of normal and dyslexic children. *Clinical Chemistry*, 27: 879–881, 1981

210. Ward N.I. Watson R. and Bryce-Smith D. Placental element levels in relation to fetal development for obstetrically 'normal' births: A study of 37 elements. Evidence for effects of cadmium, lead and zinc on fetal growth, and for smoking as a source of cadmium. *Int. J. Biosocial Res.* Vol 9(1): 63–81, 1987

211. Mackarness R. *A little of what you fancy.* Fontana, 1985

212. Davidoff G.N. Votaw M.L. Coon W.W. Hultquist D.E. et al. Elevations in serum copper, erythrocytic copper and ceruloplasmin concentrations in smokers. *Am. J. of Clin. Pathologists*, Vol 70, No 5: 790–792, 1978

213. Grant E.C.G. *The Bitter Pill: How safe is the 'perfect contraceptive'.* Elm Tree Books, 1985

214. Wynn V. Vitamins and contraceptive use. *The Lancet*, 561–564, 8 March 1975

215. Grant E.C.G. The contraceptive Pill: Its relation to allergy and illness. *Nutrition and Health*, Vol 2 No 1, 1983

216. Thomson C. and MacEoin D. *The Health Crisis.* The Natural Medicines Society, 1988

217. Medawar C. *The Wrong Kind of Medicine?* Consumer's Association and Hodder Stoughton Publ., 1984

218. Herbert V. *Nutrition Cultism*. George F. Stickley, Philadelphia, 1980
219. *The Booker Health Report: Vitamin and mineral intakes within certain population groups*. Booker Health Products, October 1985
220. *The Diets of British Schoolchildren: Preliminary report of a nutritional analysis of a nationwide dietary survey of British schoolchildren*. April 1986
221. *Social Security Consortium: Of Little Benefit. – An Update*. CPAG, 1–5 Bath Street, London EC1V 9PY
222. Levenson J. We should applaud critics of mercury. *J. of Alt. & Compl. Med.*, November 1987
223. Marshall J. Additive Alert. *Here's Health*, January 1986
224. Tainsh A.R. Beri–beri and mycotoxicosis: An historical account. *Nutrition and Health*, Vol 3, No 3, 1984
225. Tainsh A.R. Mycotoxicosis and homeostatis. *Soc. for Environmental Ther. Newsl.* Vol 6, No 3, September 1986
226. Tainsh A.R. The first medical mycologist. *Soc. for Environmental Ther. Newsl.* Vol 8, No 2, June 1988
227. Nathan-Hill A. From behind the iron curtain. *Soc. for Environmental Ther. Newsl.* Vol 6, No 1, March 1986
228. Monro J. Indian pesticide disaster fuels fears over UK food-chemical laws. *J. of Alternative Medicine*, January 1985
229. Chapman L. et al. Parkinsonism and industrial chemicals. *The Lancet*, 323–324, 7 February 1987
230. *Which?* Consumer's Association Publications, April 1989
231. Taylor G. Nitrates, nitrites, nitrosamines and cancer. *Nutrition and Health*, Vol 2, No 1, 1983
232. Best S. The electropollution effect. *J. of Alt. & Compl. Med.* May 1988
233. Hollwich F. The influence of ocular light perception on metabolism in man and in animal. *Topics in Environmental Physiology and Medicine*. Springer Verlag, 1979
234. Ott J.N. Influence of fluorescent lights on hyperactivity and learning disabilities. *J. Learning Disab.* August/September 1976
235. Ott J.N. *Health and Light*. Devin-Adair, N.Y. 1973
236. Tibbs H. *The Future of Light* Watkins, 1981
237. Kellas A. Charting the Future. *J. of Alt. & Compl. Med.*, April 1988
238. Snyder S.H. Schizophrenia. Neurotransmitters and CNS disease. *A Lancet Review*, 1982
239. Pfeiffer C.C. *Mental Illness and Schizophrenia: The Nutrition Connection*. Thorsons, 1987
240. Pilgrim D. The myth of schizophrenia. *Openmind*, No 33, June/July 1988
241. Shaw D.M. Tidmarsh S.F. Thomas D.E. Briscoe M.B. and Dickerson W. Senile dementia and nutrition. *Brit. Med. J.* Vol 288: 792–793, 10 March 1984
242. Rivlin R.S. Nutrition and ageing: Some unanswered questions. *The Am. J. of Med.* Vol 71: 337–340, September 1981
243. Millard P.H. Treatment of ageing brains. *Brit. Med. J.* Vol 289: 1094, 27 October 1984
244. Garrison R.H. Drug-Nutrient Interactions. *1984–85 Yearbook of Nutritional Medicine*, Ed: J. Bland, Keats Publishing Inc., New Canaan, Connecticut, 1985

245. Benton D. and Roberts G. Effect of vitamin and mineral supplementation on intelligence of a sample of schoolchildren. *The Lancet*, 140–143, 23 January 1988

246. Greenwood C.T. and Richardson D.P. Nutrition during adolescence. *World Rev. Nutr. Diet*, 33: 1–41, 1979

247. Laurence K.M. James N. Miller M.H. Tennant H.B. and Campbell H. Double-blind randomized controlled trial of folate treatment before conception to prevent recurrence of neural-tube defects. *Brit. Med. J.* Vol 282: 1509–1511, 9 May 1981

248. Cheraskin E. and Ringsdorf W.M. Another look at the 'ideal' serum cholesterol level. *Arch. Intern. Med.* Vol 140: 580–581, April 1980

249. Ueshima H. Iida M. and Komachi Y. Is it desirable to reduce total serum cholesterol level as low as possible? *Prev. Med.* 8: 104–105, 1979

250. Forde O.H. Knutsen S.F. Arnesen E. and Thelle D.G. The Tromso heart study: Coffee consumption and serum lipid concentrations in men with hypercholesterolaemia: A randomized intervention study. *Brit. Med. J.* Vol 290: 893–895, 23 March 1985

251. Yudkin J. Sugar and ischaemic heart disease. *The Practitioner*, Vol 198: 680-683, May 1967

252. Yudkin J. *Pure, White and Deadly*. Viking, 1986

253. Griggs B. *The Food Factor*. Viking, 1986

254. Newman W.P. Freedman D.S. Voors A.W. Gard P.D. et al. Relation of serum lipoprotein levels and systolic blood pressure to early artherosclerosis. The Bogalusa heart study. *The New Engl. J. of Med.* 138–144, 16 January 1986

255. Kuller L., Lilienfield A. and Fisher R. Epidemiological study of sudden and unexpected deaths due to arteriosclerotic heart disease. *Circulation*, Vol 34: 1056–1069, December 1966

256. Horrobin D.F. Essential Fatty Acids: A Review. *Clinical uses of Essential Fatty Acids*. Ed: D.F. Horrobin. Eden Press, 1982

257. Truss C.O. *The Missing Diagnosis*. PO Box: 26508, Birmingham, Alabama 35226, USA

258. Chaitow L. *Candida Albicans: Could yeast be your problem?* Thorsons, 1985

259. Chaitow L. *Vaccination and Immunization: Dangers, Delusions and Alternatives*. Daniel Co. Ltd., 1987

260. Yousef G.E. Bell E.J. Mann G.F. Murugesan V. Smith D.G. McCartney R.A. and Mowbray J.F. Chronic enterovirus infection in patients with Postviral Fatigue Syndrome. *The Lancet*, 146–149, 23 January 1988

261. Chaitow L. and Martin S. *A World without AIDS*. Thorsons, 1988

262. Sanchez A. Reeser L. Lau H.S. Yahiku P.Y. Willard R.E. et al. Role of sugars in human neutrophilic phagocytosis. *The Am. J. of Clin. Nutrition* 26: 1180–1184, November 1973

263. Illich I. *Medical Nemesis*. Calder and Boyers, 1975

264. Chantler J.K. Tingle A.J. and Petty R.E. *Persistent rubella virus infection associated with chronic arthritis in children. The New Engl J of Med.* Vol 313: No. 18 1117–1123, 1985

265. Ogra P.L. and Herd J.K. Arthritis associated with induced rubella infection. *J. Immunol.* 107: 810–813, 1971

266. Tingle A.J. Chantler J.K. Kettyls G.D. Larke R.P.B. and Schulzer M. Failed rubella immunization in adults: Association with immunologic and virological abnormalities. *J. of Infectious Dis.* Vol 151, No 2: 330–336, 1985

267. Miller H., Cendrowski W. and Schapira K. Multiple sclerosis and vaccination. *Brit. Med. J.* 210–213, 22 April 1967

268. Zintchenko A.P. *Zh. Nevropat. Psikhiat.* 65: 1634, 1965

269. Snead E. *Immunization Related Syndrome: Monograph.* Metro Medical Publ., San Antonio, Texas, USA, 1987

270. Scott A. *Pirates of the Cell: The story of viruses from molecule to microbe.* Basil Blackwell, 1987

271. Wilson G. *The Hazards of Immunization.* Athlone Press, 1976

272. Martin P. Psychology and the immune system. *New Scientist*, 9 April 1987

273. Depression, Stress and Immunity. *The Lancet*, 1457–1468, 27 June 1987

274. Duchateau L. Delepesse G. Vrijens R. and Collet H. Beneficial effects of oral zinc suplementation on the immune response of old people. *The Am. J. of Med.* Vol 70: 1001-1004, May 1981

275. Rippere V. The diet of psychiatric patients. *Soc. for Environmental Ther. Newsl.* Vol 2, No 1, March 1982

276. Nutrition in Medical Education. *The Lancet*, 333, 6 August 1983

277. Nutrition in Medical Education: *Report of the British Nutrition Foundation' Task Force on Clinical Nutrition*, Ed: J. Gray, 1983

278. *Promoting Better Health: The Government's programme for improving Primary Health Care.* PO Box 2, Central Way, Feltham, Middx TW14 OTG

279. Cannon G. *The Politics of Food.* Century Hutchinson Ltd. 1987

280. Walker C. and Cannon G. *The Food Scandal* Century Publishing, 1984

281. Britain needs a Food and Health Policy: The Government must face it Duty. *The Lancet*, 434–436, 23 August 1986

282. McCarrison, Sir Robert: *Nutrition and Health,* McCarrison Society Publications, London W1M 7DR.

INDEX